Women in Teacher Training Colleges, 1900–1960

Women in Teacher Training Colleges, 1900–1960 is an intricate and fascinating investigation of the lives and experiences of women in these important educational institutions of the early twentieth century. The book provides an overview of the historical context of the development of the colleges, using detailed case studies of three colleges: Homerton, Avery Hill and Bishop Otter.

Drawing on a wealth of archival material, primary and secondary sources, and on the oral testimonies of former pupils and staff, the book examines the following key themes:

- the changing social class of women students
- the colleges' 'culture of femininity' drawn from the family organization and social practices of the middle-class home
- the conflicting public and private roles of the woman principal
- the role of the college staff and the residential context of college life
- women's sexuality
- the last days of the women's colleges

Women in Teacher Training Colleges, 1900–1960 is an essential contribution to women's history and gives a unique insight into this neglected aspect of women's experiences in the twentieth century.

Elizabeth Edwards is a Senior Research Associate of Homerton College, Cambridge, and is a former librarian and archivist of the college. She has been published widely on many aspects of women's lives in the teacher training colleges.

Women's and Gender History
General Editor
June Purvis
Professor of Sociology, University of Portsmouth

Published

Gender relations in German history
Power, agency and experience from the sixteenth to the twentieth century
Lynn Abrams and Elizabeth Harvey

Gender and crime in modern Europe
Margaret L. Arnot and Cornelie Usborne

Prostitution: prevention and reform in England, 1860–1914
Paula Bartley

Crimes of outrage
Sex, violence and Victorian working women
Shani D'Cruze

No distinction of sex?
Women in British universities, 1870–1939
Carol Dyhouse

Women, work and sexual politics in eighteenth-century England
Bridget Hill

Policing gender, class and family: Britain, 1850–1940
Linda Mahood

Midwives of the revolution
Female Bolsheviks and women workers in 1917
Jane McDermid and Anna Hillyar

Women's history
Britain, 1850–1945
June Purvis (ed.)

Votes for women
June Purvis and Sandra Holton (eds)

Feminism and the politics of working women
The Women's Co-operative Guild, 1880s to the Second World War
Gillian Scott

Imagining home
Gender, 'race' and national identity, 1945–64
Wendy Webster

Sylvia Pankhurst
Sexual politics and political activism
Barbara Winslow

Child sexual abuse in Victorian England
Louise Jackson

Women in Teacher Training Colleges, 1900–1960

A culture of femininity

Elizabeth Edwards

London and New York

First published 2001
by Routledge
11 New Fetter Lane, London EC4P 4EE

Simultaneously published in the USA and Canada
by Routledge
29 West 35th Street, New York, NY 10001

Routledge is an imprint of the Taylor & Francis Group

© 2001 Elizabeth Edwards

Typeset in Garamond by
Florence Production Ltd, Stoodleigh, Devon

Printed in Great Britain by
St Edmundsbury Press, Bury St Edmunds, Suffolk

British Library Cataloguing in Publication Data
A catalogue record for this book is available from the British Library

Library of Congress Cataloging in Publication Data
Edwards, Elizabeth, 1932–
  Women in teacher training colleges, 1900–1960: a culture of
    femininity/Elizabeth Edwards.
    p. cm. — (Women's and gender history)
  Includes bibliographical references and index.
    1. Women teachers—Training of—Great Britain—History
  —20th century. 2. Women teachers—Social conditions—
  Great Britain—History—20th century. 3. Teachers colleges—
  Great Britain—History—20th century. I. Title. II. Series.
  LB2837.E39 2001
  371.1′0082—dc21   00–036627

ISBN 0–415–21476–9 (pbk)
ISBN 0–415–21475–0 (hbk)

In memory of Luis Edwards

Contents

Figures

Acknowledgements

Archival source material provided the primary evidence for my book. I should therefore like to thank most warmly the librarians and staff at Avery Hill College, Bishop Otter College and Homerton College for giving me access to their archive collections and helping me to use them.

Luis Edwards supported and encouraged me throughout the long genesis of the book, and the finished product is dedicated to his memory. Professor Jean Rudduck, Director of Research at Homerton College, has been a crucial support throughout. Professor Max Hammerton has read the whole text with scrupulous care and made helpful suggestions. Mary Tasker has constantly encouraged me especially when my enthusiasm was flagging. I should also like to thank Jenny Carr, Carol Dyhouse, Dulcie Groves, Sallie Purkis, June Purvis and my editor at Routledge, Victoria Peters, for their help and advice. I am also grateful to Scott Robertson, Gwen Seabrook-Smith and David Shorney for tracking down pictorial material.

Finally, I should like to thank all the students and staff who have recorded their memories of training college life. My book would have been impossible without them.

Introduction

The challenge of the 'new' women's history, as it has been developed from the 1970s, has been to bring women 'back into' the historical record and to present them as individuals in their own right, as active agents in the making of history.[1]

This book is a contribution to the challenge of the 'new' women's history. In spite of the fact that, throughout the first half of the twentieth century, three-quarters of the teachers in elementary schools in England and Wales were women,[2] the residential colleges which trained them have received scant attention from historians.[3] Moreover, studies on teacher training as a whole, notably L. Jones' *The Training of Teachers in England and Wales*, published in 1923,[4] and H. C. Dent's *The Training of Teachers in England & Wales 1800–1975*, published in 1977,[5] were not only largely concerned with administrative matters and government directives, but were also written from an entirely patriarchal perspective. Neither book, for instance, cites women or their training colleges as separate subjects in their indexes. The central focus of my book, on the other hand, is the experience of women living together in a particular form of community which was both residential and educational. The book's particular focus precludes it becoming a comprehensive history either of training colleges as a whole, or of women's training colleges in particular. Areas which would, for instance, be of central importance in a comprehensive history of the colleges, e.g. buildings, administration, or finance are covered only if they are germane to my central thesis. Likewise, the formal curriculum, although it is discussed briefly as part of the historical context in Chapter 1, and also forms the background to Chapter 4, nevertheless does not receive the extended coverage which would be warranted in a comprehensive history.

Martha Vicinus' pioneer study of residential communities for middle-class women in the late nineteenth and early twentieth centuries has provided valuable insights. Writing from a feminist perspective Vicinus described 'an independent intellectual life'[6] and the conflicts between 'personal life and public duty'[7] of staff in women's university colleges and private boarding schools; but her study did not include teacher training colleges. Similarly Carol Dyhouse's recent study of women in British universities[8] only mentions teacher training in passing.

The *raison d'être* of training colleges was to train women for the teaching profession, and more particularly and up to the Second World War, for them to teach in state elementary schools. Training took place in residential colleges whose organization and social customs were informed with what I have termed a 'culture of femininity'. This culture translated the social practices of the middle-class home, and importantly its family organization, into a new institutional setting. Trainee teachers, most of whom came from lower middle-class backgrounds were socialized into the customs and practice of the middle class proper. It was the training colleges' achievement not only to provide this culture of middle-class femininity as the context for students' vocational training and the academic studies associated with it, but to enhance the culture with the intellectual, cultural, aesthetic and spiritual opportunities which formed an essential part of the college's corporate life. It was the close interaction between staff and students living together in one community which made this enhancement possible.

Evidence for my study has come from many sources. Published monographs devoted to the history of a particular college[9] tend to be written from a perspective which concentrates on history 'from above'. Buildings and administration, finance and syllabuses inform these histories, rather than the actual experience of staff and students which is my central concern. Nevertheless a careful reading of these texts, including the occasional reference to the reminiscences of students or staff[10] revealed much relevant information. The historians of Lincoln, Ripon and Bedford colleges, for instance, all made incidental references to the family atmosphere in their respective colleges,[11] while the historian of St Mary's, Cheltenham gave useful evidence of the close interaction between staff and students.[12] I have made more extensive use of the histories of the three colleges which are central to my study – Avery Hill,[13] Bishop Otter[14] and Homerton.[15] Again these accounts although more concerned with institution than experience, have yielded much relevant information. Additionally, for Homerton, I have consulted a fictional account of the college at the end of the Second World War written by a former member of staff.[16] I chose the three colleges central to my study because they represented three different types of foundation. Homerton and Bishop Otter were both voluntary colleges founded respectively by the Congregational Church and the Church of England. By the early twentieth century Homerton remained a voluntary foundation but was now undenominational. Avery Hill, on the other hand, was founded by the London County Council, as a result of the 1902 Education Act (see Chapter 1) and had no religious affiliation. In practice, the culture of all three colleges was remarkably similar.

At all three of these colleges I have been able to consult a wealth of archival material which has yielded most of the evidence on which this book is based. The written archival evidence deposited in these archives included college magazines, principal's reports and other official documents, and, importantly, the reminiscences of former staff and students. At Homerton I was further able not only to consult the existing college archive[17] but to create 'new' evidence myself.[18] The additional sources which I created comprised both written and oral material. My primary focus was to obtain evidence from former staff and students of their experience of college life. Written evidence included the replies to questionnaires sent to former students of two principals – Mary Allan (1903–1935) and Alice Havergal Skillicorn (1935–60). Oral evidence was obtained from interviews with former students both individually and in groups. I also carried out, in collaboration with my colleague Sallie Purkis, a programme of interviews with some twenty-five former members of Homerton's staff.

Oral evidence has not always been accepted by historians as having equal validity to written texts – especially those texts which were written contemporaneously with the events they describe. I would argue, however, that in the absence of such texts, oral evidence provides historians with a powerful tool for accessing the past. Moreover, unlike the written record, oral history enables the interviewer to interrogate the interviewee and to ask the questions to which she seeks answers. This was particularly relevant in the research for this book when I was seeking to recover personal experience. I would further argue, that the fact that in my Homerton interviews both interviewer and interviewee belonged to the same corporate culture (albeit at different periods in its history), provided an additional asset which engendered a trust which facilitated communication.[19] Trust is of course paramount in oral interviews; and in my notes I have been particularly careful to protect individual identities.

Recent feminist historians have also provided important insights into the training of teachers as part of their wider investigations into the education of women. Penny Summerfield, in her account of girls at Lancashire secondary schools, drew attention to the second-class academic status which staff in girls' grammar schools awarded training colleges.[20] Alison Oram, in her study of women teachers and feminist politics, characterised 'social maternalism and feminine social service . . . linked with the idea of vocation' as motivating ideals for women's choice of a teaching career.[21] Diana Copelman's account of London's women teachers accepted the prevalent view at the time that training colleges were restrictive institutions with a 'low status'; nevertheless she also acknowledged that the colleges provided a nourishing environment which encouraged students' cultural and social aspirations.[22] Carol Dyhouse's study of women university students signalled the importance which the authorities gave to providing halls of residence for trainee teachers attached to universities,[23] and that furthermore 'conditions more favourable to the development of a collegiate atmosphere developed where female members of the academic staff took up residence in hall alongside students'.[24] The co-residence of staff and students in training colleges provided the essential structure for the enhancement of the culture of femininity which is the central theme of my book. Finally, Frances Widdowson's study of elementary teacher training in the early part of the period,[25] provided essential evidence on the changes in the social class of trainee teachers, which I shall be discussing in Chapter 1.

Chapter 1 outlines the historical context in which women's training colleges developed, and discusses the social class of women students. Chapter 2 describes the culture of femininity which pervaded and underlaid the academic and vocational work of the colleges. It shows how the family organization of the middle-class home, and some of its social practices, were translated from their domestic setting to provide new meanings in an institutional setting. Chapter 3 examines the conflicting discourses of the role of woman principal, as both father and mother of the institution she led. Her public and professional persona was that of a strong and authoritative father; but this public role was sometimes interrupted by the private needs of her own femininity. This chapter also details the individual careers of the principals from three colleges – Avery Hill, Bishop Otter and Homerton. Chapter 4 deals with the college staff, and describes their crucial role in enriching and enhancing the colleges' culture of femininity by transmitting to students the academic and cultural values derived from the liberal humanist traditions of the middle class. It also describes how the residential context facilitated the joint participation of both staff and students in the cultural, aesthetic, intellectual and spiritual aspects of college life. Chapter 5 discusses sexuality. In the first part of the chapter, which is concerned with heterosexuality, it shows how, within the college community, the construction of students' relationships with men friends changed over time from consensus to an area of conflict between staff and students. In the second part of this chapter I discuss the homoerotic friendships which some principals and staff formed to express the private needs of their femininity. Chapter 6 examines the last days of the womens' colleges in the 1950s. It shows how the culture of femininity gradually became outmoded and was eventually superseded, when men were admitted to women's colleges in the early 1960s. The chapter also discusses the contemporary debate on the education of women, and former students' experiences in juggling their two roles – home and work. Chapter 7 offers a conclusion.

1 The historical context[1]

The nineteenth century

Residential colleges, whose purpose was to train young women and men to teach, date back to the early years of the nineteenth century. There was, as yet, no state involvement in the provision of schools, and such provision that was made for the education of working-class boys and girls was in the hands of two religious societies – The National Society for Promoting the Education of the Poor, founded in 1811 by the Church of England, and the non-conformist British and Foreign School Society founded in 1814. The first training college as such was opened in 1805 by the British Society, at Borough Road in South London. At first only men students were admitted; but shortly after its foundation the college became co-educational. The first college for women only – Whitelands, also in London – was founded in 1841 by the National Society.[2]

In 1833, in the wake of the Reform Act of 1832, the state began, belatedly, to give indirect support to the education of the poor by giving capital grants to the National and British Societies for the building of schools. Six years later the state's involvement became statutory with the establishment of a special committee of the Privy Council to be concerned with education. The committee appointed a dynamic secretary, James Kay – later Sir James Kay-Shuttleworth – who succeeded both in increasing the amount of the government's grants to the societies and in extending their remit to include the building of teacher training colleges. By 1846 some fifteen colleges had been built, all but one by the National Society. Seven of these colleges were for women.[3]

A big impetus was given to the training college building programme by the adoption in 1846 of Kay-Shuttleworth's pupil–teacher scheme. This scheme, based on apprenticeship, was attractive to the mainly working-class pupils who attended elementary schools. Carefully selected pupils were to be apprenticed at the age of 13 to 'equally carefully selected'[4] head teachers for a period of five years. Pupil–teachers would teach in school during the day and receive instruction from the head teacher after school hours. Both pupil and head teacher would be remunerated by the state. On completion of their apprenticeship, pupil–teachers could sit an examination for the award of a 'Queen's Scholarship' which would entitle them to a place in a training college. Training colleges would receive maintenance grants from the state for each student. Between 1846 and 1870 seventeen more colleges were built – ten of them for women. These included Homerton College in London, formerly an academy for training young men to be ministers in the Congregational Church, which re-opened as a co-educational, unde-nominational training college in 1852.[5] In 1896, after its move to Cambridge in 1894, Homerton became a college for women only.[6]

The 1870 Education Act, which required all children between the ages of 5 and 13 to receive elementary education, greatly increased the demand for teachers. School Boards were set up for every Local Authority, but these Boards were not empowered to open training colleges. This put great strain on the resources of the two voluntary societies. Although the number of certificated teachers (i.e. those who had completed a two-year course at training college) increased from 12,467 to 31,422 between 1870 and 1880, and the number of pupil–teachers from 14,612 to 32,128, the fastest propor-tionate growth was of 'Assistant' teachers (i.e. ex-pupil–teachers who had not been to training college) who now compromised a quarter of all serving teachers.[7] Increasing concern with the educational standards of pupil–teachers led to the setting up of Pupil–Teacher Centres by the larger local authorities. All academic teaching for pupil–teachers was now concentrated in these centres, where they existed, with a concomitant decrease in the number of hours students were required to teach in schools. The pupil–teacher system was a central concern of the Royal Commission, known as the Cross Commission, which was appointed in 1886 'to enquire into the working of the elementary Education Acts'. The members of the Commission were divided on the subject of pupil–teachers. The Majority report recom-mended continuing the existing system, but the Minority report was severely critical of it. Among the scheme's critics was Fanny Trevor, principal of Bishop Otter College, whose evidence to the Commission I shall discuss further in Chapter 3.

Bishop Otter had originally been opened by the Church of England in 1839 as a training college for men, but it had been forced to close in 1867 through lack of support. Six years later it re-opened, this time as a college for the training of women teachers.[8] The re-opening of Bishop Otter as a college for women was in the context of the developing contemporary debate on the desirability of attracting more middle-class girls into elementary teaching rather than relying on working-class pupil–teachers. I shall be discussing the class origins of women teachers later in this chapter.

The Cross Commission had also recommended a new experiment for the training of teachers. This was the establishment of Day Training Colleges, to be attached to universities or university colleges. These colleges rapidly became highly popular, and by 1900 were catering for nearly a quarter of all trainee teachers.[9] Crucially, day college's attachment to universities, and their non-residential status,[10] made them more attractive to women from the middle class. Residential colleges, which were still provided by the voluntary colleges rather than the state, were challenged by this new type of teacher training; and women's colleges began that improvement in practice and precept which was to develop into the culture of femininity. Day colleges were later to become fully integrated departments of universities, offering a one-year teaching diploma for graduates.

1900–44

Criticism of the inadequacies of the pupil–teacher system had hardened by 1896 when a government committee was set up to enquire specifically into the system. While commending the efforts of many Pupil–teacher Centres, it was realized that the only way to improve the education of pupil–teachers as a whole was for the state to provide proper secondary schools for their instruction. This reform was set in train under the provisions of the Education Act of 1902. School Boards were now empowered not only to build secondary schools, but to provide and maintain teacher training colleges. By 1920 nineteen 'council' training colleges had been opened: thirteen for women and four co-educational. All but three were residential.[11] The residential colleges for women included Avery Hill, opened by the London County Council in 1906 on an 84-acre parkland site at Eltham.[12] The religious societies' monopoly over the provision of training colleges had been broken but, importantly, the 'belief that residence was an essential element in the training of an Elementary school teacher'[13] was to persist. Moreover, as we shall see throughout this book, there was no essential difference in the ethos of women's residential training colleges whatever the origin of their foundation.

In 1903, the Board of Education (as the Committee of the Privy Council had now become) appointed a dynamic new secretary, Robert Morant. In 1907 Morant proposed an alternative to the much criticized pupil–teacher system which was to prove its death knell:

> From August 1907 selected pupils at Secondary schools could be awarded 'Bursaries', that is, grants to enable them to stay an additional year at school between the ages of sixteen and eighteen. On completing this year they could enter training college straight away, or alternatively, could serve in schools as 'Student Teachers' for up to one year and then enter college.[14]

In practice, most 'bursars' served as student teachers for a year before entering college. No special examination was now needed for entry into training college although most students had taken one of the Local or Higher national examinations, administered by the universities and, unlike the Queen's Scholarship, not confined to students intending to teach.[15] The attraction of the 'bursar' scheme was that it ensured that students at training college had not only an adequate secondary education, but had also a year's supervised teaching experience. Importantly, the award of a 'bursary' was more acceptable to middle-class parents than the apprenticeship status of a pupil–teachership.

Nevertheless in the early years of the twentieth century, residential training colleges were negatively perceived both by the educational establishment and by the outside world. Criticisms centred on the isolation of the colleges, the inferior social class of students, the difficult balance between academic education and vocational training, and importantly 'the overcrowded character of the curriculum'.[16] Ironically, it was the increased freedom given by the Board of Education's own regulations in 1901 which had exacerbated this overcrowding. Training colleges were now instructed to draw up their own academic syllabuses and this allowed students to study certain subjects at an advanced level. Furthermore, a few students could now undertake a third year of academic study after the completion of their teaching diploma. Already by 1905 Homerton had established three advanced options in mathematics, science and French.[17] The college historian drew attention to the pressures on the timetable:

> The addition of a number of courses leading to a variety of examinations put great pressure on (the) timetable . . . The College, in effect, had to devise nine programmes to cater for students in the first and second years taking the Board of Education Certificate, some of whom would be undertaking additional work in the optional subjects, and for those taking the Matriculation and Intermediate Examinations of London University.[18]

At Avery Hill the original syllabus, drawn up by the LCC's Education Committee in 1904, gave priority to an academic course which was geared not only to the requirements of the elementary school but to students' own academic needs:

> Students should take a two-year course in which the first year was given over entirely to academic subjects including English Language and Literature and also 'masterpieces of world literature', Mathematics, Geography. a modern language, English history 'with a very general treatment of world history', and Science. Though the second year would be largely devoted to professional training, it would also contain some Nature Study.[19]

Science fell casualty to poor teaching in secondary schools until the 1930s.[20] During the inter-war years 'professional' subjects like Educational Psychology had a larger share of the formal curriculum; and, importantly (see Chapter 4), 'practical' subjects like Needlework and Music were given equal status to the 'academic' for advanced study.[21] After the Second World War the curriculum remained essentially unchanged. Students spent five hours a week on educational studies and five on curriculum studies and chose one 'main' and one 'subsidiary' subject for special study. Moreover, and of crucial importance, two periods of teaching practice (four weeks and six weeks) had to be fitted into the timetable. The principal, Dr. Consitt, 'aired her misgivings publicly in the *Avery Hill Reporter* in 1951': 'We try to improve . . . we merely overcrowd . . . Lecturers and students find the course too diffuse and full.'[22]

At Homerton the timetable in 1904, like that at Avery Hill, bore witness to 'the full and fragmented occupation of the students'. Students attended classes for 26 hours each week with Wednesday afternoons free. Instruction took the form of hour-long lectures. Four hours each was devoted to English and Mathematics. Music, General Science and History took two hours each, the Theory of Education four. The rest of the timetable comprised the practice of education and included school management and discipline, blackboard technique and other practical matters including needlework. Teaching practice accounted for three weeks in each of the two years. In their second year students were able to 'specialize' in one or two subjects. Unlike Avery Hill, professional and vocational courses at Homerton were concentrated into the first year, allowing the second year to be devoted to academic and optional courses.[23] In spite of its many critics (see below) and its seemingly prescriptive nature, the formal curriculum at training college together with the colleges' cultural ethos did in fact allow students considerable freedom to pursue their own interests, as one student at Homerton in the 1930s discovered:

> The subject which brought a new dimension into my life at this time was psychology, including the theory and practice of education. Dr. [*sic*] Waterhouse, lecturer in psychology, stood out with distinction. I found her immensely stimulating, if rather intimidating . . . her lectures were erudite and probing, and she encouraged any real interest in the working of the mind . . . I was able to join a small group to study Plato's *Republic* with her, and found her very patient and illuminating.[24]

In 1932 the training colleges were severely and intemperately criticized by a Cambridge University academic, L. C. Knights, in the first issue of the highly influential journal *Scrutiny*.[25] It is not without interest that Knights' future wife, Elizabeth, was thirty years later to become a part-time lecturer in English at Homerton College.[26] The source of the author's venom is not entirely clear. Acting on behalf of the editorial board, his article claimed to be the first of a general critique of the educational system to be carried out by the journal: 'We must begin somewhere.'[27] The examination system and the teaching of English were planned targets for the future.[28] More cogently, in view of the journal's subsequent seminal influence both on the teaching of English and on the works to be included in the English literary canon, the article reminds readers of its central concern with 'the cultural conditions that make the educational scandal possible'.[29]

The article claimed to have derived its information from the replies to 'a widely distributed questionnaire'. In a characteristic passage the author, while admitting that he has failed to distinguish between the different types of training college, nevertheless treated criticisms of both the validity of his research and his qualifications to carry it out, with lofty disdain:

> Even in publishing these notes we shall incur animadversion and objection. We have not had replies from every Training College in England and Scotland; we have not discriminated sufficiently between elementary and post-graduate Training Colleges, between Training Colleges for men and those for women; we have not mentioned the one or two decent exceptions to the general rule; and so on. In short, we presume. Our reply is that we presume to make a start, since no one else seems likely to do so.[30]

Criticisms of the training college regime were not without some validity – the overcrowded lecture programme, the lack of freedom for students to discover things for themselves, petty restrictions. Criticisms of the lack of music and art appreciation in the colleges, however, were, as we shall see in Chapter 4, very far from universally true. But it was the relentlessly dismissive attitude to the system as a whole that created such a negative impression. All the direct quotations (presumably from the replies to the questionnaire) were hostile; one of them, on women's sexuality, belonged to the realms of pornography rather than a serious treatise on women's education:

> Sometimes [attachments] existed between two pretty girls who related their adventures with their men to each other and got the thrill twice over, who slept with each other and usually walked about touching each other. . . . There were few genuine friendships as far as I knew. People made friends because it was easier to hunt men in couples.[31]

It is possible that the intemperate tone of the article detracted from the seriousness of its content. Nevertheless, having regard to the influence of *Scrutiny* and to the absence of other less polemical critiques available to the educated public, Knight's article can only have reinforced a generally critical, often dismissive, attitude towards training colleges. Dyhouse, for instance, in her study of women graduates before the Second World War, found that although intending teachers found the 'training' element in their university studies tedious and dull, nevertheless they found it 'infinitely preferable' to 'the training college route'.

Entering teaching as a graduate was seen as infinitely preferable to the training college route, both before and after the war. A degree lent cachet, and none of the women in my sample recorded any personal preference for teaching in an elementary school. One or two ... mentioned that they had refused to consider training colleges because these were associated with a narrow, illiberal regime.[32]

This attitude was still current in the highly acclaimed and influential McNair Report published in 1944 (see below).

The First World War had a drastic effect on men's training colleges, for within a few weeks of the outbreak of hostilities a third of men students had joined the armed forces. Conversely, the demand for women teachers increased dramatically. The war, like its successor twenty years later, also encouraged a climate for educational reform, the first result of which was the establishment in 1919 of national salary scales for teachers – the 'Burnham' scales. Unfortunately the downturn in the economy in the early 1920s put paid to further reforms, and the consequent reduction of expenditure severely restricted the resources available to Local Education Authorities for the maintenance of their training colleges. Voluntary colleges were also experiencing a drop in their incomes as a result of the war.

A marriage bar on the employment of married women teachers had always been the policy of some Local Education Authorities. After the First World War, and in response to the reduction of expenditure on education, the marriage bar was imposed nationwide. By 1926 three-quarters of Local Education Authorities had imposed the bar and only some 10 per cent of married women remained in teaching. There were, however, always great variations in the operation of the bar,[33] especially in London where, as Copelman has shown, some 25 per cent of women teachers were married.[34] The marriage bar began to be eased in the mid-1930s, and it was officially discontinued by the 1944 Education Act.

In 1923 the Board of Education appointed a Departmental Committee to 'review the arrangements for the Training of Teachers for Public Elementary Schools'.[35] The Committee reported in 1925, and its extensive recommendations were concerned largely with educational standards and administrative arrangements. It proposed that the Board itself should cease to be responsible for the examination of the academic side of the training college curriculum. (Responsibility for the examination of students' vocational work would, however, remain with the Board.) The examination of academic work would now be the responsibility of the universities who would set up Examining Boards to examine all students from the training colleges in their regions. Examining Boards would include representatives from both the universities and the governing bodies of the training colleges. Although Joint Examining Boards were established without difficulty in most regions, Homerton College had great difficulty, as we shall see in Chapter 3, in persuading Cambridge University to undertake this responsibility. The minimum entrance for training college was now to be a School Certificate, and importantly 'pupil–teachership and student–teachership should be discouraged'.[36] This break with all traces of the former 'apprenticeship' system and the emphasis on the desirability of a full secondary education up to the age of 18 were an indication of a perceived need to improve students' pre-college education. The report also, and unusually, singled out women's colleges for particular attention, paying tribute to the calibre of their principals and staff.[37] There was, however, extensive criticism of the report's failure to address the perennial question as to the proper balance between academic education and vocational training in the colleges. If students were better educated academically when they entered college, and if the majority of them had had no previous teaching experience, should more attention in college be given to their vocational training? Should the dual function of the training college be retained at all?

The early 1930s were a time of economic stringency and financial uncertainty for the colleges, and three Church of England colleges for women – Brighton, Peterborough and Truro – were forced to close. Dent characterized the inter-war years as ones 'of recurrent tension for the training colleges' but it would be wrong to regard them as a period of unrelieved gloom'.[38] Later, however, he admitted that 'the variety was very great'.[39] Certainly for most women's colleges this was a time of 'innovation and growing confidence',[40] of new buildings,[41] and 'increasing repute'.[42] Women's colleges increasing repute was strikingly revealed when royalty, in the person of Queen Mary, formally opened the new buildings of Whitelands College in June 1931.[43]

The outbreak of the Second World War in 1939, unlike that of the First, was a time of upheaval for women's training colleges and many were obliged to evacuate their buildings. At Avery Hill no teaching was possible from the outbreak of war in September 1939 until the end of 1940, as fear of air-raids and then the reality of the London Blitz forced the college to close its doors. Eventually the college was evacuated to makeshift premises in Huddersfield.[44] Bishop Otter's buildings in Chichester were taken over at very short notice in September 1942 to provide accommodation for the planning of D-Day, and the college was obliged to move to Bromley, where they had to share premises with an Emergency Rest Centre.[45] Homerton was more fortunate. Although it had to share its accommodation in the early part of the war with, first, Portsmouth and then Whitelands Training Colleges, by March 1942 the principal was able to announce that 'we now have Homerton to ourselves'.[46]

The McNair Report

'The impetus towards educational reform'[47] played a central part in wartime planning for the post-war world. As a corollary to planning for the Education Act of 1944,[48] a Committee of the Board of Education was set up in March

1942, 'to consider the supply, recruitment and training of teachers and youth leaders'.[49] The committee was chaired by Sir Arnold McNair, Vice-Chancellor of Liverpool University, and, of its ten members, only three were women. Moreover, although the director of London University's Institute of Education was a member, there were no representatives from teacher training colleges. The committee did consult widely among the teaching profession, including the principals of training colleges and some members of their staff, but the failure to include representatives from the institutions which played the major role in teacher education was a confirmation of 'the comparatively poor estimation in which training colleges have been held'.[50]

The McNair Report confirmed the preponderance of women in the teaching profession as a whole (some 70 per cent), and their overwhelming preponderance in elementary schools. Of the eighty-three recognized training colleges, sixty were for women only and seven were co-educational. Some 7,500 women students and 2,500 men were at training college at any one time. Training college students were trained 'almost exclusively' to teach in elementary schools, while the majority of those awarded a university post-graduate diploma taught in the secondary sector.[51] In view of these facts, it is surprising, and an indication of the patriarchal perspective of the committee's membership, that the report paid little attention to the specific concerns of women in training colleges.

The report's introductory chapter underlined the inferior status of training colleges as compared to university departments of education:

> The purpose of the training colleges has always been the preparation of teachers for the elementary schools; and the trail of cheapness . . . has also cast its spell over the training colleges which prepare teachers for them. What is chiefly wrong with the majority of the training colleges is their poverty and all that flows from it . . . [At] the university training departments . . . students and staff are full members of the university and therefore have access to all university amenities. Poverty has not, therefore, set its mark on them as it has on the training colleges.[52]

The poverty of training colleges was also related to their size: 64 of the 83 colleges had fewer than 150 students and 28 of them had fewer than 100. Such small numbers prevented 'effective staffing or economical management'.[53] Continuing its criticism of the colleges, the report recommended that the course should be extended to three years:

> A two-year course is not sufficient for students entering upon their training at 18 years of age. The studies and activities required of them and the claims of school practice are such that their day is overcrowded with things that must be done, leaving them little time for necessary recreation and reflection. An essential element in education at this stage

is a reasonable amount of leisure and a personal choice in the use of it. Many students in training colleges do not mature by living: they survive by hurrying.[54]

Turning to the question of college staff, the report made the important and valid point that staff of sufficient academic standing often 'had no experience of teaching in schools ... other than secondary schools' and consequently 'those who instructed and supervised [students] in the arts of teaching were not always themselves sufficiently acquainted with school conditions and practice'. This lack of staff with appropriate teaching experience was also the effect of the small size of colleges, where 'one lecturer must play many roles'.[55] On the question of whether or not staff should be resident in college, the report was strangely ambivalent. The relevant paragraph seems to face both ways at once:

Among the conditions of service of training college staffs, the question of residence is very important. A large proportion, especially of women lecturers, are resident. There must be resident members of staff in institutions in which students are almost wholly residential. But there is no doubt that many men and women eminently suited for training college work will not accept posts which involve residence; while some others, we fear, become in the long run so accustomed to residence that they shrink from the alternative even when, in the interests of themselves and of the college, they should cease to be resident. We suggest that, in future, residence should not, wherever it can be avoided, be made a condition of appointment and that as far as practicable there should be a residential rota so that few members of staff are required, or indeed allowed, to be permanently resident.[56]

This paragraph needs to be considered in the light of subsequent recommendations in the report. The committee upheld the frequently expressed charge that 'training colleges impose a discipline on their students which is obsolete and wholly unsuited to young people of from 18 to 22 years of age'. The report did, however, state: 'we know this to be true of some of them. But it is not true of all nor, we believe, of the majority of the colleges'.[57] Furthermore, the committee gave its unequivocal support for an increase in co-educational colleges, even though 'our witnesses were not unanimous on the question of "mixed" training colleges'.[58] I would suggest that the committee's ambivalent stance on residence (who were the members of staff who had outstayed their welcome?), coupled with their strictures on college discipline and their advocacy of co-education, was in effect, if not in intention, a subtle attack on the whole ethos of the women's college. For the co-residence of staff and students was what made the college's culture of femininity possible. Moreover, a small and multi-skilled staff only enhanced the corporate ethic, as Chapter 4 will show. The report did, however, praise the 'immense improvement' which had occurred in the education and training which students had received in training colleges during the past forty years.[59] It also praised the 'vigorous social life, expressing itself in societies of many kinds' and the social work which students undertook in the community.[60]

More generally, the report considered that the 'fundamental weakness' of the teacher training system as a whole (i.e. both training colleges and university departments) was its fragmentation into '100 institutions . . . not related to one another in such a way as to produce a coherent training service'.[61] Unfortunately, the committee could not agree how best to remedy this situation. Half of its members wanted such a service to become the responsibility of enlarged Joint Boards – the other half proposed that the universities should establish Schools of Education which would be directly responsible for all teacher training. (The committee incidentally did not propose that teaching should become an all-graduate profession.)[62]

Eventually a sort of hybrid scheme was established for the administration of teacher training. University teacher training would continue to be separately administered by University Departments of Education. The universities would, however, set up Institutes of Education, which they would staff and house. These Institutes, would be responsible for all examinations (i.e. both academic and vocational) for the training colleges in their regions. Cambridge University, as usual, refused to join the scheme. The government therefore became responsible for the Cambridge Institute of Education, which now examined all colleges in the area, including Homerton College. Homerton therefore lost its direct relationship with Cambridge University's Local Examinations Syndicate, which it had enjoyed since 1929.[63]

The post-McNair arrangements for training colleges remained in place until the end of our period in 1960 and until the coming of the B. Ed. degree and an all-graduate profession in the late 1960s. In Chapter 6 I shall discuss the 1950s and the gradual decline and final extinction of the women's training college. The McNair Report was indeed prophetic with its recommendations for a three-year course, the abandonment of residence, and the desirability of co-education. It is now time in the final part of this historical overview to consider the composition and social class of the students themselves.

Social class of students

> One of the most striking features of the history of women's involvement in elementary teaching is that whereas the profession is today unquestionably a middle-class occupation, not much more than a hundred years ago, in the 1850s, it was essentially working-class.[64]

The slow progress of social mobility for women teachers in elementary schools was initially the consequence of government policy. But the inability of the profession to attract women from the middle class proper until well into the twentieth century, even though girls from the lower middle class had been dominating the profession since the end of the nineteenth, was due, above all else, to sensitivities within the middle class itself. The working-class status of school teaching had been firmly established with the introduction of the pupil–teacher system in 1846. The secretary of the Privy Council's Committee on Education, Kay-Shuttleworth, made it clear that the state could not afford sufficient financial inducement to attract middle-class recruits to teaching, but must instead rely on 'the manual labour class and the classes immediately in contact with it'.[65] The system, which was an apprenticeship, was consonant with working-class traditions for both boys and girls. Pupils would not only receive a small salary while still at school in return for their teaching duties, but for those who qualified for admission, training at college would be subsidized by the state. It was this possibility of free higher education, together with a fixed minimum salary on qualification and a retirement pension, which made the scheme eventually attractive to girls from the lower middle class.

While lower middle-class girls were increasingly attracted to the pupil–teacher scheme, social and educational barriers prevented the participation of girls from the middle class proper. After the passing of the Education Act of 1870, there was an increasing demand for qualified teachers, and there were several attempts to attract more middle-class girls into a profession, which, on the face of it, seemed eminently suitable for them. For middle-class girls had always taught voluntarily in Sunday Schools; they were also accustomed to assist in a voluntary, part-time and untrained capacity with teaching in the elementary school. In 1858 the philanthropist, Angela Burdett-Coutts, published a pamphlet which aroused considerable interest and debate. Burdett-Coutts stressed the suitability of teaching as a career for middle-class girls, and especially for those who, through family circumstances, needed to be economically independent. Schools would benefit by a leavening of teachers from a superior social class. However, she also doubted whether middle-class girls were sufficiently well educated to pass the Queen's Scholarship for entry to training college. These doubts were justified when, in response to her pamphlet, the government set up an experimental examination to test whether middle-class girls would be able to qualify for training college. The results were 'disastrous'. For, in spite of large numbers of girls taking the examination, 'in all cases they were found to have been so imperfectly taught' that 'it was impossible to admit them to the examination for Queen's Scholarships with the slightest degree of success'.[66]

The Taunton Commission, set up in 1864 to investigate middle-class schools, confirmed the inadequacy of middle-class education for girls. Widdowson suggests that it was just this proven inadequacy of the education provided for middle-class girls in the private sector, which encouraged lower middle-class parents to send their daughters instead to the free state schools and to participate in the pupil–teacher scheme:

This revelation, together with feminist propaganda in the 60s on the need for the lower middle classes to find new areas of work for their daughters (rather than competing with destitute gentlewomen for jobs within the overstocked market of private governesses) may well have made this class respond to the pupil–teacher schemes. While the solidly middle-class girl seems to have continued to avoid the pupil–teacher schemes at the time, the lower middle-class girl increasingly came to terms with it in the late 60s and 70s and began her bid to take over the profession.[67]

This reference to private governesses is instructive. For mid-Victorian middle-class ideology was concerned above all else to shelter women from the perils of the outside world and particularly from 'contamination' with those of inferior social class. Class distinctions were rigidly enforced and sensitivities, particularly within classes, acute. Life in a residential training college would oblige middle-class girls not only to mix with their social inferiors for educational purposes, but actually to live with them as social equals. As a governess, on the other hand, a middle-class girl lived in a protected family environment with members of her own class.

The registers of Whitelands College show that, as early as 1857, although 76 per cent of college entrants were the daughters of manual workers, 10 per cent came from the lower middle class.[68] Another attempt to attract middle-class girls into the teaching profession was made by Louisa Hubbard in the early 1870s. Not only did Hubbard reiterate the arguments which had been made earlier by Burdett-Coutts, but she further suggested that a special training college should be opened for them. This was to lead in 1873 to the re-opening for women only of Bishop Otter College – a former training college for men in Chichester. The prospectus:

> drew attention to the rapidly increasing demand for schoolmistresses which had followed the 1870 Act, and to the suggestion that a fruitful field of recruitment might be among educated women of the middle and upper classes who depended for their livelihood on their own exertions, and might have a natural aptitude for teaching.[69]

Nevertheless, in spite of these intentions, Bishop Otter failed to recruit sufficient middle-class girls to be financially viable. The principal, Fanny Trevor, confessed this failure in her evidence to the Cross Commission in 1886:

Q. The college was supposed to cater for a higher social class than ordinary Training Colleges?
A. Yes – but it has been obliged in the last two years to take a few pupil–teachers who are not quite of the class that we would wish. . . . Those paying £50 p.a. [private students] are of a very superior

> social class, and those paying £20 p.a. [Queen's Scholars] are of a
> better class than the ordinary pupil-teachers, even if we have to take
> some pupil–teachers . . .
> Q. Do you have daughters of shop-keepers or artisans?
> A. I do not think we have ever had anyone of so low a class as that
> . . . We have had two or three large farmers' daughters.[70]

A significant development in teacher training in the 1880s was the opening
of pupil–teacher centres. These centres concentrated all the academic
teaching of pupil–teachers in a particular area into one place. Standards of
tuition rose rapidly, and by the end of the century pupil–teacher centres
were available in all but remote rural areas. The larger centres were 'essentially secondary schools' and the spectacular results which they achieved –
in London, for instance, by 1903, 90 per cent of pupils at the centres passed
the scholarship for entry to training college[71] – was an important factor
in the recruitment of more lower middle-class girls to the profession. By
the end of the 1880s, for instance some 40 per cent of girl pupil–teachers
at the London Fields, Hackney Pupil–Teachers Centre were lower middle-
class.[72] The days of the pupil–teacher were, however, numbered. The Cross
Commission, while still promoting the system, instituted a new form of
training college – the Day Training College. The provision of non-
residential training colleges had already been recognized as a way of allowing
'a superior class' of girl 'to enter the vocation of teaching without leaving
their homes'. The fact that day colleges were now to be associated with
universities was a further inducement for middle-class girls. Moreover, the
recognition in 1899 of other public examinations, like Matriculation and
the Oxford and Cambridge Higher Locals, as qualifying students for entry
to training colleges apart from the Queen's Scholarship, favoured middle-
class recruitment.

Nevertheless, in spite of these seeming inducements for middle-class girls
to enter the elementary teaching profession – and more particularly to enter
training college to qualify to do so – by the beginning of the twentieth
century, the majority of girls entering training college were from the lower
middle class. At Avery Hill, for instance, students: 'Came from the
Edwardian petit bourgeoisie. They were the daughters of tradesmen, artisans
and small employers, of public employees, including teachers, of clerks and
small shop-keepers.'[73]

Copelman has suggested that the continuing employment of married
teachers in London between the wars, in spite of the imposition of the
marriage bar after the First World War, was a consequence of teachers'
lower middle-class origins. For, in the lower middle class, the employment
of married women was traditionally regarded as an economic necessity and,
crucially, did not conflict with notions of respectability.[74] Lower middle-
class students remained the norm at training colleges until after the Second
World War, even, as we shall see, at colleges, like Homerton, which enjoyed

'superior' social and educational advantages. The pupil–teacher system was effectively sidelined in 1907 with the introduction of bursaries for student-teachers. Instead of a pupil–teacher apprenticeship, intending teachers were now awarded bursaries which enabled them to stay in full time education until they were 17 or 18 years old, and then, after a year as a student teacher, enter training college. This development was important for both educational and social reasons:

> The real importance of the bursar system was firstly in making it more normal for recruits to begin their pre-college teaching at 17, not earlier; and secondly, in breaking the old 'working-class' image of elementary teaching, so closely tied to the pupil teacher system. (One schoolmistress trained in the 1920s remembered that the headmistress of the private school she attended as a pupil saw nothing *infra dig* about sitting for a bursary, although to have been a pupil–teacher would have been different.)[75]

The attitude of teachers in secondary schools was an important influence on career choices for middle-class girls. Secondary education for girls expanded quickly in the wake of the Taunton Commission's damning criticisms in the mid-1860s. The Girls' Public Day School Trust, founded in 1872, set a standard of excellence for the academic education of girls, which was followed by the municipal secondary schools founded as a result of the 1902 Education Act.[76] Teachers in these schools were university graduates (as, indeed, were the staff at residential training colleges, see Chapter 4), who were concerned, above all else, that women's hard-won achievement of a proper academic education should be maintained: 'From the earliest point girls developed a strong impression that academic success and entry to higher education, especially university, but also teacher training college, were what these schools required.'[77]

Summerfield's study of two girls' secondary schools in Lancashire estimated that in the 1930s 'about three girls a year went to university and between six and twelve into teacher training'. However, 'even though teacher training was a well recognised and approved destination, the girls who pursued it tended to feel that it was second best'. Another student in the 1940s remembered':

> I think the school, we always used to feel that they were biased towards university, and latterly as you went back, they really only seemed to be particularly interested in university-trained people. Perhaps that's because they were on common ground. They were all graduates, in the main subjects, except the gym mistress.[78]

It is important to remember that it was not the teaching profession itself which held a second-class status in the eyes of these practitioners – but teaching in the elementary school, and importantly, the training colleges which trained them. For many, if not most, women university graduates throughout the period became secondary school teachers. Moreover, it was not only higher academic standards, and a shortage of places, which restricted university entrance for women; it was also the expense. Even with a scholarship life at university was expensive; students' costs at training college, on the other hand, were paid by the state. Nan Collecott was a clever girl from an impoverished lower middle-class background who had won a scholarship to her Essex high school. She decided to become a teacher because it was a secure job, and importantly, 'would give me the immediate advantage of prolonging my academic studies'. When her Higher Certificate results came out in the summer of 1931:

> Miss Hammill [the headmistress] sent for me and insisted that I should try for Girton to read for an Arts degree. She assured me that she could get me a County Major Scholarship to help with fees. My hopes began to soar as she sent for my father.

However, there was 'no way' her father could find the money 'even with a scholarship'; instead, Nan went to Homerton Teacher Training College, Cambridge with 'a hundred per cent' grant from the local authority.[79]

Statistics – Homerton College

The student registers at Homerton provide some statistical evidence of the kind of student who entered the college during the first sixty years of the twentieth century. Information includes the type of secondary school attended, pupil or student teachership, and examinations passed. Although the registers do not list the occupations of students' fathers, I have used the criterion of the schools they attended to make an estimate of social class. More particularly, the inclusion, after the Second World War of students who had attended Public Schools[80] or those belonging to the Girls Public Day Schools Trust (GPDST) is an indication that girls from the middle class proper were now entering college.

Of the ninety-six students entering Homerton in 1914, 88 per cent had had teaching experience which qualified them for free tuition at college. Some 17 per cent had been pupil–teachers and 71 per cent student teachers. The vast majority – 86 per cent – had attended state secondary schools, although some 12 per cent had been educated in the private sector. Over 60 per cent had passed the Oxford and Cambridge Senior Local Examination, or held a matriculation certificate. Fifteen years later in 1929, the proportion of students attending state or private schools had remained the same; but the numbers of pupil and student teachers had fallen dramatically. This was the result of the introduction, after the First World War, of the Higher School Certificate, which was taken at the age of 18 after a full sixth form education. The Higher School Certificate was a qualification for university entrance; but the fact that it had been awarded to many girls seeking admission to training college was a sure indication of rising academic standards. Bishop Otter's principal had already recognized and welcomed this trend:

> Higher Certificate applicants are on the increase. Some of the best LEAs are discontinuing or discouraging the Student Teacher year so students are coming straight from the 6th form with higher standards. They compare well with those who have been student teachers in their college results.[81]

At Homerton 38 per cent of students held the Higher School Certificate in 1929; 45 per cent had matriculation exemption and 15 per cent the School Certificate. (The School Certificate was taken at the age of 16 and if a student had passed well with a spread of subjects she was awarded matriculation exemption. Matriculation was the formal term for admission to a university – but, in practice, intending university students were also required to have passed the Higher School Certificate in their special subject.) The rise in the number of students who had received a full sixth form education meant that the number of student teachers had dropped to 27 per cent; 5 per cent of entrants continued to be pupil–teachers.

On the eve of the Second World War in 1939 only 82 students entered the college. The trends already evident ten years earlier had accelerated. Now only 13 per cent of students had been student teachers and there were no ex-pupil–teachers. Some 62 per cent had passed the Higher School Certificate. Significantly however 34 per cent of students only held the lower qualification of School Certificate (15 per cent of whom had also obtained matriculation exemption). The number of students who had not received a full sixth form education helped to reinforce the continuing second-class status of the training college. The proportions of students who had attended state (78 per cent) or private (12 per cent) schools had not greatly altered from previous years.

This was not the case ten years later in 1949 after the end of the Second World War. Out of an entry of 117 students, only 65 per cent of students had now been educated in the state sector; 30 per cent of students had been educated privately. Their schools now included a fair sprinkling of leading girls' public schools – like Roedean and Wycombe Abbey, as well as prestigious day schools like St Pauls Girls School and Henrietta Barnett and South Hampstead High of the Girls' Public Day Schools Trust. Examination qualifications had ceased to be listed in the registers, although school certificate with or without matriculation remained a sufficient qualification for entry to training college throughout the period.

Ten years later, in the last days of the women's college at the end of the 1950s, the middle-class status of Homerton students had become firmly established. Of the 137 entrants to the college that year, the proportions of those attending state or private schools were now – at 50 per cent and 46 per cent, respectively[82] – nearly equal. Homerton's historian commented on the changes:

> Among the groups of students who entered the College in the 1950s, two are noteworthy. One group came from families who, before the general provision of grants for higher education, were supporting sons at university and found in Homerton College a socially acceptable but cheaper course for their daughters. The other consisted of middle-class girls who were committed to teaching children of primary school age. Such students preferred the vocational relevance of a course at Homerton College to a purely academic course at a university.[83]

Middle-class status for the training college student had at last been achieved.

2 The culture of femininity

> I have seen a picture of the College, and agree with you in thinking the building very fine ... I should like to know all about everything connected with life in our college. Shall I have a room near yours? And what rules have we to obey?[1]

In this chapter I want to describe and discuss the culture of femininity which pervaded and underlaid the academic and vocational work of women's teacher training colleges. I shall show how the family organization of the middle-class home, and some of its social practices, were translated from their domestic setting to provide new meanings in the institutional setting of women's colleges. I shall also describe some other features of college life – like the May Day Ritual – which were peculiar to the training college environment.

The metaphor of the family

Mothers and daughters

The pervading metaphor of college life had always been that of the family. In the nineteenth century, when principals were usually men, colleges had been run on the lines of a mid-Victorian family in which the authority of the father was undisputed.[2] With the coming of women principals in the early years of the twentieth century, the family metaphor shifted towards matriarchal rather than patriarchal governance. I shall be discussing in Chapter 3 the woman principal's role as both 'father' and 'mother' of the institutional families she served, but the maternal model was also an important element in the organization of students themselves. As the opening quotation revealed, each first year student was allotted her own 'mother' from among the second year students. Mothers supervised their 'daughters' socialization into college life, and generally acted as their mentors and friends. Similarly, when daughters entered their second year they in turn became mothers to the next generation of students. This replication of domestic family relationships in an institutional setting was an effective method of helping students, many of whom had never been away from home before, to settle into the new environment of college life. Two students from Homerton described the system enthusiastically:

> The family system goes a great way here. To feel there is one in the college to whom you belong, one who is to be your 'mother' as a helper and guide makes you feel that Homerton is just a huge home and you yourself are one of the big family. Everyone seems willing to help and ready to answer questions, and just as you would go to the head of your family for advice, so here you go to the 'mother' for information, . . . Next year when I am a senior and a mother I shall . . . try to make those of the girls trusted to my care and guidance as happy as mine have been.[3]

> There to welcome me was my college mother, who showed me to my room and then we made a tour of the building, learning about regulations as we moved around. It was an adventure for me because it was the first time of leaving home. The next day she invited me to accompany her to Church.[4]

Another Homerton student, writing home in 1928, revealed not only how important the mother/daughter discourse was for students' initial socialization into college life, but also that over time, daughters moved away from relying solely on their mothers to form their own relationships, just as they did in the middle-class family: 'Three girls opposite to me are very unhappy but they haven't got a nice college mother. [Mine] is awfully nice and we are always together' and later: 'I'm so busy that I don't go with her [her mother] except to church but I see her at meal times. I don't need her care now.'[5]

The relationship between the two generations was inscribed into the routines of the college's social calendar. Hierarchies were strictly observed, although – as we shall see – ribbing between the generations was also evident. In January 1904 Seniors at Homerton gave a social for their Juniors: 'Our mothers presented us with flowers and programmes and at the appointed time piloted us to the Dining Hall. The Hall was cleared for dancing and everyone was in Georgian court costumes.'[6]

In May 1904 the Juniors returned their Seniors' hospitality. Their programme began with performances of Tennyson's *Foresters* and Schumann's *Gypsy Life*, followed by dancing. The evening finished 'in true Homertonian style' with *Auld Lang Syne*.[7] Later that year the college magazine recorded, somewhat 'tongue in cheek', a dispute which had arisen between mothers and daughters. Mothers complained that their daughters were lacking in respect and neglecting them. This was attributed to poor training of daughters by their mothers: 'Seniors, awake to your duties and privileges. Never let it be said that we were neglectful of training our daughters in the way they should go.' Daughters complained in turn of maternal neglect:

> Our first impulse was to rush to our mother's arms and receive her maternal welcome. What did we receive? A condescending smile and 'Well, you are my daughter, aren't you' indicating 'Keep off remember, I am a Senior'.[8]

This tongue-in-cheek exchange pointed to the dangers of a too literal interpretation of the mother/daughter discourse. At Bishop Otter family relationships, and the mother/daughter discourse in particular, reflected this college's stricter and more old-fashioned ethos. One student had vivid memories of her arrival at college and her welcome by the principal:

> She wore a rather severe blue costume with white lace at her neck and in little ruffles around her wrists. Her hair was tied back into a bun and the sunlight gleamed thinly on her steel spectacles. My heart continued to thump and bump most uncomfortably. We were marshalled into a single line and a voice hissed into my ear 'Walk up the steps, curtsey and say your name'. The line moved forward, now was the moment. 'Miss Forster Ma'am,' I stuttered. 'I welcome you into our family.'[9]

In the 1920s Bishop Otter's mother/daughter discourse ran into trouble because the system itself was too strict and interpreted too literally. A student writing in the college magazine describes the problem with interesting frankness:

> It is not surprising that in many cases the old system didn't work. Once chosen mother and daughter had to sit together for tea and supper for the whole year. If either of the two forgot and talked too much to her neighbour, to the neglect of her duty, the other was jealous, and meal times became periods of strife and boredom. The poor daughter often felt the problem more acutely than her parent, for she was feeling horribly strange and had no-one with whom she could discuss the position and meanwhile she was getting further into the mire as regards her filial duties. For the first few nights her mother would visit her to bid her good night, perhaps they would kiss each other, but after that the duty devolved upon the daughter.

The old system had encouraged an over-exclusive interpretation of the mother/daughter discourse which was inimical to the cultural freedom which the experience of college aimed to provide. The new system sought to remedy the situation by matching the sort of arrangements which prevailed at Homerton:

> Each 2nd year takes a newcomer under her wing at the beginning of term but the adoption lasts for a short time – as long as the two parties concerned like to make it. . . . The slavery of the mother/daughter discourse has been abolished.[10]

Throughout the period, there were sporadic attempts to modify the system. The aim was not so much to alter the system itself but to move the language away from its family connotations. In 1948 the Homerton Union of Students passed a resolution, which had the principal's approval, that the terms 'mother' and 'daughter' should be dropped and replaced by '1st year' and '2nd year'. In a fictional account of Homerton at the same period, the system was still in place; and although it was recognized as functional, it was also regarded as a little 'silly':

> 'We're to have a college mother it seems,' said Katharine, making a small face.
> 'Yes, it sounds rather silly, I think, but I suppose it's a useful idea – saves time getting to know the ropes. I knew mine at school last year as a matter of fact.'

Jane's 'mother' was an old girl from her own school; Katharine's was a stranger who had sent her a helpful but rather didactic letter. The two girls decided that she was no doubt 'very worthwhile' but hopelessly 'old-fashioned'.[11] Nevertheless, the discourse lingered on at Homerton and even as late as the 1970s it was still functional: 'The college mother system was a nice touch. It gave someone to contact as the nerves set in just before starting college.'[12]

In the late 1950s, Bishop Otter was addressing the same problems with the mother/daughter discourse which, on the face of it, the college had overcome back in the 1920s.

> The main consideration was breaking down the family system – not to forcibly divide up groups but to make responsibility to each other in general rather than in particular. We hope we no longer need the terms 'mother' and 'daughter' although many of our number are still much attached to them. This does not discourage 2nd/1st year friendships but leaves students to choose friendships freely. There will still be some form of 2nd Year 'helping hand' for 1st Years on arrival.[13]

Interestingly, the mother/daughter discourse at Bishop Otter 'didn't really stop until the men came'[14] in the early 1960s and the college became co-educational. Similarly, at Homerton, the system faded with the arrival of co-education in the late 1970s.

The extended family

Mother/daughter pairs frequently joined together to form larger family groups. In the 1920s at Homerton, for instance, one 'family' group organized bicycling trips for its members,[15] while another joined together for birthday parties.[16] In the 1940s new students were welcomed with a family party: 'On the first evening one's mother and her friends invited their college daughters to supper in one of their rooms and we soon felt part of a family.'[17] The metaphor of mothers and daughters was broadened out into that of the extended family An article in the *Schoolmistress* of 1890 had explained an early adoption of the metaphor at Hockerill College:

> Each new student thus becomes a member of a 'family' when she enters the college, as she is the daughter of her mother, who in turn is the daughter of her mother. . . . Family gatherings are sometimes arranged at which daughter, mothers, grandmothers and greatgrandmothers meet together for social intercourse.[18]

Colleges' extended families were institutionalized in the early twentieth century with the formation of Old Students Associations, and these associations quickly became a powerful means for promoting corporate identity and loyalty. Immediately on her appointment in 1903, Mary Allan, Homerton's first woman principal, transformed the small groups of former students who had been meeting informally in London into a formal Homerton Association. She created the annual Whitsun Reunion which gave the association both a focus and a corporate identity. Moreover, by holding the reunion at college and in term-time, it was possible for all members of the college's extended family to gather together. Current students were able to 'tender a hearty welcome to mothers and grandmothers',[19] and 'large numbers of past students could partake of college hospitality and renew their youth'.[20] Allan underlined the importance she attached to the Association's role in promoting the college's reputation: 'She often spoke of her pleasure in, and the values of the Homerton Association, for members had in their hands the status and reputation of the college.'[21]

At Bedford Physical Training College old students were also incorporated into an extended family. The Old Students Association, founded in 1906, proved the 'culminating feature' of the college's 'family image'.[22] In its annual Holiday Week for old students, the college harnessed its family metaphor to promote both professional standards and corporate loyalty:

> July 1906 saw us all back at College – the guests of Miss Stansfeld [the principal], for what was to be the first of yearly holiday courses. What a week of talk and work and play it was. It was naturally a very small meeting, in fact a large family party. The amount of work Miss Stansfeld put into that week is realised when you hear that we had a

whole day on the river, taking lunch, tea and supper, besides many buns for odd moments. Two other picnics, five lectures, gymnastics every day, dancing, vaulting and a tennis tournament.[23]

An Avery Hill student, returning to college for the Whitsun Reunion in 1952, encapsulated the enduring strength of the family metaphor in women's teacher training colleges. 'Little notes and flowers' had been left in rooms vacated for the occasion by their present occupants. 'The joy of coming into contact with the youngest of the "family"' made this old student feel 'more like a very dear aunt than a stranger'.[24]

Ceremonies

The family ideology of training colleges was further enhanced by the invention of traditions, such as the annual Ceremony of Carols at Christmas time, and the festivities of May Day. Both ceremonies had a symbolism which harnessed the domestic context of college life to endorse the wider values of an educational community. Three generations of Homerton students bear witness to the Carol Ceremony's enduring significance:

> Carols for Christmas. 2nd year students all in dressing gowns and each carrying a candle sang their way round all the rooms and corridors at Homerton between midnight and one o'clock.[25]

> We were awakened by something far more lovely than a siren. It was the sound of carol singing coming nearer and nearer. Soon a procession of 2nd years each carrying a candle passed along the corridors of blocks ABC and D and E.[26]

> Every year on the night before we broke up for Christmas we would get up about 3am and taking candles waken the first years and process all around the college singing carols. We finished up with hot soup and rolls at about 6am. It was quite magical and never to be forgotten.[27]

Informal singing on Christmas Eve around the Christmas tree in the middle-class home had been transformed by its institutional setting into a ceremony which not only underlined the intimacy of college family life, but also bore witness to the seriousness and spiritual purpose of the college community.

May Day

The May Day Ceremony, which was a re-creation of the ancient festivities of May Day, owed its revival in the context of women's colleges to John Ruskin. In 1881 Ruskin persuaded Whitelands Training College to initiate May Day celebrations. Other training colleges adapted the idea to suit their own particular needs. Ruskin's original ideas had been simple. He suggested that students elect a May Queen by secret ballot and then 'present her to the Principal in a crown of primroses and violets at breakfast'. Whiteland's principal, however, instituted far more elaborate festivities, which included a church service, processions and dancing around the maypole. Until 1940 the entire student body was 'outfitted in May Day dresses at the college's expense'. The May Queen's robes were particularly elaborate: 'Satin and silk chiffon with french knots, beading, and, always, exquisite embroidery, usually of flowers with symbolic connotations, but sometimes incorporating butterflies and birds.' The ceremony continues to this day, when former May Queens, clad in their original robes, join their successors in the 'Revels'.[28]

Similarly, at Avery Hill, May Day was celebrated with elaborate 'rustic' ritual. A crowning ceremony, when last year's queen placed a crown of lilies on her successor's head, was followed by dancing round the maypole, led by the maids of honour clad in white muslin. The day's festivities ended with a pageant performed by students.[29] Students were aware that their May Day revels at college were resuscitating old customs to form a new corporate tradition.

> As I saw the happy groups dispersing I hoped that May-day festivities would ever continue at Avery Hill even though the quaint custom has disappeared entirely elsewhere.[30]

> We hope to hand down these revels as a tradition which shall last as long as Avery Hill.[31]

During the First World War, profits from the revels were handed, appropriately, to the fund to establish the Star and Garter Home for Disabled Service Men – the Women of Britain's Memorial.[32]

Homerton's interpretation of May Day moved the occasion away from Arts and Crafts nostalgia and rustic revels to a festival which, as with the Ceremony of Carols, combined the college's family ideology with a celebration of its commitment to ideals of professionalism and service. There was no May Queen, or elaborate costumes and processions; and verse speaking and singing rather than maypole dancing and pageants formed the cultural traditions of the day. The occasion made an indelible impression, as two students recalled:

> May morning is unforgettable. The college hall was gay with bunches of cowslips one by each plate. At prayers Miss Allan [the principal] read as only she could, from the Song of Solomon the passage that begins: 'Rise up my love, my fair one, and come away.' Then after breakfast the finest singer went with her accompanist to the piano, and sang the May morning song: 'Come out, come out my dearest dear,

Come out and greet the May.' How surprised and delighted were the juniors, from whom the secret had been kept. The privilege of going out early to pick the cowslips was handed down from generation to generation of seniors. Later in the day the flowers were sent to a London hospital.[33]

I have always remembered the unbearable beauty of coming down on May Day to find everywhere decorated with greenery, cowslips, primroses and violets all done by the Seniors without us hearing a sound.[34]

Not every student however was so enthusiastic:

May Day was a pagan revival at Homerton. I never quite came to terms with it. On the last day of April we were expected to trail out into the countryside and come back laden with greenery, even branches from trees, to decorate the stairways and public spaces. Then, on the day itself, we all wore white and had our photographs taken in year groups on the lawn. It seemed a complete anachronism to me, but everyone seemed to go along with it as an almost sacred ritual, which was strange under a strictly religious Principal.[35]

This ritual functioned at several levels. Mothers were surprising their daughters with a special treat. The principal's choice of the Song of Solomon, the greenery and flowers which decked the hall, and the performance of the May morning song, all reflected May Day's origins as a spring fertility rite, as did the 'virgin' white dresses[36] which students wore. This coded expression of eroticism was particularly interesting in an institution that otherwise frowned on any expression of sexuality. Above all, the ceremony was a celebration of youth and its aspirations in which all the college family expressed, in more lyrical and festive terms than usual, the ideals of professionalism and service for which the college stood. The May Day festival and the Ceremony of Carols remained essentially unchanged at Homerton, until both traditions came to an end in the early 1960s, when a new dining hall was built.

Mealtimes

The ritual of mealtimes was an essential component of the social practice of the middle-class home. Its role in enforcing the lack of educational opportunities for women had been given classic expression in Florence Nightingale's pamphlet *Cassandra*: 'If she has a knife and fork in her hands for three hours of the day, she cannot have a pencil or a brush.'[37] Nevertheless the discourse of mealtimes was adopted by women's colleges and adapted to their needs. As in the middle-class home, the discourse functioned not only to promote the socialization of individual students into college life but also as an important element of social/family control. Most training college students had not experienced in their own homes the formality with which college meals were conducted:

> College had its formalities: dinner was a college meal for which every-body changed and Grace was said, though at other meals one table did not wait for another but each student stood to say her own thanks before departing.[38]

> To train us (I suppose) in social graces a member of staff sat at the head of each table at the mid-day meal.[39]

Meals at training colleges were not as elaborate as those in university women's colleges. This lack of social status was further underlined in prac-tice. Training colleges usually treated the mid-day meal, which was styled 'dinner', as the most formal of the day, while the evening meal, styled 'supper' was comparatively informal. In the universities, in contrast, evening dinner, as in the upper middle-class home, was always the most formal and elaborate of the day.[40] Attendance at meals was compulsory and punctu-ality strictly enforced. Students who were late for a meal had to apologize formally to the principal. This could be embarrassing as a Homerton student in the 1940s recalled: 'Could I forget the morning I didn't make it to breakfast on time. As I stood on High in my grey Gor-Ray skirt and wind-jammer apologising to the Principal for being late, my pyjama legs unrolled simultaneously.'[41] Another student recorded real anxiety when late for a meal:

> She told us that we had been 'reported out'. That means that the prefect at our table had reported us 'out' to the lecturer who was sitting on high. We were scared. We'd missed prayers and part of supper. We ran downstairs and the lecturer was just leaving. I hurriedly explained to her why we were late – we hadn't heard 'Big' – the bell – go and she said it was all right.[42]

In 1952 the staff at Bishop Otter entertained students with a play – *The Mystery of Bishop Hamster College or Who put the Bishop in the Basement*. The play 'showed keen insight into the most hidden corners of student life and how much Staff enjoyed the embarrassment of the poor unfortunate who has to bow after late entry to meals.'[43]

A student at Bishop Otter in the 1950s, who described herself as from a 'a socially-deprived home' and with 'no cultural background' revealed just what an ordeal the ritual of mealtimes, both formal and informal, could be:

> Too often, I seemed also to be waiting to catch her [the principal's] eye from the High Table in the dining hall, waiting to bow to her

because I was late again for the meal. Entertaining her 'to coffee' in my horsebox [her dormitory cubicle] was also a tense hour while I strove to serve coffee to the others present, and cold water only to her – for she drank no tea, no coffee and no milk either.[44]

At Homerton every meal, except for tea which the students had informally among themselves, was preceded by prayers. The staff then filed into hall and took their seats at the high table.[45] After meals the staff retired to the combination room – 'the door being ceremoniously opened by the head prefect'.[46] The socialization of students was further enhanced by the requirement that: 'The Senior Prefect had to find a victim each day to eat on High Table with Prin. and the lecturers. She [the principal] ate very quickly and left you struggling with food and trying to be intelligent.'[47] Students taking turns to make conversation with the principal and lecturers at high table, had translated into an institutional setting the middle-class requirement that daughters be equipped to make polite dinner party conversation with their parents' guests. One student remembered her social embarrassment for over sixty years: 'Seniors sat on either side of Miss Allan. My pastry flew onto her plate. "Yours I think Miss Jones," she said, returning it to me.'[48] A student at Bishop Otter in the 1950s had similar memories:

> One vivid memory is of sitting next to the Principal on my first ever High Table dinner (paralysed with fright that a half grapefruit would feature on the menu). We all had horrors that an indiscreet jab to separate the segments would project a smarting jet-stream of juice into a lecturer's eye or onto their clothes.[49]

Socialization between students themselves was also encouraged by formal mealtime procedures. Bedford Physical Training College had a system called 'following', 'whereby at meal times you moved each day to the place where the student ahead of you in the alphabet was sitting the previous day'.[50] At Avery Hill student 'hostesses' booked seats at their tables. Students themselves acknowledged that this was 'a grand way to get to know many students of both years'.[51] Interestingly, it was a male student at Bishop Otter in the 1960s, who recorded an awareness of the importance of formal mealtimes in maintaining the college's corporate ethic:

> In the formality of the evening meal, the coming together of staff and students, for example, the dignity of human contact was firmly emphasized. For those of us who turned up late, or who had to leave early, the necessity of bowing to the High Table seemed at the time to be oddly anachronistic but, with hindsight, it now seems a way of emphasizing meal times as more than a cafeteria style 'queue up'.[52]

Food

The actual food that students ate revealed a diet that was substantial, if somewhat stodgy by modern standards. Nicknames abounded, as an Avery Hill student from the Edwardian period recalled: '"Niger" Toes [prunes] and cold rice Thursdays. Boiled fish and suet pudding Fridays.'[53] Similarly, a Homerton student from the same period recalled: 'Sausages for breakfast on Tuesday morning, cold meat and pickles and cold apple pie at noon on Sundays; and a cornflour pudding called "whitewash".'[54]

A student in the 1930s drew attention both to the inappropriateness of some college food and to its incorporation into college mythology:

> Supper even on a cold, cold night with a bitter wind blowing across the Fens would be cold meat pie and shaking jelly. As some people had had a Sunday exeat and been out with undergrad friends this meal was always known as 'love-cooler'.[55]

Students at Edge Hill also incorporated their food into college mythology:

> The menu for meals was quite good though not exciting. The cooking at one time was shocking . . . Wednesdays and Fridays were known as 'Psalm, Fish and Mystery' days because we sang psalms instead of hymns at Morning Prayer and at dinner we had what we called 'Mersey Whale' (a whole fish sent to table swimming in a sea of greasy water), and Mystery, a revolting sloppy mixture of flour, breadcrumbs, dried fruit and huge lumps of suet.

Interestingly, when students complained to the principal she 'Was most annoyed that the complaint had not been made before. Henceforth the fish was cooked in an appetising way and very good fruit pudding was served.'[56]

A more serious criticism of college food was revealed in an internal report carried out in 1936 by Bishop Otter's Council. The college was found to spend only six shillings and four pence per week per student on food, in contrast to the eight shillings and twelve shillings per week at other church colleges. Moreover, the recommendations that milk should no longer be watered, less tinned meat be used and more mechanical aids provided in the kitchens, showed that students' diet had fallen victim to economic stringency.[57] Even as late as 1950 students' diets could still be deficient: 'Food was still rationed but it was quite good . . . I remember the great dishes of macaroni cheese and how they had to introduce some grapefruit when we all came out in boils.'[58]

Students were always able to augment the basic diet provided by college with food parcels from home. At Homerton they could also look forward to the weekly treat of 'Saturday afternoon tea in town'. For one student in the early 1930s, who came from a rural background, going out to eat in a restaurant was a new experience:

> Entering a restaurant freely was entirely new to a country girl. We always walked into town, never spending a penny on bus fares, so that we could spend an hour having waffles and maple syrup at The Waffle; helping ourselves to a luscious slice of cake at the Copper Kettle; or dallying with a pot of tea at the Dorothy.[59]

College routines and domestic duties

Middle-class standards for the close supervision of daughters were upheld in the college setting by a timetable which was strictly regulated and enforced. Most of the student day was accounted for and opportunities for 'free' leisure were limited. A 'mother' writing to her 'daughter' in 1945 described the regime:

> Now I'll just say a wee bit about the daily routine of college. Rising bell goes at 7.15 a.m. but no-one gets up then. Breakfast is at 8 a.m. and since we have to be punctual there is usually a lot of hectic washing and dressing at the last minute. Lectures 9–1 o'clock. Dinner 1.15 p.m. Afternoon lectures begin at 2.15. Tea 5.30 p.m. Sometimes evening lectures. After supper we are free to go out so long as we are back by 10 p.m.[60]

By 1945 some students were beginning to chafe at their strictly regulated lives. I shall show in Chapter 5 how control of students' sexuality became a contested arena. Other restrictions such as the compulsory wearing of college hats and gloves when going out, were more trivial, if irksome.[61] A 1902 student, reminiscing 60 years later pointed out that 'to the modern student it must sound a very grim regime but it did not seem so to us as we were used to control'.[62] This close supervision – in contrast to the relative freedom enjoyed by contemporaries in university women's colleges – was due both to the training colleges' vocational orientation and to the humbler social origins of their students. It is interesting that students from 'superior' training colleges like Homerton, Avery Hill and Bishop Otter, considered that while there were 'many training colleges with a more restricted life, we were far more restricted than University Students of our own age'.[63]

Students were sometimes intimidated by the middle-class standards of femininity embodied in the colleges' domestic regime. Even as late as the 1950s, a student at Bishop Otter felt at a disadvantage: 'Coming, as I did, from a socially-deprived home and no cultural background, as the whole country was emerging from wartime deprivation, I was uncomfortable at College, though delighted to be there.'[64]

Students' own rooms and dormitories, as I shall show below, were usually spartan. Public rooms, on the other hand, while reflecting some of the traditional grandeur of men's colleges, softened this grandeur with an appropriate femininity. Avery Hill was located in a converted late Victorian mansion, where, as a visitor in 1914 reported, 'students have the pleasure of working among surroundings designed for the pleasure of a millionaire'.[65] At Homerton, the college hall encapsulated this feminine interpretation of a traditional masculine ambience: 'The Hall was a most impressive feature with its brick walls and the High Table for members of staff[66]; 'Hall in those days was dimly lit, the tables were spread with white cloths and we always had flowers on them.'[67]

The entrance hall at Homerton, in the fictionalized account of the college in the 1940s, was described as allowing students access to 'another world':

> Here was a large square hall, with two fine Persian rugs on the floor, a semicircular alcove housing a great jar of yellow chrysanthemums, one or two pieces of obviously genuine Chippendale furniture. and a curving staircase, carpeted in dusky blue . . .[68]

A curious discussion at Homerton during the Second World War centred around the appropriateness of spending money on flowers for the college during wartime. It was a sign of the insularity of training college culture, and of Homerton's good fortune to be still, unlike other training colleges, on its own site, that an emphasis on traditional feminine standards took precedence over the needs of those suffering as a result of the war. In May 1941 at a meeting of the newly formed Homerton Union of Students, the following 'interesting proposal' was put: 'That five shillings to seven and sixpence per week for flowers is a scandalous extravagance when thousands are starving and homeless and that the money be directed to the Red Cross.' After heated discussion, it was resolved that: 'College was in sympathy with the idea but regarded the expense as justifiable on the grounds that civilisation must be maintained amid the destruction of today.'[69]

Domestic work

In the nineteenth century, it had been usual for students to undertake a considerable part of the domestic work of training colleges themselves. Students in 1890 at Southlands College, for instance, had the following domestic duties: 'Each student is responsible for the cleanliness and neatness of her dormitory, and all in turn take charge as monitors of class-rooms and lecture hall, but no scrubbing or laundry work is done by them, nor any cooking.'

At Lincoln College, duties were heavier and included mangling and the preparation of food.[70] As the majority of students at this period, and earlier, were from the working class, it was considered not inappropriate that they should combine domestic work with their studies. But as the class origins of students shifted upwards towards the lower middle class (see Chapter 1) and, importantly, the middle-class standards of the culture of femininity began to take hold, attitudes changed. By the early years of the twentieth century, it was no longer considered appropriate for students to undertake domestic duties, and, therefore, most of the domestic work in college began to be carried out by servants, as in the middle-class home. Students tidied their own rooms or dormitories, which were inspected weekly.[71] A crisis arose, however, during the Second World War, when compulsory conscription for unmarried young women led to a shortage of maids. The consequent imposition of domestic duties on students aroused acute feelings of hostility. That students should rebel about such a seemingly trivial issue, and at a time of national emergency, showed just how important was the maintenance of their newly acquired middle-class standards. The imposition of domestic duties was a threat to this status and reminded students only too clearly of their lower middle-class origins. A student at Edge Hill college described students' hostility:

> Apart from cleaning our own rooms (banging threadbare mats on the steps on Saturday mornings) twice a term one would have a day on 'housework' with one's room-mate. We were excused lectures while we swept and dusted, cleared the tables and set them again, doled out tea and buns in the afternoon and milk in the evening. Housework was not very popular but even less so was work in the main kitchens which was necessary once for a few weeks when there was a strike of kitchen staff. Oh, those horrible pans to scrape and piles of lettuce to wash and search for caterpillars, but the kitchen work was only temporary, thank goodness.[72]

This crisis was particularly acute at Homerton, which unlike Edge Hill, Avery Hill and Bishop Otter, remained on its own site throughout the war. A system was devised whereby first year students were assigned to 'A two day household duty rota when the students cleaned the college in turn and this included bathrooms and toilets.'[73] It was entirely in keeping with the college's family and community ethos that domestic duties were referred to as 'household' rather than the low status 'housework'. Nevertheless, it was a sign of how well Homerton students had assimilated the college's interpretation of middle-class femininity that this imposition on students of domestic duties, formerly performed by servants, was so deeply resented. The principal recognized this: 'We have all more than we wish of domestic chores, but we are deeply grateful to Miss Knox and her Staff for their splendid organisation and catering in face of a continual shortage of domestic help.'[74]

In 1940 the Homerton Union of Students (HUS) had been formed with official blessing. HUS provided students for the first time with a public arena for the collective airing of grievances and soon after 'household' was imposed in 1943, the issue was raised:

> *Payment for household duties.* Much discussion on this point arose. The Head Student reminded College that many other training colleges had been doing similar duties since the beginning of the war, and that we in Homerton had been comparatively lucky. The general feeling was that payment to the individual ought not to be asked for. Finally the meeting decided that an enquiry should be made and if the money normally paid to the maids was not being used then we might ask if all or part of that money could be given to any of the following:
> 1. A charity such as the Red Cross.
> 2. To the general college funds to provide for the increased costs of living which were sending fees up.
> 3. To the students' entertainment fund which was in need of money.[75]

This debate exposed the tensions which the imposition of 'household' had aroused. The Head Student, appointed by the principal, attempted to hold the official line by implying that it was students' duty to shoulder household chores. Most students recoiled from payment to individuals because payment was only suitable for those whose job it was to do housework, i.e., working-class domestic servants. Domestic servants, incidentally, all received a tip from each student at Christmas time. Nevertheless, there was a strong feeling that students should be rewarded in some way for shouldering extra duties. Giving to charity was socially acceptable, as was financial reward which would benefit the community as a whole rather than students as individuals. The debate rumbled on. Some paid cleaning staff remained in college, and in 1945 a dispute arose as to who should do the really dirty work, i.e. disposing of used sanitary towels: 'The cleaning staff refused to empty sanitary bins as long as students did not wrap the towels in paper. As students had neglected to do this the people on Household Duty would have to empty the bins.'[76]

Such sharp class antagonism in public was quite contrary to the college's community ethic. It showed the depth of students' resentment – a resentment which still crackled in students' memories forty years on.[77] 'Household' remained into the post-war period because of the continuing shortage of domestic staff. Voluntaryism as the only possible attitude to housework for educated middle-class women received explicit recognition in 1952. By this time there were some graduates resident in college. It was ironic that the following HUS resolution foreshadowed only too clearly the domestic duties which students would undertake 'voluntarily' in their own homes when they left college, as Chapter 6 will show: 'It was suggested that graduates should do household, but it was agreed that Homerton was privileged to have graduates and that they should only do household voluntarily.'[78]

A 'room of one's own'

A 'room of one's own' was one of the crucial experiences for personal development which college could offer women students. This central feminist tenet had been given classic expression by Virginia Woolf in the late 1920s.[79] Training colleges, however, with the notable exception of Homerton, did not provide every student with her own room until the end of the period. Students slept in dormitories, divided into cubicles, which were spartan and crowded. This failure to provide students with the privacy of their own space and the freedom to enjoy it was another manifestation of the strictly supervised training college regime. Students from Avery Hill in the early years of the century described their experience in vivid detail:

> Oh that dormitory. Dress tables and washing stands seemed to wander about at their own free will and beds grew out of walls at all angles. We dared not use too much water for fear of splashing.[80]

> Dormitories divided by curtains pulled back for ventilation at night, horrible little iron basins, fetch hot water in cans from bathroom down corridor. No PRIVACY [her capitals] was the worst of all.[81]

Even at Homerton, where students had their own rooms, conditions at this period were equally spartan:

> Our rooms were cold in winter and lighted by candles. Sometimes we had to break the ice on our water cans before washing in a bowl. There were no showers, no entertaining rooms, no student kitchen.[82]

> On the ground floor gas lighting was in use, but above, except for lights on the corridors there was no lighting or heat in any bedroom.[83]

The lack of adequate washing facilities and the consequent difficulty in maintaining middle-class standards of feminine hygiene were not confined to students. Florence Johnson, Bishop Otter's principal in the 1920s, had to petition the College Council before she was granted her own private facilities:

> It is very important, if you want to prevent the principal getting 'nervy' to *provide her with a really good bathroom and pantry* [her underlining] which can be reached from her own private corridor, without making her go out and wander about among the students. Convenience and comfort in bathrooms is really the most important item for everybody, staff and students.[84]

The dormitory culture underlined the frequently expressed comment that training colleges had 'the atmosphere of a girls school'.[85] A Bishop

Otter student in the 1920s captured this atmosphere in a vignette entitled 'Lights Out':

> Running down the cloisters towards the upstairs dormitories, the half hour on the Cathedral clock struck. At 9.30 p.m., lights out, the principal throws a lever in main fuse box of the recently installed electricity system. I fumbled for the latch. 'Who is it?' hissed a voice. 'Forster' I mumbled. 'Get in, get in' commanded the Dormitory Prefect showing me towards my cubicle. 'Prin will be doing the rounds any minute now, put your night-dress over your clothes and pretend to be asleep.'[86]

The most important restriction which dormitory life imposed was that students were not allowed to read in their cubicles. Second year students at Bishop Otter were given this privilege in the late 1920s but ten years later the conversion to study bedrooms for all students was still incomplete: 'It would be good to make our cubicles more like study bedrooms by the addition of a desk and a chair but at present first year students have to do their private reading in classrooms or the Library.'[87]

In 1949 the college enlisted the financial support of its old students to 'replace the remaining dormitories by study bedrooms'.[88] But it was not until 1957 that the Church of England gave 'among all its other pressing needs' a million and a half pounds to its training colleges to complete the conversion. By then, even the most conservative colleges had to acknowledge that dormitory accommodation could not provide adequately for students' needs:

> As opportunity offered, accommodation in single rooms replaced dormitories (inspected for tidiness and divided into a series of cell-like apartments, each sparsely furnished with a 'coffin' cupboard, a bed – not to be used as a seat, and a chair).[89]

> It is not possible to grow in spiritual and mental stature without a certain amount of privacy and the leisure to use it. The closing of dormitories will contribute to the wise use of study periods.[90]

Nevertheless when the 'coffin' wardrobes and iron bedsteads had been carried out and the old wooden partitions torn down, there were still 'some people who mourn the free and friendly atmosphere of the "horse-boxes" in the dormitories'.[91] The conversion of the dormitories coincided with the breaking of the 'family' tradition at Bishop Otter. Both events were symptomatic of the decline and increasing obsolescence of the training colleges' traditional ideology – a decline which became increasingly evident as the 1950s progressed (see Chapter 6). The old ways still had many defenders. Some students found the camaraderie of the dormitory culture more comfortable than the lonely freedom of a room of their own.

Dormitories were prominent in the culture of the upper middle-class boarding school; and it is possible that lower middle-class girls at training college, who had avidly read boarding school stories while at day school, saw the college dormitory system as an embodiment of their own fantasies.[92]

Homerton had inherited the buildings of Cavendish College when it moved to Cambridge in 1894. (Cavendish College had been a short-lived experiment by Cambridge University to provide accommodation for undergraduates who could not afford full collegiate membership).[93] After Homerton had moved to Cambridge, therefore, Homerton students were able to have their own rooms – a facility which was recognized to confer a distinct advantage over other training colleges: 'I think Homerton was unique among training colleges in that each student had her own room, an inestimable satisfaction to most of us both for the privacy so given and the chances of entertaining.'[94] Homerton students, however, did not enjoy unfettered freedom in their rooms for either study or entertaining: 'The corridor prefect had to knock on each study door at 10 o'clock every night and we inside had to answer 'In and alone, goodnight', before we put lights out at 10.30 p.m.'[95] Any student showing a light after 10.30 ran the risk of being spotted by the college porter on his nightly rounds and subsequently fined.[96] Cambridge University's women students at Girton College, in contrast, were allowed to work and talk all night if they wished.

> We can stay in our rooms for days and no-one knows. We have to sign our initials in a book night and morning, but we can get somebody else to do that for us and simply not appear if we don't want to.[97]

The possession of a room to themselves also gave Homerton students the opportunity to express their femininity in the arrangement of their rooms. The importance of this opportunity is manifest in a student's letter home in 1928:

> My room is ever so sweet and I have just about the nicest view in college. . . . My window opens on three sides. . . . On my large window sill I have two small mats with a little photo on each . . . I have my clock on a larger mat on the mantelpiece and a blue box with snaps at one side and my scent spray at the other . . . my shoes are in the recess called a wardrobe and my hats are on top of the recess. My tunic, apron and dressing gown hang at the back of the door.[98]

Twenty years later, our fictional heroines at Homerton also described their rooms as 'sweet'. Their rooms reflected the increasing sophistication of students' artistic taste:

> 'It's like a biscuit box. So is yours. But,' said Jane firmly, 'I think it's *sweet.*'

'One's own little nest. I intend to make mine very cosy indeed – piles of cushions, and one very impressive picture – not van Gogh's "Sunflowers", however.'

'I've got the "Doge of Venice",' said Jane, 'a really good print that mother gave me last birthday. And I shall get rid of the green casement cloth curtains, and put up some printed cotton that my brother brought from India when he was demobbed.'

'Good. Let's vie with each other to have the most original rooms in college.'[99]

Not every student was so enthusiastic. While most students valued the privilege of 'a room of one's own', the furnishings provided by the college were basic. One Homerton student in the 1930s compared her room unfavourably with those provided by the university women's colleges:

> My first room overlooked the kitchens and maids' bedrooms, so that there was a constant stream of returning footsteps after ten o'clock . . . The room was not very comfortable, but adequate, and I was uncritical. There was a tradition that every student on leaving donated one pound of her first salary to a fund used to provide extra furnishings for students' rooms. They must have been very basic originally; we all went to Woolworths and fitted up our own reading lamps . . . When I visited Ruth and Joan at Girton I was envious of their two rooms each, carpeted with open coal fires and with facilities for making tea in their rooms.[100]

Dress

A close watch was always kept on students' clothes and their general appearance. At Avery Hill, for instance, the information given to the college's first students was detailed and prescriptive:

> It is requested that the dress of students be as neat and simple as possible. A serge or tweed coat and skirt with a shirt of washing material are most suitable for everyday wear. One better dress is desirable for Sunday. On the occasion of College festivities it is hoped that students will wear white. . . . A supply of underclothing for three weeks is necessary. It should include woollen vests or combinations. . . . Students will be expected to wear a white sailor hat with a College ribbon.[101]

Some items of clothing – like college blazers, scarves and hat bands – functioned as uniform – enabling students not only to 'advertise' their collegiate membership to the outside world but also to be identified as such.

> Students in Edwardian England accepted readily that, even when walking a distance of 30 yards . . . they were obliged to wear a long

skirt down to the ankles, a hat, with a hat band in the college colours of blue and yellow, gloves and a coat.[102]

Students were always concerned that these collegiate emblems should be adapted to display an appropriate femininity. In 1950 a keen debate at Homerton followed the announcement by the college tailors (also and significantly tailors to Cambridge University) that the Homerton scarf could be confused with that worn by students at the local Technical College.[103] At the next meeting of the Homerton Union of Students there was 'much heated discussion with regard to blazers and scarves'. The meeting finally agreed on royal blue with white stripes but only after a plea for more femininity in college uniform had been discarded as open to misuse:

> To a question that there might be a more feminine scarf available the Senior Student stated that royal blue silk squares could be provided, rayon costing 22/6, pure silk 39/6. In that case there would have to be some regulation to prevent students using them as head squares.[104]

Students at Avery Hill were rebuked by their principal in the late 1920s when she discovered at a play rehearsal that 'we wore no bras or corsets'. Her injunction that students should 'look to our figures'[105] betrayed the principal's old-fashioned concern with deportment and the constant worry among college staff that students show respectability in their dress at all times. A Homerton student recalled a similar incident:

> We usually wore white dresses [for Country Dancing] and light stockings. One evening I was wearing lighter stockings than usual and apparently Miss Allan [the principal] wondered if I had dared to attend the dancing without any! So she asked someone to come close enough to me to find out. ... She was very strict on etiquette and suitable dress, as this little story illustrates.[106]

Even students' leisure wear was not immune from scrutiny. The debate on the wearing of slacks at Homerton revealed, in miniature, the tensions between individual freedom, middle-class standards and professional propriety which lay at the heart of the college's culture of femininity. The HUS minute book charted the debate. In November 1941 a proposal that slacks be worn outside college in the cold weather was not accepted. Two years later a proposal that slacks be worn in Hall, was, not surprisingly, also lost by a large majority. Clearly if trousers were not acceptable for informal leisure wear still less could they be deemed suitable as formal wear. By 1943, however, women's experience of war work had made the wearing of slacks more generally acceptable, and later that year a partial relaxation of the ban on slacks was allowed:

Slacks out of college. This question aroused much discussion. Several people felt that slacks were not suitable for general wear though there was some use for them outside in cold weather. Students were asked, if the motion were passed, to wear only neat and well-fitting slacks out of College. It was pointed out that other women's colleges of both London and Cambridge Universities were allowed to wear slacks. Finally the motion that students should be allowed to wear slacks in the evenings in cold weather and also on expeditions into the country connected with the Environment course was carried.[107]

This debate showed that class and gender concerns continued to be of central concern, even during the social upheavals of the Second World War. It was not without significance that the motion was passed only after reference to the practice of university women's colleges had reassured students that the wearing of slacks would not endanger their middle-class status. Even so, the relegation of slacks to the status of protective clothing and the concern that 'only neat and well-fitting' slacks be worn out of college, were an indication that training college students' vulnerability to local middle-class opinion was still a potent force.

Everyday wear in college was neat and serviceable. Our 1928 correspondent, for instance, reported home that 'My navy skirt is lovely and my green jumper too. I nearly always wear them every day.' For the Saturday Night Entertainments however, (see below) she expressed her femininity in more elaborate and competitive fashion:

> You can make my dress semi-tight but for goodness sake not too slack round the hips. I see girls here wearing georgette dresses on Saturday nights and they look like sacks on them. I want to look simply a dream.[108]

By the 1940s students were, on special occasions, attending dances outside college. The fictional students at Homerton dressed in appropriate finery to attend the end of term dance at the 'agricultural college'. This account is interesting as 'the agricultural college' in reality would have been a May Ball at a Cambridge University college (see Chapter 5). The principal was also displaying the feminine side of her role when she admired students' finery and dispatched them to 'the gaieties ahead' with her maternal blessing:

> The last Friday of term brought the agricultural college dance, and the Circus was dark with young men in dinner jackets who had called for their partners. Susan Emerson aroused the envy of all by appearing in a white fur cape, Roberta Lauderdale looked a perfect dream in flame-coloured georgette; the rustle of Meg Foster's taffeta petticoat was considered the last word in elegance, and the principal gratified the entire college by coming to see every one's finery, and by graciously pronouncing a blessing on the gaieties ahead.[109]

Entertainment

In-house entertainment on Saturday evenings for both staff and students was a tradition which lasted in women's teacher training colleges up to and beyond the Second World War. Students were not allowed out late in the evenings, except by special exeat, and Saturday nights was the time when the whole college family, as in the middle-class home, could relax together. Dancing was particularly popular. No men, of course were allowed into college on these occasions, and the 'sedate all-female dances'[110] evolved curious rituals which echoed the courtship customs of the middle-class home:

> On Saturday evening there were concerts and best of all dancing. In the 2nd year I had the privilege of taking a lecturer to the dance and called for her at her room. My favourite was Miss Glennie – she was very sweet. I always felt she had a soft spot for me and I certainly had for her.[111]

At Avery Hill students carried 'dainty' programmes to their dances and 'drew for partners' for the Affinity Waltz. There were courtship echoes too in Musical Arms for 'it was so much more exciting to rush for a Senior's "arm than for a chair"'.[112] In the 1920s, Bishop Otter, at a time when the mother/daughter discourse was being liberalized (see above), decided to make its dances more informal: 'A student still brings a lecturer down to dances and takes her back but between the first and last dance there is no booking . . . the "grab" system is now in vogue in place of booked programmes.'[113]

Avery Hill invented tradition by incorporating dancing into a ceremony to mark the passing of the generations: 'In 1929 a new ceremony – a Farewell Dance among the trees with fairy lights twinkling to the sound of Old Man River – seniors pass their badges of office to their successors.'[114]

'Theatricals'[115] always played a prominent role in the Saturday Evening Entertainments. At Homerton these occasions were attended by the principal in appropriate style and with hierarchies carefully observed:

> We had some kind of entertainment every Saturday evening arranged by the students (plays, sketches, country dancing etc.). Miss Allan attended most of them. She was given a special printed invitation each week by the Students Entertainment Committee and the Senior Student would escort her to the Gym where the entertainments were held.[116]

> She always wore evening dress. A Representative was assigned to accompany her, bringing a knee rug, a cushion and sometimes a box of chocolates.[117]

By the 1930s the Saturday Night Entertainment was beginning to flag. For Homerton students more opportunities had become available 'both in the town and at the University', providing 'a feast of education and entertainment'.[118] Earlier, attempts had been made to make the evenings 'as festive as possible by wearing evening dress' and inviting friends to attend.[119] More one-act plays were performed to 'allow a greater time for dancing'.[120] In 1935, for instance, students were 'charmed' with a miracle play *The Deluge* and a Jewish play *They went forth*.[121] But although the Committee had decided in 1934 that their function was to be 'an organ of real dramatic value', their first hypothesis that the committee 'was primarily to help College to fill up what would otherwise be a boring and unprofitable Saturday evening' seems to accord more with reality.[122]

Friendship

A universal comment on the training college experience is that it was a place where 'lifelong friendships were made'.[123] Avery Hill's historian recorded student friendships spanning the whole of the college's history. These ranged from the 'Inseparable Five' of pre-First World War days, 'who remained lifelong friends into the 1960s and 1970s' to the twelve students of 1949–51 vintage who were still holding informal meetings and exchanging letters in the mid-1980s.[124] Friendships between groups of students, as well as those between individuals, were an interesting feature of college life. Friendships were an extension of the colleges' family ideology, and just as daughters in the middle-class home progressed from relationships within the family to friendships outside the home, so at college students progressed from their 'mother's' care to friendships which they had chosen for themselves.[125]

A Homerton student, writing in the college magazine during the First World War drew attention to the transforming effect of students' relationships with each other:

> Very few girls can live in a College of two hundred students, and remain unchanged. Some shy retiring souls are enticed out of their retreat under the freshening influence of a sunshiny friend; by rubbing shoulders with their fellow students the obstreperous folk become less assertive and more pliant. Some gain in force of personality, and others lose, and yet others give away part of their old powers in exchange for new.[126]

Later in the same article she wonders how students will keep up with each other during the summer holidays. Interestingly, at this early date, friendship is constructed within the framework of the family system:

> 'Will the members of the College families be scattered broadcast up and down the country, or will they often meet together?' we ask. Then

we inquire what has been done by students of other years. Some circles of friends make a point of joining up once again for short holidays, while others keep in touch through the post.[127]

Residence in college was a great facilitator of friendship. A early day student at Avery Hill 'felt shut out from the communal life of college' and crucially that 'it was not so easy to make friends'.[128] Conversely, a Homerton student in the early 1940s, describing the overcrowding when Homerton was sharing its premises with Portsmouth Training College, shows how this enforced propinquity could lead to a lasting group friendship:

> Single rooms were made double, and we were put in the Rabbit Warren, at the top of ABC, three to a room. We were known as the Rabbits, and seemed to be called on fairly frequently to provide sketches or other entertainments at short notice, on Saturday evenings. We also had a gas fire – our only heat – so were very popular for drying hair. We were then reprimanded by Glennie (the deputy principal) for the size of the gas bill! The six of us are still in touch.[129]

Friendships were also forged in subject groups and during leisure activities. A group of four students, whom I interviewed when they re-visited Homerton together 'forty years on', had formed their friendship when they all specialized in divinity at college. Two of them went on to be head and deputy head at the same grammar school in Kent.[130] Twelve students from 1940–42 met through the Cambridge Inter-Collegiate Christian Union (three of them also met their husbands there). On leaving college they started to write to each other in 'round robin' fashion. These circulating letters, in which each member adds her news in turn, were still going strong when I interviewed the group in 1990.[131]

The ability to get on with fellow students was a central, if unstated, requirement of college life. In *First year up* the heroines Kit (Katherine), Jane and Alison 'rapidly became known as special friends', and they gathered around themselves an outer circle of lesser friends.[132] The novel also contained an interesting portrait of a student who was a misfit at college, and who did not relate well to her fellow students. Throughout the novel Grizelda is portrayed in a transgressive light. She stole students' exeats, dismissed the end of term college entertainment with scorn, and, most crucially of all, was revealed, in spite of her pretensions, to have a mother who was of inferior social class.[133] Eventually she tells Kit that she never wanted to go to training college, but was desperate to get away from home. She 'loathes' children and would like to be a fabric and dress designer.[134] Clearly the victim of poor career advice, she was nevertheless condemned because she offended against the college's corporate ethic – 'She had given nothing to college and college promptly forgot her'.[135]

Reunions provided, and still provide, additional opportunities for friend-ship groups to meet together within a college's extended family. At Homerton it is a tradition for such groups to target particular anniversaries – twenty-five, forty, or even fifty years on. The re-living of college experi-ences and the sharing of memories is additional proof of the lifelong significance of the 'friendships that have lasted all these years'.[136]

3 The role of woman principal

Her rendering of 'Stern daughter of the voice of God' said it all.[1]

In Chapter 2 I drew attention to the woman principal's role as both father and mother of the institutional family she served. In this chapter I shall examine this role in more depth, paying particular attention to her public and professional persona.

Principals' private emotional and sexual needs will be discussed in Chapter 5. I shall first provide a theoretical framework and then illustrate this from the experience of the three colleges which provide the central evidence in my story – Bishop Otter, Avery Hill and Homerton. (Brief sketches of the two male principals will also be included.)

Heward has argued that the appointment of women principals in the early twentieth century, to replace the clerical principals of the nineteenth, was both a question of government policy and of professional authority. The small but growing number of women graduates were now able 'to claim professional authority on the basis of academic qualifications'.[2] The Board of Education, for its part, was concerned to reduce the power of the Church of England and its clergy in training colleges. In 1909 the Board introduced a new regulation which legitimated the professional role of women and particularly that of woman principal in the training college:

> In view of the large number of questions arising in the administration of Training Colleges confined to women students that are best dealt with by women and the large number of capable women now available for such posts, the Board will in future require that vacancies occurring in the headships of such colleges shall be filled by women.[3]

Avery Hill and Homerton, as we shall see, anticipated the Board's new regulation. But the reluctance of Bishop Otter to appoint a woman principal in 1919, although the first principal of the college had been a woman, showed the necessity for a statutory ruling on the matter.

The role of woman principal was always problematic. If the college was organized as a family, the principal, as its head, must of necessity take on the role of a strong, powerful and authoritative father. But this paternal role was always intersected and sometimes interrupted by principals' maternal and feminine concerns. For the enforcement, by her own example and precept, of the college's culture of femininity was bound to conflict with a patriarchal style of leadership. Principals attempted to solve this conflict by dividing their lives into public and private spheres. On public occasions they would adopt the role of a powerful authoritative father; privately they could show maternal concern for both staff and students.

Each principal had to make her own resolution of these conflicting discourses of masculinity and femininity, gender and power. Some principals were able to soften the masculine discourse of their public role with feminine concerns and interests. Other principals preferred to separate the public from the private as sharply as possible. Their exercise of public power made as few concessions as possible to the normative constraints of femininity. I would argue that no woman principal achieved an entirely satisfactory resolution of this conflict. The period which Steedman has called the 'fragile hegemony of women principals'[4] was a transitional one, bridging the narrow authoritarianism of nineteenth-century male principals and the full professionalism of women principals in the late twentieth century.

Principals carved out their new position by developing the traditional feminine and maternal role of service to others. Service to one's own family was translated outwards into a wider and institutional sphere. The crucial difference was that women principals wielded, in their colleges, the ultimate authority and power which in the family belonged to the father. Principals established their authority with a sense of vocation and dedication, which was often expressed in religious terms. By expressing this authority in a spiritual language of idealism and service, these principals were again using a traditional feminine discourse for a wider purpose. Other principals, no less dedicated to the service of their colleges, followed a more male pattern of autocratic rule, which needed no external justification for its legitimacy. In contrast to their male predecessors, women principals were always resident in the colleges they served. Residence allowed them to maintain constant vigilance and control over all aspects of college life. Vigilance could sometimes degenerate into feminine 'fussing', but more importantly it allowed principals to monitor closely the academic, social and cultural standards on which the college's reputation depended. Similarly, the comparative frequency of principals' enforced retirement through ill-health could be interpreted as a resort to a traditional female strategy when faced with a difficult situation. In fact, however, the complete dedication and constant vigilance required of women principals inevitably took their toll, and this could lead to real physical breakdown and emotional exhaustion. Principals' backgrounds and education varied greatly, and it was often difficult, especially in the early days, for colleges to make suitable appointments.

Some principals were women of outstanding ability who found in this new career a satisfying and all-absorbing outlet for their talents. For some, a charismatic personality greatly facilitated the exercise of their principalship. Certainly, the success or otherwise of a college depended very largely on the principal's performance.

The power which principals enjoyed within their institutions was very great – but it was a power which was inoperable outside the narrow confines of the training college world. This circumscription of power was both a strength and a weakness. It allowed women of outstanding ability an absorbing and dedicated life which, although outside a family context, was officially sanctioned. But the narrowness of the teacher training world and its invisibility to the public gaze encouraged stagnation and resistance to change. It also discouraged principals from developing a true professionalism which would have allowed them to step outside the training college into positions of authority and power in the outside world. By the 1950s the ethos and practice of women's training colleges were seen as increasingly outmoded, both by their own students and by the outside world. Women principals found it difficult to adapt to changing social and sexual mores, which contradicted many of the ideals of the culture of femininity established so successfully by their predecessors. The days of the women's training college were numbered and with it the fragile hegemony of their principals.

Bishop Otter College

Fanny Trevor (1873–95)

When Bishop Otter re-opened as a women's college in 1873, it took the then highly unusual step of appointing a woman as 'Lady Principal'. Fanny Trevor, described as a 'gentlewoman' of independent means, was, in spite of her lack of formal educational qualifications, a woman of outstanding ability. But the conditions of her appointment, and her subsequent treatment by the college governors, denied her the complete authority which later women principals were to enjoy. Trevor was appointed at a salary of £100 per annum – a salary which initially she declined to accept. Such altruism was not unknown in these early days. Margaret Stansfield, for instance, founder and first principal of Bedford Physical Training College, in 1903 bought, with her own money, the house which was to provide the college's first home.[5] Trevor's altruism did nothing to enhance her authority. For not only did the governors award the college's chaplain a salary of £120 per annum – £20 more than the principal's notional stipend – but they extended his duties beyond the chapel to include responsibility for the college's finances and all its correspondence. Later the principal's authority was still further undermined when the chaplain was given entire responsibility for students' religious instruction.[6]

The governors were eventually obliged to accept that the success of the college was in 'great measure' due to Trevor's 'invaluable services';[7] but this lukewarm tribute only underlined their customary dismissive attitude:

> It must have made great demands on the patience and tact of an able and honorary Lady Principal to lead the academic work of the college while being obliged to defer in many respects to a chaplain ... who had less nominal authority but more real power.[8]

Trevor's position was acknowledged nationally when she was asked in 1886 to give evidence before the Royal Commission to Enquire into the Working of the Elementary Education Acts (the Cross Commission).[9] Her evidence shows that, even at this early date, the promotion of a middle-class culture of femininity in training colleges was the deliberate policy of women principals. Trevor's encouragement of middle-class girls to train as teachers, and her forthright condemnation of the pupil–teacher system, were couched in terms of educational efficiency, but her evidence also revealed her central concern with social class and middle-class values:

> *Commissioner* You find that they [pupil–teachers] are less intelligent than those who come in from the other classes, not being pupil–teachers?
>
> *Trevor* It is difficult to find the right word, they are less receptive ... we cannot do much with them, they go out very nearly as they came in, beyond having learnt a little more by cram ...
>
> *Commissioner* I suppose you are aware that a very large proportion of the pupil teachers come from educated and good homes?
>
> *Trevor* I think not. I think a very small proportion. My experience is quite in the opposite direction.
>
> *Commissioner* You object, I see, to the pupil–teacher system entirely?
>
> *Trevor* Entirely ... and I think that any parents of better position would do everything they could to hinder their children from going through the drudgery of pupil–teachership.[10]

Trevor's insistence, moreover, on the importance of denominational teaching in training colleges was expressed in terms of the familial values of the middle-class home.

> *Commissioner* Have you a strong opinion as to whether it is wise to have denominational teaching for those who are going to teach the youth of the country?
>
> *Trevor* I do not think so much of that, as that it is necessary when you are living in a household that you should all be of one mind in the house ... we are like a family.[11]

It was entirely in keeping with the governors' attitude to Trevor that no reference was made in the college's official records either to the Cross Commission itself, or to their own principal's pioneering and influential role in its proceedings.[12]Trevor resigned as principal in 1895. The college's annual report recorded cryptically that 'the reasons assigned to Miss Trevor for her resignation were such that they could not ask her to continue in office',[13] but it is likely that her most compelling reason was the continuing undermining of her authority by the duties assigned to the college chaplain.

Edwin Hammonds (1897–1919)

The problem of the principal's authority at Bishop Otter was eventually solved in 1897, when the college appointed a male, non-resident clerical principal and placed all authority in his hands. The Rev. Edwin Hammonds was to prove a popular and energetic principal for the next twenty-two years. But his paternalistic and patriarchal attitude to the students, and his lack of concern both with new developments in other training colleges and with wider educational matters, meant that by the end of his principalship the college was falling behind best contemporary practice. When Hammonds finally retired in 1919, the college governors, much against their will, were obliged by a Board of Education ruling[14] to appoint a woman principal to succeed him. They chose Florence Johnson, an Oxford MA, who was vice-principal of Furzedown Training College in London.[15]

Florence Johnson (1919–30)

So much is owed by so many to this great lady.[16]

This tribute, by a former student, reflected Johnson's charismatic personality and the universal esteem in which she was held. Blessed with great charm and good looks (see Figure 3.1), she was able to temper the exercise of her masculine authority and command with a feminine warmth and sense of fun.[17] The central concern of her principalship was the need to raise the standing of the college by the promotion of the highest academic standards and cultural enrichment for her students. But equally important for Johnson was the nourishing of the ideals of service to others, and mutual commitment, on which the college as a women's community depended.

Johnson set about raising the college's academic standards by giving preference to those entrants who had the highest academic qualifications. Like Trevor before her, but unlike Hammonds, she gave preference to students who had completed a full secondary education, rather than to those who had served an apprenticeship as a pupil or student teacher.[18] The status of the staff was raised by changing their title to 'lecturer' from the now obsolete 'governess'. Johnson also encouraged more specialization in the

Florence Johnson

Photograph taken by S. Westaway.

Figure 3.1 Florence Johnson, Principal of Bishop Otter College, 1919–30.
Source: Courtesy of University College, Chichester.

curriculum with the far-sighted aim to equip students 'to move onto a University degree after college'.[19]

Johnson's personal authority was never in doubt, and she was always prepared to 'fight for what she wanted'.[20] This included the maintenance of her own standards of domestic femininity. She was not happy with the living accommodation which had been allocated to her. In Hammonds' day it had belonged to the Lady Superintendent – a post which Johnson had now re-styled 'Matron' to indicate its domestic responsibilities.[21] Johnson asked the chairman of the Council to install a bathroom for her. His reply revealed the grudging reluctance with which the college's clerical trustees conceded an appropriate status to their woman principal: '"The Lady super-intendent never had a bath," he growled. "Why does she want one? Oh well let her have it."'[22]

Johnson spoke 'little of her religious conviction',[23] and it is noticeable that during her principalship the *Bishop Otter College Magazine* devoted far less space to the college chapel than it had in either of her predecessors' time. Rather, Johnson expressed her religious faith in her dedication to the service of the college – a service which, she told students at the end of her principalship, 'has been a joy indeed'.[24] She encouraged students to work with her in this service, and to come together within the community 'in the spirit of St. Francis'.[25] In 1929 a window was dedicated to St Francis in the college's old common room (significantly, not in the chapel). Money for the window was subscribed by all those students 'who brought to their college life something of the spirit of Franciscan fellowship'.[26]

An ethic of service required students to develop 'a greater sense of respon-sibility'.[27] Johnson encouraged this by moving the college away from a practice which was acknowledged to be 'reminiscent of schooldays' towards one that promoted individual responsibility and greater maturity. College matters were now discussed by students at open meetings, and the 'police duties' of prefects were abolished.[28] Importantly, friendships between first and second years were facilitated by the abolition of the 'slavery' of an exces-sively rigid interpretation of the mother/daughter discourse (see Chapter 2). Not all her reforms were well received by the more conservative of her students, especially if they concerned religious observance. When, for instance, she decreed that 'it was not necessary to wear a hat in chapel' it proved 'difficult' at first to get girls to follow'.[29] Johnson's 'youthful outlook' startled some students. It allowed her, however, to relate to them on matters of mutual feminine concern, e.g. an interest in clothes. Beautifully dressed herself, and a skilled dressmaker – students even remembered the silk suit the principal wore at a post-war reunion – she also 'noticed and took great interest in what students wore'.[30] The exercise of this quintessentially feminine discourse, on equal terms between principal and students, was unusual. Johnson's charismatic personality gave her the confidence to relate to students in this feminine way, without fear that it would compromise the masculine authority of her public role.

For all her ability, charm and warmth, Johnson remains an enigmatic figure. In 1930 she took the 'difficult decision' to leave Chichester and return to London as principal of another Church of England Training College, St Gabriel's, Kennington. She held this post until her retirement in 1943.[31] Although Johnson spoke of how 'hard it is to brace myself to a new venture' and others referred to 'the intrinsic sacrifice the principal is making',[32] she had never been really happy in Chichester. It was common knowledge that she 'missed city life in London',[33] and throughout her principalship she would refer delicately to the cultural drawbacks of 'the little Cathedral city'.[34] Her resentment of the Chichester clerical establishment must also have influenced her decision, as was her desire to live nearer her sister Mary. Johnson continued, however, to cross swords with the clerical establishment even after her move to St Gabriel's, as the Bishop of Peterborough, chairman of St Gabriel's governors, revealed at her memorial service. 'He admitted he had not always seen eye to eye with Miss Johnson but although she was 19 years older than him she was always far less square.'[35]

Johnson always kept in touch with Bishop Otter and she attended most of the Chichester reunions; St Gabriel's, in turn, became Bishop Otter's 'London home'.[36] We have no evidence of Johnson's private emotional life. But it is likely that her life-long devotion to her sister, who was an artist, gave her the emotional support which enabled her not only to do 'magnificent work',[37] but to be so 'well loved' by her students.[38]

Elsie Bazeley (1930–5)

By the 1930s, there were more women than earlier in the century well qualified to become women principals. All the six candidates shortlisted, from a field of twenty-two, to succeed Florence Johnson were university graduates; three held university or training college lectureships; one was vice-principal of a training college; and one taught divinity at a well-known girls' public school. Elsie Bazeley, an Oxford science graduate, had taught at three schools before taking up a lectureship at Whitelands Training College. She then became principal of three training colleges in succession – Warrington, Sunderland and the Home and Colonial, before accepting her current post as a lecturer in education at King's College, University of London.[39] Bazeley did not immediately accept Bishop Otter's offer of the principalship. With a confidence befitting the rising status of women principals, she told the College Council that she had already been shortlisted for an inspectorship with the London County Council, and that she would accept that post if she were offered it. Bishop Otter agreed to hold the principalship open for her, and their patience was rewarded when a month later Bazeley withdrew her application to the London County Council.[40]

Like her predecessor, Bazeley was an attractive woman who dressed well. Her official photograph (see Figure 3.2) can be read as emblematic of the

Figure 3.2 Elsie Bazeley, Principal of Bishop Otter College, 1930–5.
Source: Courtesy of University College, Chichester.

woman principal's dual role. The principal's private femininity was displayed both in the embroidered jacket which she wore over her plain blouse and skirt, and also in the small vase of flowers which she had placed on her working desk. Conversely, the official files which she is shown to be consulting and the presence on her desk of a telephone bore witness to the masculine authority of her public role. Bazeley came to Bishop Otter with 'a high reputation for her knowledge and support for new methods of education'.[41] She was particularly concerned that students 'should understand the children we have to teach'. Consequently, the study of child development, drawing on the new insights of psychological research, became a central focus in students' study. Soon after Bazeley arrived in Chichester, she was able to use her extensive connections in the educational world to host a conference at which the recently published second Hadow report (on primary education) was discussed. The distinguished delegates included Sir Henry Hadow himself.[42]

In emphasizing a child-centred approach to teacher training, Bazeley was bringing Bishop Otter into line with advanced contemporary practice. She likened the training college to a 'workshop' rather than an academic institution, and stressed that as students now came straight from the sixth form it was 'not quite so necessary to concentrate on high level scholarship'.[43] Bazeley's model of the college as a workshop should not, however, be interpreted as a return to narrow vocationalism. Rather, like Johnson before her, she was concerned that students should develop themselves not only by academic study but in service to others. Bazeley's concept of service reached beyond the college community to include those, and especially children, less fortunate than students themselves. In 1932 she opened a play centre in the college grounds for local children 'especially those living in tin huts at the bottom of College Lane'.[44] Here students could apply their theoretical studies of child development in a practical fashion. In her concern for disadvantaged children, Bazeley, like her contemporary Freda Hawtrey at Avery Hill (see below), was employing a feminine discourse as part of her public masculine role. Although her concern for children's welfare was not as overwhelming as Hawtrey's, it was nevertheless central to Bazeley's interpretation of the principal's role.

Bazeley's principalship was cut short when, after less than four years in post, she developed cancer. She had already been in pain for some time when she went into the Middlesex Hospital in August 1934.[45] In June the following year she applied for sick leave and this leave was later extended to Easter 1936.[46] In March 1936 she resigned as principal, and a month later she was dead.[47] Bazeley's illness sadly undermined her performance as principal. In her own words 'although we do everything we can to keep our standards up', she was clearly finding it difficult to perform her customary leadership role. Crucially, in her inability to interview all candidates personally, she was failing to ensure that middle-class standards of femininity were maintained: 'I am more determined than ever to interview all candidates before admission. Two students at present were not interviewed. One has a malformation of the mouth so she does not speak clearly. One never stops talking.'[48]

Bazeley's final message to her students poignantly revealed not only her exhaustion but the centrality to her principalship of her maternal concern for the children her students taught:

> Miss Westaway [Acting Principal] has to go to School Practice and my brain is now exhausted, so we say goodbye and love to you all. Our purpose is I suppose, to become not pure pedagogues but friends and guides to the children.[49]

Dorothy Meads (1936–47)

The rising status of women principals was further confirmed by the appointment of Doctor Dorothy Meads to succeed Elsie Bazeley as principal of Bishop Otter. Meads' high academic status was matched by her extensive training college experience, which had included a lectureship at the Diocesan College, Brighton, and her current position of senior tutor at Crewe Training College.[50] Bishop Otter trawled widely in its search for a new principal. It advertised the appointment three times in the *The Times*, the *Daily Telegraph*, the *Guardian*, *The Times Educational Supplement* and the *Church Times*, with the offer of an attractive salary of £600 (rising to £750 per annum). From thirty-one applicants the selection committee, which included two women, drew up a long list of seven. This was eventually whittled down to three and Meads was chosen after a ballot.[51]

The relationship between the college and the cathedral establishment had improved with the elevation of Bishop Bell to the Chichester See. Bell took his duties as chairman of Bishop Otter's Council more seriously than his predecessors,[52] and he was particularly helpful during the difficult wartime period, when the college was evacuated to Bromley (see below). Meads continued her predecessor's policy of underpinning the academic and cultural enrichment of college life with an ethic of service to others. But Meads' concept of service was more intense than Bazeley's and was informed by a devotional austerity which was religious in origin. Her constant concern, for instance, that students should have a 'sense of vocation' and be prepared for 'sacrifice of self' prompted her warnings against the hedonistic values of contemporary society: 'All is artificially and gaudily lit . . . and the Scenic Railway desecrates England's Day of Rest.'[53]

Nevertheless Meads was remembered for her friendliness and vitality.[54] Austere in her personal habits, she, nevertheless, enjoyed taking trips in her Baby Austin car[55] and was devoted to her two small dogs (see Figure 3.3). Meads was to need all her vitality and courage when, in August 1942, at the height of the Second World War, she received the following 'urgent' telephone call: 'Can you come to Bromley tomorrow? We are going to lose

Figure 3.3 Dorothy Meads, Principal of Bishop Otter College, 1936–47.
Source: Courtesy of University College, Chichester.

the College in Chichester. It must be given up in the interests of the war.'[56] This was Meads's first knowledge of the decision which was to have such a drastic and deleterious effect on her own life. The Air Ministry had requisitioned the Bishop Otter site for the planning of D-Day. As a consequence, and without consulting the principal, it had been decided that the college should move near London, to the Old Bishop's Palace in Bromley. It was ironic that Stockwell Training College had been evacuated from the same site earlier in the war to a place of greater safety.[57] Meads had accepted this lack of prior consultation without comment at the time, but her loss of control over subsequent events was seriously to undermine her confidence in the authority of her public role.

The college moved to Bromley in the autumn of 1942 and almost immediately Meads went into hospital for a 'serious operation'. Bishop Bell found the time for frequent visits to Bromley, 'in spite of his heavy commitments elsewhere'.[58] At first the principal could report that everyone was 'playing up well'[59] but the strain of the 'very difficult conditions' soon began to tell on her health and composure. The college was obliged to share its premises with a Rest Centre for the homeless and wounded, and broken nights and air-raids made study difficult. Nevertheless, in spite of these difficulties, both students and staff continued to serve the wider community; they were largely responsible for organizing and staffing the Rest Centre, as well as helping in the local youth clubs and at the hospital.[60] Students were well aware that 'the principal wants them not only to be good teachers but useful in society'. This obligation was, however, lightened for students by their improved recreational facilities, due to Bromley's proximity to London.[61] But for Meads the continuing stress severely undermined her morale: 'I have felt as though the college was disintegrating. I am powerless to retain domestic staff and I cannot maintain a religious atmosphere.'[62] It is interesting that Meads uses the word 'powerless' in this context. For whatever the circumstances, principals were always aware of the masculine power discourse they needed to employ in their public role. For Meads the 'disintegration' of the college, as she saw it, was particularly stressful because she could no longer maintain the 'religious atmosphere' which was so central to her ethic of service.

By September 1944 the Rest Centre had taken up all available teaching space at Bromley, and the college was forced to move again, this time to the congenial surroundings of Lady Margaret Hall, Oxford. A year later, at the end of the war, the college finally returned to Chichester.[63] Now that the wartime crisis was over Meads was relieved that she could 'look back with a considerably better sense of proportion at the experiences which befell the College in Bromley'. Recognizing the need, in the changed post-war world, to give students more responsibility for running the college, she set up a Joint Committee of Management, representing both staff and students.[64] But Meads' confidence and health had been fatally undermined by her war-time experience, and although she tried valiantly to cope with the practical difficulties of the post-war years, and particularly with the necessity to repair buildings ravaged by their wartime occupancy, the task was too much for her. Querulous complaining began to replace her positive commitment to service: 'Many obstacles hampered our efforts to make the college speedily habitable once more. At first there was pleasure in their overthrow, but later the fatigue and irritation engendered by frustration and the deadly monotony of steady overwork went far to kill all the pleasure.'[65]

A year later Meads was forced to resign through serious illness.[66] She admitted that she was worn out with 'the gadfly of bureaucratic control, which accords ill with the ideal of Freedom, which had stimulated us in the war'.[67] Quite literally, she had 'sacrificed herself to her work'.[68] Her last years were 'extremely sad' and when she died eleven years later the college 'could only be thankful that she had been released from suffering.'[69]

Elisabeth Murray (1948–70)

> Miss Murray was the first principal of the college since Miss Trevor, seventy-six years before, who had not come from another training college; but she brought to Bishop Otter valuable experience of the academic and residential standards of Girton, of Ashbourne Hall, University of Manchester and of Somerville College, Oxford.[70]

With the appointment of Elisabeth Murray as principal, in the difficult post-war period, Bishop Otter was reverting to an older tradition, which seemed to many of those concerned to be anachronistic, even unprofessional. For Murray had no experience of the training college world and had never taught in school. From an academic background – her grandfather James Murray had been editor of the *Oxford English Dictionary* – she obtained a degree in history at Somerville College, Oxford, in 1931; she then embarked on historical and archaeological research. In 1934 she was appointed tutor-warden of Ashbourne College, University of Manchester. She left Manchester after two years to return to research work in Oxford, and in the early years of the Second World War was appointed Assistant Tutor and Registrar of Girton College, Cambridge. She remained at Girton until her appointment to the principalship of Bishop Otter in 1948 (see Figure 3.4).[71]

Murray's strengths and experience lay in the maintainance of the traditions and practices of corporate life and in upholding the middle-class values of the culture of femininity. It was her achievement that she maintained these traditions throughout her time at Bishop Otter, which spanned the coming of the three-year course, and the introduction of men students. The details of her appointment, which are well documented, reveal the reasons why her appointment caused anxiety. For her attitude at interview appeared cavalier, and she seemed unconcerned at her lack of professional expertise. Nevertheless, her university and collegiate experience, her

Figure 3.4 Elisabeth Murray, Principal of Bishop Otter College, 1948–70.

Source: Otter Memorial Paper, *Flints, Ports, Otters and Threads* (1998), courtesy of University College, Chichester.

academic qualifications, and the crucial support of the chairman of the governors, Bishop Bell, awarded her the job:

> The college received 22 applicants, and seven aspirants were invited for the initial interview. 'I wore', wrote Miss Murray later, 'my green "kitchen equipment" outfit for the interview and was just about as green myself – it did not help my displaying a total ignorance of the recently published McNair Report'. By the time of the final selection, however, the Report had been read and Miss Murray had some knowledge about what faced the College – although staff were less sure of what faced them. 'Bishop Bell', recorded Miss Murray, 'had consulted the staff as to which candidate they would prefer. They were not enthusiastic about either: my rival had dropped her cup of tea and smashed it, and I had shown eccentricity in declaring that I never drank tea or coffee' [*Murray autobiograpical notes*]. But Bishop Bell's view, the wish to appoint a candidate from a university, triumphed – although not, as one suspects he might have hoped, by a unanimous decision, Council voting 13 to 5 in Miss Murray's favour [*minutes of College Council*]. What was of issue, of course, was not Miss Murray's knowledge of universities, but her limited experience of schools and, more importantly, lack of experience in training teachers.[72]

It was as well that future members of Murray's staff did not know her opinion of school teachers, recorded in 1933. They display a disdain which was typical of upper middle-class attitudes at the time:

> Really one wonders how these people get their jobs. One looks as if she came off a chocolate box and has an awful affected simpering manner – like a cinema heroine . . . I never did see such a collection of aged and halt and dull females, each one I am introduced to is worse than the last.[73]

Nevertheless, in spite of these seemingly unhelpful attitudes, Murray's 'energy and vision transformed the college'.[74] She presided over an extensive building programme, including the replacement of dormitory accommodation with individual student bedrooms. Her concern with 'the furnishing and decor for these new rooms',[75] reflected not only her interest in art, which I shall discuss in Chapter 4, but also the importance which she gave to creating middle-class standards of domesticity in college. Murray also 'had the humility to know there were gaps to be filled' in her expertise, appointing, for instance, experienced staff to cover 'the school aspect of teacher training'.[76] Her ability to know from the first every student's name and background was legendary,[77] as was her enthusiasm for, and participation in, the college's corporate life:

The College was small enough for people to know each other, and to live in community. Miss Murray took part in corporate events, as College dances, the Chapel service, the Chichester Gala, where her ancient bicycle might be found waiting to see the student float pass by.[78]

It was usual for women students in training college to see the principal as a remote and austere figure. One student at Bishop Otter remembered the principal in her public masculine role as head of the college:

I lived in awe of Miss Murray, and usually felt on edge and uncomfortable in her presence . . . she seemed a remote and very austere Principal (with her angular frame topped with hair parted in the centre and drawn tightly into a bun).

Interestingly this same student, after she left college, developed 'a real friendship' with the principal.[79] Other students also recorded the difference between the principal's austere public persona at college, and her friendliness in the private sphere after they had left: 'Once I had left College and returned for Otter Reunions and other special occasions, I have found it easier to converse with her.'[80] 'Over the years, whether I have called unexpectedly or by arrangement, I have always been warmly greeted and made most welcome.'[81]

It was a male student, towards the end of Murray's principalship, who drew attention to the importance of the principal's aloof persona in maintaining her masculine control of the college:

For me the lady remains an enigma. The Vice-Principal, it was asserted, 'dealt with the men'. There are those who can speak of individual acts of kindness on Miss Murray's part but, paradoxically, it was the aloofness and austerity of her demeanour which ensured that her will and her regime prevailed.[82]

Murray set great store on the maintenance of all aspects of middle-class femininity, and this was usually appreciated by students. The requirement, for instance, that all students should have private interviews with the principal 'in which we had to make all the conversation' although reckoned 'a great trial', was nevertheless recognized as 'an excellent lesson for life ahead'.[83] Murray was normally careless about her everyday appearance, but she recognized the importance of appropriate dress for formal occasions:

On special occasions she would dress very carefully, almost richly, another sign, perhaps, of her pleasure in beautiful things; though it was probably more to do with her sense of a duty to uphold standards, even some unfashionable ones.[84]

Curiously, in view of the importance of the family metaphor in college she moved swiftly to 'stamp out' the system of 'mothers and daughters'. She was not entirely successful in this, and the system lingered on until the advent of men students in the 1960s.[85] Possibly Murray considered the system immature and inimical to the wider social and cultural values she was seeking to emphasize in the college.

The private needs of Murray's femininity can only be glimpsed. Sheila McCririck, lecturer in art and a close friend, characterized 'her more private side' as 'naïve and intuitive'. She was much influenced by her elder brothers and her academic inheritance.[86] She was 'a devout churchwoman',[87] and the chapel was central to her college life. Throughout her principalship she attended morning service in the chapel, escorted by the president of the Students' Union.[88] As befitted her role as principal of a church college, and like her predecessors in office, her service to the college was an expression of her religious faith, which she expected the whole college community to share: 'All the rich experience of two years here is of little lasting significance unless it bears fruit in life and the quality of the fruit depends upon the strength of the College as a worshipping community.'[89]

Later in her principalship she was worried by the introduction of programmes to extend students' social and personal skills. She disliked the secular ethic of these programmes – no mention was made of 'the fruits of the spirit' or 'the love of God'. This episode was also an example of the difficulties which Murray encountered when forced in the 1960s to move from the sheltered life of the women's college, to adjust to the changed climate of the co-educational college.

After her retirement Murray devoted her energies to writing a biography of her grandfather, and to a number of cultural, ecclesiastical and archaeological activities in the Chichester area. Agnes Sibley, Murray's old friend and academic colleague came to live with her, when Sibley retired in 1974. This was a close and supportive relationship, and when Sibley died in 1979 Murray's loss was acknowledged to have 'diminished' her vitality.[90] Murray died in 1998, at the age of 88. Her obituary in *The Times*[91] complete with a picture not only of Murray herself but, significantly, one of her grandfather surrounded by his editorial team – devoted only one paragraph to her work at Bishop Otter. This would seem to be in keeping with Murray's own estimate in 1989 of the place in her life of her principalship at Bishop Otter: 'I feel that what I have done in retirement is what I would wish to be remembered by rather than anything I did at Manchester or Cambridge and most of what I did at Bishop Otter.'[92]

Avery Hill College

The first two years: 1906–8

An inauspicious beginning.[93]

We have seen at Bishop Otter that ill-health was a common problem for women principals. At Avery Hill, no fewer than five different women were to guide the college in its difficult first two years, and the first three resigned within the college's first year.

Mary Bentinck Smith (1906–7)

Mary Bentinck Smith was selected as the college's first principal from a field of ten applicants. Bentinck Smith, who held a first class degree and a doctorate, was currently director of studies at Girton College, Cambridge and lecturer in medieval and modern languages. Previously she had taught at Royal Holloway College, London. But first-class academic credentials were not necessarily a sufficient qualification for the principalship of a newly established teacher training institution. Lacking experience of teachers in training, Bentinck Smith expected students to reach academic standards more appropriate to university undergraduates. Moreover, her lack of administrative experience was severely tested by the LCC's last minute decision to increase the number of students admitted in the college's first term. To add to her troubles four matrons came and went in the first year.

Nevertheless, in spite of these difficulties, Bentinck Smith established good traditions at Avery Hill. Unlike Bishop Otter and Homerton, most of the college's first students lived out. The principal, recognizing the importance of residence in establishing the college's corporate life, successfully persuaded the governors to provide more residential accommodation within college. Her efforts to raise academic standards included banishing knitting and sewing from the library and holding Sunday evening poetry readings in her own rooms. Importantly, and radically, she encouraged students to run their own affairs. Unlike Homerton, for instance, students elected their own senior student and prefects. This early training in leadership and democracy fostered a student body, which was more politically and socially aware than at most training colleges.[94]

1907–8

Bentinck Smith was taken ill in February 1907 and resigned, only six months after taking office. The college's science lecturer, D. A. C. Marshall was appointed acting principal, but after only a month she too was taken ill. Nor was the fate of the college's second principal, A. B. Collier any happier. For within three months, in spite of a promising beginning, she too was taken ill and forced to resign. It could be argued that these women were using a well-sanctioned feminine strategy to retreat from an impossible situation. With the college at crisis point, the LCC was forced to mount a rescue operation, and assign one of its own staff – Phillipa Fawcett – to become acting principal.

Phillipa Fawcett, daughter of Henry Fawcett, Gladstone's blind Post-Master General, and Millicent Fawcett, the suffragists' leader, had had an outstanding career at Newnham College, Cambridge. Her placement above the Senior Wrangler in the Mathematics Tripos was a landmark in women's long and difficult progress to win full recognition from the university. Perhaps surprisingly for one so gifted academically, Fawcett chose a career in educational administration. As principal assistant in the LCC's education department in charge of secondary schools and teacher training, she was admirably qualified to undertake the task of restoring morale and confidence at Avery Hill.[95] Fawcett was popular with the students who found her 'kind and capable'.[96] She was also very effective – 'When we were a ship without a rudder, she pulled us through'.[97] When a new principal was appointed in the summer of 1908, the college with its morale restored, could look to its future with increasing confidence.

Emily Maria Julian (1908–22)

Not the least of Phillipa Fawcett's services to Avery Hill was her crucial influence over the appointment of the college's third principal. After the traumas of the past two years, the LCC's Education Committee was seriously concerned lest the principalship was too onerous for a woman. Fawcett was able to persuade the committee that now the college's administrative structure had been reformed, and, crucially, that the principal had been freed from domestic responsibilities, this was no longer the case. Nevertheless, the closeness of the vote (12 to 11) showed that the appointment was far from uncontroversial. Nor was the actual choice uncontested. The LCC initially offered the post to Miss Hughes, the 35-year-old headmistress of the Colston Girls' School, Bristol. Miss Hughes declined the offer, and, after a second set of interviews, the post was offered to Emily Julian. At the initial interviews Julian had only received six votes to Hughes' twenty-eight.

It is likely that Julian's age – she was nearly 50 when appointed – had been seen as a drawback. Otherwise, although she did not have the academic distinction of Bentinck Smith, she was well qualified for the post. With a Cambridge degree and a solid teaching career behind her, she was currently headmistress of Tunbridge Wells High School for Girls. She had had no experience of teacher training, but the qualities of toughness, firmness and stability, which she had shown as a headmistress, were to prove equally effective at Avery Hill.[98]

Julian built on the foundations which had been laid down by Bentinck Smith. She understood the need to enhance students' academic and cultural

Figure 3.5 Emily Maria Julian, Principal of Avery Hill College, 1908–22.
Source: Courtesy of the University of Greenwich.

experience within the corporate and feminine framework of college life. Physically she was a tall, statuesque woman, with a dignity which commanded respect (see Figure 3.5). Under her leadership Avery Hill acquired a well-qualified and dedicated graduate staff. The crucial post of vice-principal was filled from within by Edith Waterhouse, mistress of method. Waterhouse was later to move to Homerton[99] where she became, as we shall see, closely attached to the principal, Mary Allan. Julian also did all she could to encourage cultural and artistic appreciation among the students. At the summer reunion in 1909, she welcomed former students' gift of pictures and expressed the hope that a tradition had been set 'until the bare walls of the Dining Hall are filled with things of precious beauty'.[100]

Julian was able to temper her dignity with flexibility and humour. One student reported that, although Julian was vigilant in maintaining standards of behaviour – she herself was reprimanded by Julian for laughing too loudly at meal times – the senior student was able to negotiate with the principal 'to get rid of some of the tedious rules'.[101] Another student recalled an incident when local villagers had objected to students sleeping outside in the hot weather 'on mattresses in flannelette nighties. The principal told the villagers not to look'.[102] Of Julian's private and inner life we have little evidence. It is likely, however, that as a woman already in middle age when she became principal, her private life would have been established outside the college context. One student gave intriguing evidence that Julian was a supporter of the suffragettes. Such support was not, of course, respectable behaviour for middle-class women, let alone the principal of a training college. Consequently this feminist, let alone feminine, discourse could only be safely expressed in coded terms: 'Our Edwardian upbringing by Victorian parents bade us view so unfeminine a movement with prim disgust even when the principal appeared at lunch with green and purple tie.[103] Later we changed.'[104]

Julian had the confidence and *savoir faire* to indicate a subversive feminist discourse without disturbing the masculine authority of her public role. Her life as principal was dedicated to the college. She was concerned to maintain and foster links among former students and would travel long distances to attend regional reunions.[105] Ever mindful of the college's financial needs, and as a keen gardener herself, she encouraged the sale of produce from the college estate on the local market.[106]

Avery Hill, with its proximity to London, was deeply affected by the 'realities' of the First World War. Julian showed her leadership qualities, combining both the masculine and feminine sides of the principal's role, throughout this difficult time. During the air-raids she ordered both staff and students to shelter in the cellars. She herself, on the other hand, kept watch on the open roof, refusing all company with the words – 'You must go down, my dear, its much too dangerous for you up here.'[107] When the armistice was declared in November 1918, she allowed students to go up to London to join in the celebrations, and, far from reprimanding late returners, she invited them to join her for a cup of coffee.[108] She also showed unusual and unconventional understanding, when she allowed a student, whose fiancé was returning to the Front, the privacy of her own room for their farewells.[109] Like Florence Johnson at Bishop Otter, Julian did not feel the need to separate the public from the private as sharply as some principals, notably Homerton's Alice Skillicorn (see below). Perhaps, as an older woman, she could express a maternal discourse as part of her public role with more confidence than a younger principal would find possible.

Freda Hawtrey (1922–38)

In spite of Emily Julian's efforts, which included staying on as principal for an extra year at the LCC's request, Avery Hill's fortunes were at a low ebb in the early 1920s. This was partly the result of decreased government spending on education, but it was also due to the college's poor examination results and inadequate residential accommodation. It was fortunate therefore that the LCC chose Freda Hawtrey, a woman of outstanding ability, as its fourth principal.[110] One of Hawtrey's students summed up the impact she had on the college: 'A marvellous "Prinny" who encouraged us in social service, pride in our profession, and appreciation of the arts.'[111] The order in which Hawtrey's attributes were listed is instructive for, like her contemporary principals at Bishop Otter, Hawtrey saw service to others as the most essential part of the corporate ethos of the training college. As she herself wrote in the college magazine: 'The beauties of the College itself, set amidst lawns and trees, its sunny spacious rooms . . . have their right value when they form a background to strenuous work in dingier surroundings.'[112]

Hawtrey, like Bentinck Smith before her, was already well into middle age when she became principal. After graduating from Royal Holloway College, London, she taught at St Leonard's School, St Andrews, before returning to her studies at Somerville College, Oxford. She then took up the post of warden of women students at Bangor Normal College, before her appointment as principal of Darlington Training College in 1912. Hawtrey was thus the first principal of Avery Hill to have had training college experience. She was also the first to have won recognition at the national level. She was one of a dozen principals convened by the government in 1920 to discuss forming closer links between the colleges and the universities. Later, in 1923, she was chosen – one of only two training college principals to be so – to serve on the Board of Education's Departmental Committee on the Training of Teachers for Public Elementary Schools.[113]

Hawtrey's reign at Avery Hill was that of an autocrat. A tall, slim elegant woman (see Figure 3.6), she had a commanding dignity which could both charm and intimidate.[114] Unlike Freda Johnson at Bishop Otter, however, she had 'no unbending friendliness' towards students who regarded her 'with awe'.[115] She 'did not suffer fools gladly'[116] and 'if she wanted something

Figure 3.6 Freda Hawtrey, Principal of Avery Hill College, 1922–38.
Source: Courtesy of the University of Greenwich.

. . . she always got it'.[117] On her appointment Hawtrey immediately 'began to stamp her character on the institution'.[118] Although she was said to have had 'no great love for administration'[119] she quickly persuaded the trustees to upgrade the standard of the college's residential accommodation and to improve the quality of the students' food.[120]

Hawtrey's previous training college experience and wide connections in the educational world enabled her to make equally crucial improvements in the academic and pedagogic standards at Avery Hill. She insisted that matriculation should be the minimum entry for students; unusually she required all the staff – most of whom had only taught in secondary schools – to gain experience in the primary sector; and, looking to the future, she urged the Departmental Committee to extend the training college course beyond two years. By 1930, academic standards had risen sharply.[121] Cultural activities were also encouraged and Hawtrey was able to use her family connections in the artistic world for the benefit of students. Jelly d'Aranyi, the well-known violinist, who was Hawtrey's niece, gave concerts in college. Hawtrey was also related to the famous actor Charles Hawtrey[122] and in encouraging student drama she was carrying on a family tradition. She directed and cast the annual nativity play and even played Father Christmas at a party held in college for orphans from the Chailey Homes.[123] The principal was always concerned to maintain the middle-class standards of behaviour in college. Students were impressed by her 'queenly beautiful voice'[124] as she addressed them, after morning prayers, on a variety of cultural and topical subjects.[125] Even in the comparative informality of the Green Room standards of deportment and decorum were enforced. Students were reprimanded, for instance, when they abandoned their usual underwear when rehearsing in seventeenth-century dress.[126]

It was universally acknowledged that, in spite of her outstanding work as principal, Hawtrey's most central concern lay outside the college – in her 'passion' for the 'welfare of under-privileged children'.[127] For not only did she introduce welfare work with children as a core element in the college curriculum, but she was closely involved in many pioneering child welfare projects at national level. She took a keen interest in the nursery school run by the Macmillan sisters in Deptford and campaigned tirelessly for the establishment of a child welfare project on the old Foundling Hospital site in London. In 1933 she was invited to sit on the Board of Education's Consultative Committee on Infant and Nursery Education, and two years later she was given leave of absence to study nursery school provision in France.[128] So strong were these interests that students noticed that her concern 'for very young children' led her 'to be neglectful of her job sometimes in her quest for the welfare of children'.[129] Her resignation as principal in 1938 was in order that she could devote more time to the Foundling Hospital project.[130]

An overwhelming concern for children themselves rather than for those being trained to teach them was also a characteristic of Elsie Bazeley,

Hawtrey's contemporary at Bishop Otter. The emotional drive which fuelled this concern was an interesting example of how some principals were able to compensate for the lack of their own children by concentrating their energies on deprived children in the community. Again, a central discourse for women in the middle-class home – looking after children – had been translated into an institutional context. These principals were able to use the masculine authority of their public role to satisfy the private emotional needs of their own femininity.

Frances Consitt (1938–60)

Dr Consitt's principalship – like Alice Skillicorn's at Homerton – took Avery Hill through both the difficult period of the Second World War and the quiet 1950s, to the threshold of the three-year course and the coming of co-education. The college did not find the appointment of its new principal straightforward. From the first advertisement eleven candidates were interviewed. Judged 'a distinctly poor bunch', the post was re-advertised and Consitt was appointed unanimously.[131]Consitt was well qualified for her new post. Her previous career had combined academic research with a wide experience of teacher training. A lectureship in history at St Gabriel's College, London had been followed in 1933 by her appointment as principal of Bingley Training College. Moreover, like her predecessor Freda Hawtrey, she had already won national recognition with the presidency of the Training Colleges' Association. Described on her appointment as a woman with 'a keen intellect, a bright alert mind, and a rich geniality of disposition',[132] her valedictory tributes twenty-two years later stressed her leadership qualities, her spiritual values, and her fighting spirit (see Figure 3.7).[133]

Immediately on appointment, Consitt was plunged into plans for the evacuation of the college in the event of war. Plans to move the college to York did not materialize, and Consitt spent the whole of the first year of the war scouring the countryside for possible locations. Meanwhile, back at Eltham, students, because of the bombing, stayed at home, while the staff maintained such contact as they could by post. Eventually, in December 1940, accommodation was arranged in Huddersfield – but it was very far from ideal. Students had to be 'billeted' out in lodgings; no-one had a study bedroom; and meals had to be taken at the local British Restaurant. The college was thus deprived of the residential community life which was such an essential part of the training college experience.[134]

That the college flourished during these difficult years and increased its reputation was largely due to Consitt's indomitable leadership. Without it, 'the college might have disintegrated'.[135] In Huddersfield, students were soon immersed in social service throughout the town running clubs for children and young people; social work continued to be an integral part of the curriculum. Other innovations – particularly in work with younger children – won national attention and the college was visited by the McNair

Figure 3.7 Frances Consitt, Principal of Avery Hill College, 1938–60.
Source: Courtesy of the University of Greenwich.

Committee.[136] Consitt argued that the college's wartime exile had forged 'a partnership of difficulty' between herself and the staff and that 'the sense of common understanding and purpose has often brought me a feeling of singular happiness'.[137] These comments encapsulated all that was best in the principal's role. Strong masculine leadership was warmed by the principal's personal commitment to, and pleasure in, a shared feminine community of aspiration to excellence and service to others. Consitt's unflagging energy, and persistence in pressing the authorities, enabled the college to return to its blitzed London site in the autumn of 1946, although it was three years later before all the necessary restoration work had been completed.[138]

Principals were able to draw on a supportive female network. This included principals in other women's training colleges and members of the female inspectorate. Dr Dorothy Sergeant, an HMI, and partner of Homerton's principal Alice Skillicorn, reported to the Ministry of Education that the 'degree of improvisation' which Consitt had employed at Avery Hill in the immediate post-war years was 'quite remarkable'. Privately, Consitt was able to confess to Sergeant that 'It's no joke being the most blitzed college in England'.[139] This opportunity to 'drop her guard', in private and to an equal, was an important safety valve for principals. Consitt was also well aware of the importance of salary level in maintaining the principal's status. She pointed out to the governors that her salary was £150 p.a. less that those paid to the principals of Homerton and Whitelands, although these colleges were smaller.[140]

Consitt gave an account of her policy as principal in a letter she wrote to the Ministry of Education in 1946. In this account she revealed how integral to the training college experience were the middle-class standards of the culture of femininity. She interviewed all candidates personally, and although she preferred students to have spent two years in the sixth form, 'it was not so much their academic qualifications which influenced her as their personality and character'. In her own words – 'We look for soundness, vigour, vitality, sensitiveness. We attach quite as much importance to fitness in character and temperament as to academic attainment.' Experience with children, e.g., with Cubs and Brownies, was important. Tellingly, 'she also paid heed to [applicants'] appearance, dress and speech'.

As the 1950s progressed, Consitt, in spite of her energy and charismatic leadership, seemed to mirror the stagnation and failure to 'to keep up with the times' that was to overcome the training college world (see Chapter 6). As early as 1952, although Avery Hill itself was continuing to attract good candidates, she drew attention to the lack of purpose and moral conviction among young people in the post-war world: 'We are all gravely concerned at the national insufficiency of candidates of the necessary calibre. Do young people fear responsibility? Is their idealism insufficient.'[141]

The following year, at the time of Queen Elizabeth II's coronation, her enthusiasm for 'the stimulation of a community of young women preparing themselves for the ministry of teaching' and the 'inspiring example of the Queen' seems in retrospect to be striking a valedictory note for an age that was already passing. The principal was also beset by many administrative difficulties which she found increasingly irksome. Non-teaching staff were difficult to find, and the governors' insistence on close supervision of petty cash seemed to her quite inappropriate.[142] The college celebrated its Jubilee in 1957. On Jubilee day, the college was addressed by Lord Hailsham, Minister of Education, and he and the principal both extolled the traditional values of the women's training college. However, rapid change was on the way, and in the following year the principal was told to prepare not only for a rapid expansion in numbers but the introduction of men students. Well might she comment, 'We have reached the end of an epoch at Avery Hill College.'[143]

Consitt retired in 1960. Tributes to her seem rather formal with few personal reminiscences, except a feminine mention of her 'legendary hats'.[144] Consitt had given inestimable service to the college, but with the dawning of the co-educational era the values of the residential women's teacher training college, of which she had been such a staunch upholder, would be submerged, if not entirely lost.

Homerton College

John Charles Horobin (1889–1902)

When John Horobin was appointed principal of Homerton in 1889, the college was still on its London site (see Chapter 1). Horobin was to be the crucial influence both in moving the college to Cambridge[145] in 1894, and in transforming it into a women's institution in 1896. Unlike Edwin Hammonds, his contemporary male principal at Bishop Otter, Horobin was a forward-looking principal, alive to new education developments and, interestingly, sensitive to the needs of his women students. A former student at Homerton, he had had a wide experience of teaching in school, before entering Cambridge University as a mature student in 1885. A man of stupendous energy, always 'racing against the clock', he was active in Liberal politics and the National Union of Teachers, in addition to his college duties. At Homerton he widened the college curriculum – paying particular attention to improving the sports facilities and encouraging students' literary and cultural activities.[146] At Cambridge he persuaded the Trustees not only to build a new practice school near the college but to enlarge the college estate by 23 acres.[147]

The difficulties which Horobin encountered in trying to reduce the segregation of the sexes, which had always pertained at the college in spite of its being co-educational, throw interesting light on the problems which women students faced in a patriarchal world. These problems – which encompassed both class and gender – deeply influenced subsequent women principals' determination to socialize their students into a securely middle-class culture of femininity. Horobin described his attempts at mixed meetings:

> We get our students so mixed in mental calibre and preparatory training that mixed classes do not pay. I have had to stop mixed meetings [of the Literary Societies] at the request of the girls – they could not speak freely before the men and therefore did not enjoy the meetings; some of the men seemed to forget that the girls did not go to the meetings to be stared at – 'made eyes at'. Some of the girls [at the social evenings] complained of their own sex forgetting themselves.

In spite of the principal's liberal leanings, double standards were rigidly enforced. Two students caused a scandal by their sexual relationship. The woman was suspended from college; the man continued his education unpunished.[148] These difficulties with 'mixed events' 'discouraged' Horobin, and made him 'determined to transform the College into a single sex institution'.[149]

Horobin died suddenly in July 1902. For the next year the college was run by his wife Maud. This was not a success, and in 1903 the Trustees invited applications from women only for the post of principal.[150]

Mary Miller Allan (1903–35)

With Mary Allan's appointment as the college's first woman principal in 1903, Homerton began to acquire a national reputation for academic and professional excellence. Her appointment, however, was not without its critics. Allan had worked her way up from humble origins, via a pupil–teachership, to obtaining the Government Teacher's Certificate from Dundas Vale Training College, Glasgow. A lectureship at the Church of Scotland Training College, also in Glasgow, had been followed in 1895 by her appointment, at the early age of 26, to the headship of the Higher Grade Central School in Leeds. The lecturers at Homerton were disappointed that Allan's academic standing was not higher. Allan had already studied, in her spare time, for the LLA (Lady Literate in the Arts) from St Andrews University[151] but this qualification had always had a somewhat equivocal reputation,[152] and in a town like Cambridge the comment of the college's HMI was not unexpected: 'The degree she holds will not be considered of any value in Cambridge society.'[153]

Allan's concern that Homerton should be acceptable to the academic and middle-class conservatism of Cambridge society was one of the central themes of her principalship. From her earliest days at the college, Allan was to confound all her critics. A woman of outstanding ability and determination, by her forceful leadership, she soon brought 'all the work of the College under her personal control'.[154] Her leadership showed formidable masculine qualities, but it was also informed by the concerns of middle-class femininity:

> Miss Allan had a very strong personality, awe-inspiring, rather unapproachable. She was dignified, just and a disciplinarian.[155]

> She held Homerton in her hand. A very strong character both mentally and physically she never allowed any misdemeanour to go unchecked – she criticized her students' accents, the way they walked, and always expected us to behave with dignity and a sense of our vocation as teachers.[156]

Allan quickly set out to enhance the academic curriculum at Homerton. Suitable students were encouraged to study for a further post-certificate year, which included the possibility of reading for Part 1 of Cambridge University's Geographical Tripos.[157] She herself conducted students' voice and speech training. This was an interesting combination of the principal's masculine and feminine discourses. The acquisition of a good clear minimally accented voice was essential vocationally for all teachers in training – but it was also an essential quality for the middle-class culture of femininity:

> Our first morning 'lecture' was a meeting with Miss A. She told us to stand round the room with our backs to the wall. Each student had to read a poem from [the] 'Oxford Book of English Verse', but first to give our names. It was uncanny how she pin-pointed the exact part of the country we each came from – Cockney, Welsh, Norfolk, Cornwall, Bradford, etc. Quite an ordeal for most of us.[158]

Allan was anxious to encourage students to share her own love of poetry, and her Sunday afternoon readings and discussions, were remembered and appreciated by many students: 'Notices were put up. "Miss Allan will speak at 3 p.m. on Sunday" – they were known in College as "Will Speaks". Wide variety of subjects. Morals, poetry (Browning's poems), drama, health.'[159] Allan's favourite poem was Wordsworth's *Ode to Duty* and the poem's opening words – 'Stern Daughter of the Voice of God' – became emblematic of Allan's power and authority over the college.[160]

Political astuteness and the ability to persuade and convince all those who were concerned with the work of the college were essential components of the principal's public role. Some principals – notably those at Bishop Otter – had difficulty with their trustees. Allan, on the other hand, was always able to exercise strong paternal authority both with the college's trustees[161] and with the Board of Education[162] and even with difficult parents.[163] Her dogged determination not to be intimidated by opposition was revealed in her long campaign in the 1920s to get the University of

Cambridge to take over responsibility for the final examination of Homerton students. For in 1926 the Board of Education had announced that it was proposing that local universities should take over this responsibility from the Board. Oxford and Cambridge universities, however, were exempt from this obligation because they were deemed to be 'national' rather than 'local' universities.[164] Allan described her anxious and difficult campaign to persuade Cambridge University to make an exemption for Homerton in a report to the Trustees a year later:

> The absorbing question still is the approach to the University with regard to the Final Examination of the Students. The matter was first mooted in December 1925, and was discussed first with the Vice-Chancellor in February 1926 – but still there is little progress to report, indeed but for the kindness and assistance of the Master of Trinity Hall there would have been none. Since I last reported to you on the matter Dr Cranage has formally brought the subject before the Extra-Mural Board. . . . The decision come to was 'that no action be taken at present'. Dr Cranage unofficially advised that a direct appeal should be made to the Council of the Senate. The Master of Trinity Hall kindly arranged that I should meet a member of Council, who advised my again seeing the Vice-Chancellor, with whom, I had a long interview on the 10th inst. Finally he advised that a careful memorandum should be prepared on the matter and signed by some influential members of the University, both Governors of this College and others interested.[165]

Eventually a year later Allan's long and patient campaign bore fruit and in 1928 the university's Local Examinations Syndicate signalled that they were 'prepared to undertake the work'.[166] This link with the university was of very great advantage to Homerton, as Allan herself reported to the Trustees in 1930:

> There is little doubt the standard of the examination has been raised since it has been taken over by the Examinations Syndicate. The syllabus being much more clearly defined, and the external examiners being in touch in almost every case with the actual work done.[167]

Allan attended Emmanuel Congregational Church in Cambridge.[168] In college she 'maintained an unobtrusive religious atmosphere which was entirely undenominational'.[169] Unusually for a training college principal, she supported the Labour Party; and in 1918 she signed the nomination papers of Cambridge's first parliamentary Labour candidate. Her more general concern for the working class was on public record: 'She told us of her growing conviction that the roots of the nation are fixed in the working classes whose children we teach.'[170] These words were delivered soon after Allan had taken leave of absence during 1919 and 1920 for a world-wide tour, which included participating, as its only woman member, in the Commission of Inquiry into Village Education in India. Her first vice-principal and obituarist, extolled the value to Allan of this experience:

> She came up against some of the big world problems . . . and met far more interesting and important people than most of us may hope to see in a life-time . . . it added to Miss Allan's stature in thought and wisdom, giving her a background of ideas based on newer and far older civilizations than our own'.[171]

I would argue, however, that in spite of this ecumenical experience, Allan's total absorption in her principalship, and her overwhelming concern that the college should be acceptable to the academic and middle-class conservatism of Cambridge society, led her 'to keep quiet' about her more radical concerns. It is in this context that Allan's lack of emphasis on an ethic of social service to others outside the college community, which was such an integral part of other principals' interpretation of their role, needs to be assessed. Welfare work with children was not introduced into the college's curriculum, and there is little evidence of students' voluntary participation in such projects in the town. For such activities, which would have exposed students to the town's critical gaze, could have compromised the respectability on which Homerton's reputation depended. Within the college community itself, however, Allan could encourage students to raise money for good causes. In 1928, for instance, 'special efforts' were made 'for the miners distress fund'. These efforts included a Gilbert and Sullivan night, a waxwork show and 'people volunteered to do things and they charged for them and gave the money to the miners'.[172]

Allan's concern for Homerton's respectability was made more acute by the college's marginal position in Cambridge society. Cambridge was a town dominated by the male values of its university, which barely tolerated its own women students, let alone those in an obscure teacher training institution. The university's misogyny had been underlined by a privilege which it had only been forced to relinquish as late as 1894. This was its right to imprison for up to three weeks women walking in the town – who could well have been Homerton students – whom its suspected of being prostitutes.[173] It is in this context that Allan's legendary annual homily to her students on the importance of avoiding sexual encounters with undergraduates needs to be understood: 'It was Miss Allan's proud boast that for years she had had two hundred women students among four thousand men [university] and had never had any trouble.'[174]

I shall be discussing Allan's concern about students' sexual behaviour in more detail in Chapter 5. This concern was understandable in the context of the earlier years of her principalship, but towards the end of her service, her 'fussing' became increasingly irksome to students. Moreover, her obsessive concern with respectability was not confined to sexual matters:

Miss Allan was always very keen that students upheld the reputation of the College. I remember her denunciation of students who went to the 'Littles' (the row of shops on Hills Rd. quite near to College) to buy cakes and pastries. She said she's seen a succession of students coming along carrying confectioner's bags which must give near-by residents the impression that we didn't get enough to eat at College – and she didn't want the College to get such a reputation.[175]

Allan's former students are unanimous in bearing witness to her formidably stern and authoritarian public persona, and to her overwhelming concern with their academic progress and social and sexual respectability. There is less agreement about her private persona:

Strong seemed very unbending, but could do so if you were in trouble, or at Prefects' Teas – on the rare occasion. She wasn't the kind of person who would get alongside the student but she could be gracious. I was terrified of her in my first year, but understood her better in my second, when I was a prefect. I held her in high regard.[176]

Being gracious to students on informal college occasions was an extension of the principal's public role. Allan was always motivated in her actions by her concern for the well-being of the college as a whole, and I would argue that her help for students in difficulties was driven more by this concern than by a feminine sympathy for students as individuals: 'She had a strong sense of self-discipline and expected this in the students. She resented anything such as illness, which was a hindrance to their progress.'[177]

Another student drew a warmer picture of Allan, drawing attention to her sympathy with poorer students and, interestingly, using a maternal metaphor to describe her behaviour:

Sympathetic to students whose opportunities in education had been halted after the General Strike of 1926. . . . Understanding and directive of personal problems. Did not suffer fools gladly. Tolerant to youth's exuberation and mistakes. Encouraging to all efforts. Quick in correction. A Mother figure when sickness confined one to the Sanatorium.[178]

Not every one agreed about Allan's tolerance: 'I found her completely devoid of the milk of human kindness. She did her best to suppress any liveliness or gaiety in her students, you had to be serious and dowdy to win her approval.'[179]

Allan, however, was, unlike her successor Alice Skillicorn, far from being dowdy, and she was acknowledged to dress appropriately at all times. Her dress signalled her dual gender role. Daytime clothes were chosen to enhance her public dignity and status as head of the college, and were the feminine equivalent of the masculine suit. She wore dark well-cut tailor-

Figure 3.8 Mary Miller Allan, Principal of Homerton College, 1903–35.
Source: Courtesy of Homerton College.

made dresses and jackets of good material[180] 'without much attention to current fashion'.[181] When she entered the private sphere she wore more feminine attire. For evening supper with the staff for instance she wore 'a deep blue mandarin robe',[182] and for her retirement dinner in 1935 her dress was elaborately feminine: 'On the occasion of her retirement … we saw the real Miss Allan, dressed in a beautifully cut gown of black lace with a high Medici collar and a corsage of red roses.'[183] This student's perception of the 'real' Miss Allan as feminine was also evident in Hugh Riviere's portrait, commissioned in 1913.[184] Riviere shows Allan in an embroidered velvet dress, displaying a necklace, bracelet and ring, and with her hands decorously folded in her lap (see Figure 3.8). The perception of the 'real' Miss Allan as feminine, by both students and portraitist is interesting. Clearly the principal's 'masculine' public role, however effective in practice, was not seen as an integral part of her personality. Because she was a woman, she was 'really' feminine.

Allan's private femininity was crucially expressed in her homoerotic friendship with her second vice-principal Edith Waterhouse. I shall discuss this relationship, which was immensely supportive to Allan, in more detail in Chapter 5. This partnership between a principal and her deputy could have raised many problems 'when distance was lost but inequality remained'.[185] But both women, united in their devotion to the college, overcame any potential problems by a combination of personal compatability and flexible role reversal. In the public sphere, Waterhouse accepted that as vice-principal she was necessarily subordinate to Allan's power as principal. Allan rewarded Waterhouse's devotion by frequent public tributes to 'her work as vice-principal which I particularly prize'.[186] In the private sphere, however, both women were able to set aside the inequality of their professional life, to form a flexible, equal partnership in which 'it was uncertain as to who dominated who'.[187]

Allan's reports to the Trustees and her occasional contributions to college magazines give us some access to her own words and thoughts. At the end of her principalship, she was persuaded to write a few words on her life in the college magazine. Although we have no direct evidence that she was a feminist, or a supporter of women's suffrage, she was certainly aware of the disadvantages women suffered from their lack of educational opportunities:

> At 18 years of age I went up to Glasgow Normal Training College. But a strange question had to be debated first. Would Glasgow University *that* year open its doors to women undergraduates? But alas two more years were to pass before work was begun there.[188]

In a letter Allan sent to the London re-union in February 1920, while she was in India, she expressed her feelings with an emotional intimacy which was far removed from her public self. She names her two deepest impressions of foreign travel:

1   The quite extraordinary beauty of the world everywhere.
2   (and much harder to express) The extraordinary worth and interest of all man's labour wherever it is free from selfishness. The highest worship of God is the service of Man . . . (This may hardly be coherent stated briefly, and would need to be enlarged upon on Sunday afternoons).

Allan showed a rare warmth and humour in this letter. She also expressed in religious and aesthetic terms her ethic of service to others, beyond the college community. However much she 'downplayed' this ethic in the Cambridge context, it was central to the woman principal's role. Later in the letter Allan revealed just how central Homerton and the women in the college community were to her emotional life and security:

> The price one pays for a great experience such as I am having now, is the interruption of the companionship that had made life worth living, of the daily exchange of good offices between those we live with. Some loneliness is inseparable from a Wander-jahr. But how can I thank those of you who banished even this feeling by the cordiality of the greeting which reached me in Christmas week . . . I am tremendously proud of your great Christmas card, and carry it on all my journeyings . . . I cannot make you understand how much it meant to me.[189]

Allan retired in 1935. She remained living in Cambridge and shared a house near the college with her sister and nieces. She died in 1947. To the end 'she retained her lively interest in the College and in all associated with it'.[190] For thirty-two years she had moulded Homerton into one of the foremost women's teacher training colleges in the country. Her work was carried on and enhanced for the next twenty-five years by her successor, Alice Havergal Skillicorn.

Alice Havergal Skillicorn (1935–60)

In the career of Alice Havergal Skillicorn, the problematics of the woman principal's role are perhaps most clearly displayed. Skillicorn's solution to the conflicting discourses of the role was to separate the public from the private as sharply as possible. In her public role as head of the college she exercised a power wherein masculine discourse made few concessions to the normative constraints of femininity. This marginalization of feminine discourse in her public role was the key to its success – but, as we shall see, its consequences for her life in the private sphere, especially in old age, were not happy.

Skillicorn, like her predecessor Mary Allan, came from a humble background. Her father was a shoemaker and her mother ran a bakery from the family home. Skillicorn became a pupil–teacher and then went onto Hereford

Figure 3.9 Alice Havergal Skillicorn, Principal of Homerton College, 1935–60.
Source: Courtesy of Homerton College.

Teacher Training College. At the age of 30 she obtained a BSc at the London School of Economics and subsequently became a lecturer at St Hild's Training College, Durham. While there she took a master's degree, and eventually returned to London to become an HMI.[191] Skillicorn's early life and academic career were to affect deeply her interpretation of the principal's role. Her parents' business skills gave her a financial acumen which she was to employ to great effect during her principalship. Publicly she 'kept quiet' about her humble origins and her hard won academic success. In her entry for *Who's Who*, for instance, she failed to mention either her pupil–teachership or her time at the Hereford Teachers Training College.[192] In private, however, she was devoted to her family and visited them frequently in the Isle of Man.[193] She was very surprised to be appointed principal of Homerton and, throughout her principalship, took great pride and pleasure in the contacts she made with distinguished academics at Cambridge University.[194]

Unlike the other principals discussed in this chapter, Skillicorn was a strikingly ugly woman (see Figure 3.9). However, this handicap to her femininity was deplored not so much in itself, but because she took no action to remedy it:

> Quite unforgettable, alas. She was small, dumpy, dowdy . . . with piercing eyes and protruding teeth. She made little effort to be attractive in any way.[195]

> Not a pretty woman. Her teeth protruded. She wore her hair drawn back in a severe way. She wore very plain tweedy clothes which were in no way stylish.[196]

A more telling criticism of Skillicorn's appearance concerned its effect on her status as principal: 'My mother thought she was one of the cleaners.'[197]

Nevertheless, however much her appearance fell short of the standards of middle-class femininity, even to the point of compromising her status as principal, she had no difficulty in projecting this status and her masculine authority as head of the college through her transgressive body: 'Small, unprepossessing, I remember her most with shoulders slightly forward in her black gown walking into Hall – when she was there, one never looked at anyone else.'[198]

There was only one item of her clothing to which Skillicorn attached any importance – and that was her academic gown: 'When wearing her gown, she often stood holding the lapels and walking about holding one lapel.'[199] This posture was enshrined in Henry Lamb's portrait of Skillicorn, painted in 1953 (Figure 3.9). I read this posture as Skillicorn's desire to cling onto and wrap herself round in her academic status. Her gown was to her not so much an item of clothing, about which she was unconcerned, as the emblem of the academic/masculine authority with which she directed the affairs of the college. Skillicorn inherited and improved upon the political strategy of her predecessor, Mary Allan, to make Homerton the best institution for the training of women teachers in Great Britain. Her single-minded devotion to furthering the best interests of the college at all times was universally acknowledged, as was her power:

> Miss Skillicorn's career as principal of Homerton College was driven by an overriding purpose: that the college should be the outstanding women's college in its field. She was of that last generation of college principals who exercised autocratic power.[200]

Skillicorn's financial acumen was one of the most formidable masculine qualities which enhanced her ability to perform her public role. On her appointment, she immediately saw the necessity to improve the college's financial position by the better investment of its capital, then largely on deposit in the bank. Early in 1936 she persuaded the college trustees to purchase government stock, and four years later, at the beginning of the Second World War, she seized the opportunity to invest a substantial sum in defence bonds and war stock.[201] One of her canniest investments was the purchase in 1946 of a large hostel in North London for only £5,500. Millbrook House not only provided the opportunity for Homerton students to gain teaching experience in inner city schools, but it also saved the college some £1,000 a year in teaching practice travelling costs.[202]

Skillicorn had the ability to combine a 'masculine' strategic perception of new educational potential for the college with a tactical and tactful 'feminine skill' in turning such potential into actual opportunity. Her wartime campaign to build a nursery school at Homerton, for which she persuaded the government to foot the bill, showed these qualities in full measure. In the autumn of 1938, in the wake of the Munich crisis and Homerton's first experience of evacuees, Skillicorn 'floated' the idea of a nursery school to the trustees:

> It might be well during the present session to review the educational policy of the college, and to consider the wisdom of developing the non-academic and professional side of the work, particularly that which is concerned with training for teaching in nursery, infant and junior schools. Such a policy, if adopted, would involve the provision of a nursery school on the college premises.[203]

By March the following year Skillicorn had obtained the co-operation of the Cambridge Borough Council, who agreed to pay one-quarter of the maintenance cost of the nursery, which would provide the Borough with a valuable facility for its less advantaged children. When the necessary approval from the Board of Education was slow in coming, Skillicorn was able to employ her tactical skill and take advantage of her female network to expedite matters. She persuaded the Board's female medical adviser to visit Homerton with the result that she gave her endorsement to the scheme. The well-known architect, Maxwell Fry, was retained and tenders for the building work invited. The Board of Education gave its final approval to the plans in October 1939 but by this time the Second World War had broken out. The Board consequently advised that, because of the shortage of building materials, the scheme should be put in abeyance. Skillicorn, however, immediately saw that the wartime situation, far from signalling the defeat of her plan, in fact provided an enhanced opportunity for achieving her purpose. She urged the Board to reconsider its advice, 'as some anxiety had been recently expressed as to the educational provision for smaller children who had been evacuated'. Work on the building was started in the summer of 1940 and by January the following year the school was ready to receive its first pupils. It was then that Skillicorn crowned her achievement with a final tactical manoeuvre. Having already indicated that some of the nursery's pupils could be evacuees, she now proposed that they all should be – the places 'could be filled with most advantage by evacuee children'. This 'master' stroke resulted in all financial provision for the school, except for the salary of the superintendent who became a member of the Homerton staff, being transferred from the college to the government to become the responsibility of the National Evacuation Account.

Skillicorn had thus secured not only a valuable facility for the college at minimal cost, but she had also won an enhanced reputation nationally for herself by her patriotic action.[204] The nursery school was also the occasion for Skillicorn to give a rare display of a feminine discourse as part of her public masculine role. When she described the school to the trustees as 'delightful' with the children making 'a picturesque and happy addition to the college', she revealed the pleasure she could take in the company of children – a pleasure she normally only showed when 'off-duty' in the private sphere.[205]

The day-long visit of the President of the Board of Education, R. A. Butler, in October 1941 when he was planning what was to become his great Education Act of 1944, was another 'feather in Miss Skillicorn's cap'[206] and further proof of the influence she had attained in the training college world:

> He asked if the training colleges were satisfied that the preparation for scripture teaching in the schools was adequate. He thought much of the present difficulty could be removed, if he could assure the deputations which came to him that the training colleges were doing their share satisfactorily.[207]

Skillicorn's success in her public role depended crucially on her ability to wield masculine authority over the community she served. Her professional relationships with her staff were autocratic, brusque and entirely instrumental. There was no place in her public role for a feminine desire to be liked. As she is reported to have said: 'I am the principal of this college, and I do not discuss my decisions with the staff.'[208] All of Skillicorn's relationships with the staff were subordinated to, and directed towards, what she perceived to be the good of the college as a whole rather than what was necessarily in the best interests of individuals themselves. Once she had assured herself that a member of staff was competent, she left her alone to carry out her work undisturbed; incompetent staff, on the other hand, were harassed until their work reached the standard that Skillicorn demanded. If it did not, staff were either persuaded to leave or were summarily dismissed.[209] Skillicorn's managerial style was bolstered by what one of her staff referred to as a court. An inner core of loyal courtiers enjoyed the principal's confidence and favour and stoutly defended her against the criticisms of disgruntled outsiders.[210] Nevertheless, Skillicorn was too astute a politician and too dedicated to the well-being of the college to be corrupted by sycophancy. She was always keen to promote her staff's career prospects. During the course of her principalship no fewer than eleven members of her staff went on to become principals of other women's colleges; others became HMI and county advisers.[211] Skillicorn's pivotal role in this female network was crucial both in enhancing Homerton's influence and in extending her own personal power.

The masculine impersonality and instrumentality of Skillicorn's professional relationships were, however, sometimes interrupted by the imperatives of her own femininity. She had favourites who were, interestingly, always young and attractive women. One member of staff, described as a 'live wire' whom Skillicorn 'appreciated every minute of', was allowed by Skillicorn – contrary to all the regulations – to live in the college sanatorium with her two godsons who had been bombed out. Conversely, Skillicorn also had her victims – 'always insignificant people whom she trampled on with venom'.[212] I read this behaviour as one of self-hatred. Skillicorn saw mirrored in unattractive and insignificant people her own lack of physical attractiveness, and also her social incompetence which I shall discuss below. She privileged attractive people because they compensated for her own lacks. As one of her own staff commented:

> Miss Skillicorn was a complex character. She could behave in a way that was wounding, and was by no means popular with all . . . I think she was ambitious and thwarted – partly because she was a woman . . . and perhaps because she was personally unattractive.[213]

Off-duty in the private sphere, without the protection of her professional persona, Skillicorn 'did not find personal relations easy'; 'She was intensely shy' and 'seemed unsure of herself socially'.[214] This social unease was greatly alleviated by the warmth and relaxed personality of Skillicorn's partner, Dr. Dorothy Sergeant. Sergeant, who was an influential HMI, had never been a member of the Homerton staff,[215] and thus Skillicorn avoided any possible conflict between the discourses of gender and power in her private life. I shall discuss Skillicorn and Sergeant's homoerotic partnership in more detail in Chapter 5.

Skillicorn separated the masculine and feminine discourses in the construction of her principalship as sharply as she could. The subordination and marginalization of femininity in the interests of the masculine power discourse of her public role was the strategy adopted by most successful women principals, but in Skillicorn the strategy was seen at its most extreme. Skillicorn's doctrine of 'separate spheres' was even evident when she displayed a feminine sympathy as part of her public role:

> She was capable of great sympathy in the real crises of life, never sentimental but offering strong support. . . . It was characteristic that these acts of sympathy and generosity were undertaken secretly. . . . Professional austerity and strong feeling existed side by side, almost in separation.[216]

Similarly in her relationship with her students this same separation was felt. It was rare for students to have more than one personal interview with Skillicorn throughout their college careers; occasionally a student would be signalled out for more individual attention but only 'if they did something special which brought them to her notice'.[217] Once she had retired, however, Skillicorn began to enjoy socializing, with Sergeant's invaluable support, with some of her former students. They found her 'altogether a different person' now she was in the private sphere: 'As a student I saw a formal impersonal "head of college" figure, only in later life did I get to know her as a warm friendly, normal person.'[218]

As with Mary Allan, the masculine power discourse of the principal's public role was not seen as 'normal'. But for Skillicorn normality consisted largely in this public role and without it she found life in the private sphere difficult. Moreover, fate was not kind to her. Sergeant died suddenly, and in Skillicorn's absence, in 1969.[219] Skillicorn was to live another ten years but the loss of Sergeant, on whom she had relied to provide the feminine skills she needed for her life of retirement in the private sphere, meant that her 'gnawing feeling of loneliness'[220] was never properly assuaged. Her twilight years were spent in a local nursing home, still loyally visited to the end by a faithful few of her former students.[221]

4   The staff

Academic and cultural enhancement

The lecturers held a conception of the teacher shaped by their membership of a professional middle-class section of society, the unmarried status of women in teaching, and their commitment to a career. The interaction between the lecturers and the students in the residential community was close and continuous, creating the conditions for the students to acquire the values and standards of their lecturers.[1]

There are those of my time who remember with gratitude the Sunday afternoon Bible class taken by Miss Allan, and the Browning lessons, during which she turned a magic key to the understanding of so many of his poems. We shall never forget the Tuesday Emerson evenings, when we sat on the floor of Miss Allan's sitting room and read with her some of the Essays.[2]

In this chapter I shall describe some of the ways in which the culture of femininity was enriched and enhanced by the transmission to students of the academic and cultural values of the liberal humanist tradition. The influence of college staff was of paramount importance in the transmission of this tradition. In the first part of the chapter I shall show how the staff, by their dedication and high educational standards, forged residential college communities in which liberal humanist values flourished. I shall then concentrate on three areas of the curriculum – art and craft, music, and literature and drama. I have chosen these areas for their pivotal role in college life. Unlike other subjects in the formal curriculum, e.g. arithmetic or geography, they had a valency beyond the pedagogic. For not only did they enrich individual students' general development and personal fulfilment, but, importantly, they provided the opportunity for that staff–student participation in shared activities which lay at the heart of the corporate culture. Furthermore, these were areas which had always been accessible to middle-class girls in the Victorian home. Crucially, however, in the home they had been deemed mere 'accomplishments', fit only to entertain others on social occasions, or to while away the time; at college they were transformed into serious activities with professional standards. Equally important for the maintenance of corporate values, was staff encouragement for other student activities, which, although not part of the curriculum, addressed cultural, political and spiritual concerns. In the last part of the chapter, therefore, I shall discuss students' political and religious activities and particularly their involvement in the peace movement between the two world wars.

Qualifications and social class

The enhancement of students' educational and cultural standards was due, above all else, to the staff's superior social class and higher academic qualifications. In the nineteenth century women staff in training colleges had normally received a vocational qualification only. By the early twentieth century, and with the encouragement of the Board of Education, women graduates were beginning, in increasing numbers, to be appointed to training colleges. Their change of title from the nineteenth-century's 'governness' to the twentieth-century's 'lecturer' signalled this crucial development in training college culture.[3] While students were typically clever girls from the lower middle class, whose education had been in the state sector (see Chapter 1), the staff were now typically daughters of the professional middle class, who, after private schooling, had received a university or other form of tertiary education. At Homerton, for instance, of the 172 women appointed to the college staff between 1897 and 1960, 157 had received some form of tertiary education; 97 had been to a university (45 to Oxbridge), 45 to teacher training college, and 15 to art school or music college.[4] Information on the staff's schooling is less well documented, but for those for whom it is known, 70 per cent of those appointed between 1900 and 1935 had attended independent or private schools. This proportion remained at no less than 50 per cent throughout the period.[5] Similarly, at St Mary's College, Cheltenham, 'The appointment of graduates became the norm.' Already by 1922, six of the eleven staff at Cheltenham were graduates, three had been to teacher training college and two to art or music college.[6] At Avery Hill, in the late 1930s, seventeen out of the twenty-two members of staff were graduates.[7]

The collegiate atmosphere in training colleges, where academic staff and students lived and worked together in a residential community, was widely acknowledged as beneficial. The Departmental Committee on the Training of Teachers for Public Elementary Schools, set up by the Board of Education in 1923, 'argued persuasively that the common life of the training colleges was much richer than that of the newer universities because, like Oxford and Cambridge, their students lived and worked in the same collegiate environment.'[8] Halls of Residence for women at the newer universities did foster some of the domestic and social mores of the culture of femininity, but crucially 'conditions more favourable to the development of a collegiate atmosphere' only 'developed where female members of the academic staff took up residence in hall alongside students'.[9]

Former members of staff remember 'a tightly knit community' which, although it could be 'claustrophobic – almost closed' nevertheless 'shone with real quality and worth'.[10] Staff had 'personal respect in everyone's professional skills'.[11] Another member of staff commented that she 'couldn't have done the job if I didn't live in'. Importantly, staff were 'supportive of each other' in personal as well as academic matters.[12] The college, in effect, 'was their family'.[13] Critics of the residential community drew attention to its claustrophobic tendencies and lack of sophistication. One member of the Homerton staff, recently demobbed from the ATS after the Second World War, found it 'difficult to settle into a female institution' after the 'sophistication of the Army'. Cups of tea were offered rather than gins and tonic. Although she found the college 'in many ways very civilized', the evening meal 'when you had to make conversation when you were tired', was 'awful'.[14] Others felt they were under constant surveillance and 'never quite had privacy'.[15] Even the McNair Committee (see Chapter 1), which reported in 1944, although largely critical of the staff in training colleges had to admit that 'the immense improvement in the content and conduct of elementary education during the past forty years 'was 'largely due to the education and training given to students in training colleges'.[16]

Staff lived in considerable comfort at Homerton. Each had a bedroom and sitting room with a bathroom to each corridor.[17] Until the Second World War, there was a full complement of maids to perform all domestic chores. Even when it became difficult to get servants, and both staff and students had to help with the less onerous tasks, like the washing up, there were still sufficient servants to maintain domestic standards. There was always a male chef and a resourceful handyman – 'there was nothing he could not do'.[18] Staff appreciated 'the tradition of eating together at High Table, as at other Cambridge colleges' and being waited on.[19] At weekends maids brought staff a cold supper in their own rooms.[20] The principal had her own personal maid, who was reputed to pack her clothes, darn her stockings and even tell her 'what to wear'.[21] Although the staff were free of domestic responsibilities, they had additional administrative duties which were a consequence of their residence. One weekend out of every three they had to remain 'on duty' at the college to answer the phone. For it was the principal's belief that 'parents would not like it if they could not get in contact with a member of staff at any time'. This requirement, which was still in force in the late 1950s, was an example of the stagnation and outmoded ethos which was afflicting the training colleges in the 1950s (see Chapter 6) – 'Even ten years later no-one would have put up with it.'[22]

One of the central advantages which living in a residential community afforded staff was the opportunity for sharing leisure pursuits with congenial companions. At Homerton, the college's location in the university town of Cambridge was an additional attraction for the staff. One member 'loved to walk into Cambridge to the theatres and lectures'[23] For another, going out to Cambridge to the theatre or tennis club was 'what made' her college experience 'enjoyable'.[24] The staff frequently went to the theatre or cinema in Cambridge as a group, including one memorable occasion when the principal joined them for a drink at the Garden House Hotel to celebrate her birthday. The next year the staff celebrated the principal's birthday with a theatre trip to London to see the smash hit *My Fair Lady*.[25] From 1950, the staff's social life was largely organized by Dorothy Westall, the college's domestic bursar. Westall was an interesting woman. Although not a member of the academic staff (she had previously been housekeeper at Repton, a boys' public school), through her powerful personality and domestic and diplomatic skills she quickly became a central figure within the college community. Her housekeeping standards were 'terrifically high' and her taste reigned supreme. She insisted, for instance, on cut flowers rather than house plants inside college; the plants, so carefully reared by the college handyman, were banished to his greenhouse. The college benefited from Westall's 'good artistic eye' and her 'interest in everything';[26] but she used her skills not only for the good of the community as a whole but also to enhance her own love of power. Very little escaped her notice and nothing was too small for her attention. A key weapon in her armoury, for instance, was the staff's table napkins. By personally allocating these napkins to mark where staff should sit at meals, she was able to manipulate and control their conversations.[27] 'Westy's' powerful personality and autocratic ways could have been a disruptive influence in the community, but the contrary was in fact the case. Her central role in domestic and social life was in fact one of the key factors in maintaining the college's residential ethos, as its traditions began to erode, as with other training colleges, in the 1950s (see Chapter 6).

Dedication to the service of their college, strong ethical principles, and a close involvement in many aspects of corporate life, characterized successful, long-serving members of staff. Avery Hill's historian described Lena Ellaby, who was one of the college's earliest members of staff:

> Miss Lena Ellaby taught History from 1908–1927. Her untimely death in 1928, a year after ill-health forced her to retire, caused a shock wave to pass through generations of students who remembered her not only as a very fine and dedicated teacher but as an early advocate of women's rights and a loyal and staunch supporter of the Christian Union.[28]

The espousal of a 'political' cause (women's suffrage) through the lens of religious faith was characteristic of the training college culture. This perspective was to be evident, for instance, in the peace movement between the wars (see below). Ellaby's obituary in the college magazine also drew attention to her sympathetic nature, her sporting prowess and her love of the magazine *Punch*. More intimately it portrayed a woman for whom college, with its 'congenial company, occasional lectures, and visits to theatres satisfied her and made up her life'.[29]

Stella Westaway gave Bishop Otter distinguished service for forty years from 1897 to 1936. Originally appointed as governess and mistress of French and music, she was later successively, lecturer in history, vice-principal, acting principal and for her final half-year principal.[30] Such versatility of role was not uncommon among training college staff and was to prove an important element in the promotion of the corporate culture. When Westaway died in 1956 her obituary was written by Miss Hammonds, daughter of Edwin Hammonds, principal at her appointment. Miss Hammonds painted a vivid picture of the young and very feminine Westaway: 'She was very young, very charming and very pretty. As a child I loved her at once and admired her looks and elegance. I picked rose buds for her.' Hammonds also drew attention to Westaway's enthusiasm for, and skills in, a wide variety of activities, her vivid personality and her availability 'at all hours'. Like Ellaby 'she lived her loyalty to college'.[31]

Elizabeth Glover was lecturer in Divinity at Homerton from 1950 to 1964, and she aroused the passionate admiration of some of her students. The daughter of a well-known Cambridge academic, she was not resident in college, but lived in her parents' home where she looked after her 'elderly' and 'formidable' mother. Glover's non-residence in college meant a lack of status and the loss of the constant support of colleagues, which she felt keenly, although by the late 1950s staff residence was becoming less common. Her involvement with her students was unusually close. Students visited her at home and she joined them on rambles. A Quaker, with a 'burning faith', she was felt by students to have unusual spiritual power; this 'genuine goodness' was, however, tempered by her lively nature and 'sparkling sense of humour'.[32]

Academic and cultural enhancement: art and craft; music; English and drama

> An English lady without her piano, or her pencil, or her fancy work, or her favourite French authors and German poets, is an object of wonder, and perhaps of pity.
>
> All accomplishments have the one great merit of giving a lady something to do.[33]

These two quotations, from a mid-Victorian male writer, point to the ambivalent status which cultural achievement held for the Victorian middle-class woman. Indeed, 'accomplishments', although they could give great pleasure and satisfaction to the woman concerned, were never recognized as personal achievements at all, but merely as harmless ways for an idle woman to pass her time. In this section I want to examine how three of these 'accomplishments' – art and craft, music, and literature and drama – were enhanced and transformed for students by their college education and experience. The 'professionalization' of these accomplishments and their legitimation in the public sphere, formed a key theme linking staff and students in the construction of the college's culture of femininity. All three subjects were essential components of teachers' professional skills. They also played a major part not only in the academic side of the curriculum, but in the leisure activities which enriched college life. The skills and knowledge which students acquired could also provide them with life-long interests and pleasure.

Art and craft

Art and craft had always been obligatory subjects for teachers in training, and throughout the period they continued to be core components of the vocational curriculum. In the liberal humanist tradition, craft had always been awarded an inferior status, largely because it depended on purely manual skills. Art appreciation, on the other hand, along with the ability to create works of art, was an attribute of elitist high culture. This culture was only available to those – almost invariably men – who had been appropriately educated. A cultural dichotomy therefore lay at the heart of the inferior status awarded to the accomplishments of the middle-class woman. It was the training colleges' achievement that they not only bridged the cultural gulf between art and craft, but gave to their women students the educational and cultural knowledge to appreciate fine art.

The difficulties which early students faced in adapting the conventions of domestic accomplishment to the academic and cultural standards of college life were described by an Avery Hill student:

> In the library, where we were, of course, supposed to read, students delighted to sit with the needlework or knitting Miss A. K. Smith demanded from them (as part of their course work) and have a cosy chat. This comfortable custom came to the notice of the Principal. Lacking in sympathy, she ruled that there must be inviolable silence in the library to make reading possible for all.[34]

Avery Hill was one of the earliest training colleges to encourage students to appreciate works of art. In 1909, only three years after the college's foundation, the principal started an Art Gallery of reproductions of famous works of art. Two pictures – by Raphael and G. F. Watts – were the gifts of the first cohort of old students. In encouraging succeeding generations of old students to continue this custom, the principal was not only both promoting students' appreciation of art and enhancing the beauty of their surroundings, but she was also inscribing old students (grandmothers) into the college's extended family.[35] At Homerton students were already admiring an original Pre-Raphaelite oil painting by a woman artist – Jane Benham Hay's *A Florentine Procession*. This had been purchased, in the principal's words, 'for its decorative value' and as a 'good example of a woman's work'. It still hangs in the college's dining hall and has proved inspirational for succeeding generations of students.[36]

First Year Up[37] gives interesting glimpses of the artistic education of Homerton students in the 1940s. Alison goes to a local bookshop to look at an exhibition of 'reproductions of French painting'. She examines each print carefully and chooses a Sisley. The visit to the exhibition is also the occasion of her first encounter with the man she will marry. He is impressed by her confidence in her own judgement:

> 'You do know something about painting, I'm sure.'
> 'Well, just a little, because I'm interested, and it's part of my course at the training college.'[38]

The appointment of Miss Payne, as head of art, at Avery Hill in 1911, 'set a standard' and 'upheld an ideal' for subsequent art teaching. Art always had a moral dimension within the training college experience. It was one of the means by which teachers could bring beauty and hence goodness into children's lives. Payne was an artist herself. In describing her work as 'delicate', bold with colour, and 'with a spiritual quality', her obituary bore witness to the importance not only of academic and technical skill but also of moral authority in the relationship between staff and student in the training college.[39]

Moral authority was also an essential component of two outstanding teachers at Homerton. Eileen Delany came to Homerton in 1919 as lecturer in handwork and needlework and played a pivotal role in the college's culture until her retirement in 1942.[40] Students remembered her 'wonderful character' and 'moral lectures' as well as her 'very high craft standards'.[41] She was also 'large, homely and kind'.[42] In keeping with the corporate ethos of the college, she often took prayers in Hall, in spite of being a Roman Catholic! The fact that she was reputed 'to have had to do penance afterwards'[43] only added to the affectionate esteem in which 'this character in our lives'[44] was held. Delany's teaching was inspirational as well as highly professional. One student describes how her attitude to craft work was transformed from a hated chore into a life-long interest. She was also able to take bookbinding and woodwork as her advanced subject, illustrating how, in the training college curriculum, manual craft skills were given equal status with academic subjects:

> I had done no needlework or craft since elementary school days when I had hated it, spending two years hemming a pillowcase! But with Miss Delany I discovered I had a talent for many crafts so that I made it my Advanced Subject (Bookbinding and Woodwork). All my life since I have enjoyed using my hands and still do counted thread embroidery for pleasure.[45]

Kay Melzi was appointed lecturer in art at Homerton in 1938, and like Delany, remained at the college until her retirement in 1970. Melzi was a quieter, more introverted character than Delany, but her teaching was equally inspirational. Students reported that 'she made one believe that one could achieve far more than one had ever thought possible',[46] and that 'she always found something to praise however poor the artistic attempt may have been'.[47] Melzi's philosophy of 'never being negative'[48] was recognized by students as 'wonderful psychology' and her comments 'very interesting Miss . . .'[49] or 'very jolly colour'[50] became legendary. Under Melzi's guidance, students were not only encouraged to reach higher artistic achievements themselves but their whole aesthetic perspective was widened: 'She made me look at colours in an entirely new way and at pictures which I might never have enjoyed so much without her teaching.'[51]

Melzi's education of students in the artistic values of high culture was greatly facilitated by her connections in the art world. As a former student at the Royal College of Art, it was her influence that persuaded the eminent painter, Henry Lamb, to paint the principal, Miss Skillicorn's portrait in 1954.[52] Melzi's friendships with outstanding women artists like the painter Nan Youngman and the sculptor Betty Rea,[53] who taught at the college from 1948 till 1964,[54] added to the enrichment of students' cultural experience. Rea – 'a passionate ardent character'[55] – and Melzi were remembered by students as 'special spirits' whose 'spiritual stimulus' 'changed students' direction'.[56] Youngman's memoir on Melzi also bears witness to the transforming effect of art education on students' lives and development: 'Students were expected to develop their own powers of expression through the practice of the visual arts. This experience we believed had a definite connection with their development as people.'[57]

It was Youngman's belief that 'The period post World War Two was the best time for training colleges' emphasis on the creative possibilities of art for children'.[58] At Bishop Otter, this was an exciting period for art education with the beginning of the college's Permanent Art Collection of original works by modern artists. The collection was the brainchild of the college's new principal, Elisabeth Murray, who took office in 1948. During the Second World War the college had evacuated to Bromley and 'an association rapidly became established with the Art School at Bromley'. The college authorities were also influenced by the national commitment to furthering the arts in both public and educational contexts which dated from the foundation of CEMA (the Committee for the Encouragement of Music and the Arts) in 1940. CEMA was succeeded by the Arts Council of Great Britain in 1945. Eleanor Hipwell, became head of art teaching at Bishop Otter in 1944, and she not only appointed part-time specialist staff in craft skills, but bought three modern paintings which she gave to the college. Her successor, Sheila McCririck, was well connected in the art world, as was the principal. Murray's uncle had been a founder member of the Royal Society of Painter Etchers, and her brother was a sculptor and

Director of Antiquities in Nigeria. The principal could also rely on the support of sympathetic members of the College Council and especially the Dean of the cathedral, Walter Hussey. At first she planned to ask contemporary artists to lend pictures to the college, but, emboldened by the suggestion of the well-known painter, Ivor Hitchens, she subsequently began a policy of buying original pictures in instalments.

I would argue, however, that although students undoubtedly benefited from being able to study original contemporary art within the college walls, the collection was regarded more as a hobby of the principal's than as a resource which belonged to all. At first, students had no say in purchasing policy, but in 1957 the purchase of an abstract by the young artist, Patrick Heron, 'provoked restlessness amongst students' and enquiries as to the wisdom of spending the government-funded block grant for such a purpose. Eventually a 'democratization' of purchasing policy took place, and more works by women, and more craft work began to join the collection. The foundation of the art collection, which was originally hung all about the college, was also part of the principal's tactics for educating students in middle-class domestic taste.

> Miss Murray was indefatigable in promoting an awareness of a total living environment, and she spent much time and energy in selecting furniture, carpeting, curtains, and interior decorations that were in accord. A similar care was exercised on the physicalities of the whole College site.[59]

However, the imposition of the principal's elitist taste inevitably aroused hostility as the domestic bursar recalled: 'She was very friendly to the art teachers and chose all furnishings. No-one else was given a say. . . . She wanted to be arty crafty with everything and not necessarily practical.'[60]

Music

There were many aspects to the experience of music in the training college. Vocationally students continued to the end of the period to receive 'piano lessons to equip them for the exigencies of morning assemblies and the demands of music and movement in its many manifestations'.[61] Music could also be studied academically to an advanced level. One student at Homerton for instance, in the late 1940s, reached such a high musical standard during her Homerton career that she 'won the Open Scholarship for singers to the Royal College of Music in London'.[62] Music also played a very important part in the colleges' leisure activities. Practices and taste evolved over time.

In the early years of the twentieth century, musical entertainment at college translated into a new corporate setting the conventions and taste of the Victorian and Edwardian middle-class home. In such a home, for instance, my mother and her sister would frequently sing duets to entertain my grandparents and their guests. Bishop Otter recreated this family atmosphere in 1903 when 'the Principal and his family entertained students with songs, recitations and a duet *Babes in the Wood*'.[63] Saturday night musical entertainments at Homerton also had a domestic flavour at this period:

> Oct. 23rd. – On Saturday we had the pleasure of witnessing a performance peopled partly with 'babes', who were the performers in a charming operetta entitled 'Childhood Days'.

> Nov. 13th. – The musical item from the Easter Social, 'The Rose of Persia', was repeated to the delight of all.[64]

Singing could also be harnessed to inscribe corporate values as well as providing the opportunity for individual performance. Specially composed songs were a feature of college life:

> I shall never forget the first Hockey Day when First Year Students played the Seniors. We marched round the field singing the 'Hockey Song' to the tune of Drake's Drum. The last verse was:

>> The Wide world's a calling to a sterner strife
>> Forwards are you ready up the field?
>> Summon all your forces to play the game of life
>> Backs your steady sticks, prepare to wield,
>> Backs your steady sticks, prepare to wield.[65]

College songs were part of a masculine collegiate tradition, which women's colleges adapted for their own needs. Two Homerton students set their own words to music for their College Song. The song recorded the cosy femininity of college life, as well as its academic rigours and corporate pride:

College Song

Let us sing the joys of College, country rambles, teas in town.
Hard fought battles, splendid victories, coming up and going down.
Sorrows of examinations, Terror of inspection days
Are forgotten and forgiven when they bring our College praise.

Homertonians, Homertonians, Send the echo far and wide.
Raise your voices loud in triumph, lift your heads in pride.
Sing the glories of your College, feeling 'this is mine'
Say it now and sing it always for the sake of Auld Lang Syne.[66]

Like their male counterparts, women students could also use parody and humour. This verse from a parody of *Much Binding in the Marsh*, a popular radio show of the 1940s, mirrors students' feminine concerns:

> At Homerton College on the Cam
> Care of Individuals is our duty
> At Homerton College on the Cam
> We're more concerned with culture of our beauty.[67]

National events were also celebrated with communal singing. At Bishop Otter, in 1912 'The students marked the Coronation [of Edward VII] by singing round the college at 10.30 with Japanese lanterns',[68] while on Armistice Day in 1918 Avery Hill students, 'led by Miss Henley marched round the village singing God Save the King'.[69] Another early Avery Hill student used the musical skills she had honed at college to form her own orchestra during the First World War. In keeping with the college's service ethic, the Roslake Orchestra – all of whose members were women – 'went round the hospitals entertaining soldiers'. The orchestra's repertoire reflected popular taste being 'equally at home with straight music and jazz music for dance'.[70]

Singing was also an integral part of the May Day Ceremony (see Chapter 2); changes over time in both performance and repertoire reflected the evolution and increasing sophistication of student taste. At Homerton in 1906, 'the finest singer went with her accompanist to the piano and sang the May morning song: "Come out come out my dearest dear, come out and greet the May"',[71] while at Bishop Otter in 1910 students sang a popular ballad *May Dew* 'on the terrace as the snow falls'.[72] By the 1940s the singing of popular ballads had been replaced 'by the singing of madrigals by the 2nd year music group'.[73] Similarly, post-war Homerton students, by 'singing the Boars Head carol at the Christmas lunch, while chef walked down Hall with a silver salver' were transforming this domestic occasion into a re-creation of a medieval Oxbridge ceremony.[74]

The influence of the staff was crucial in widening students' musical appreciation. As music was a leisure activity as well as an essential part of the college curriculum, it was entirely appropriate that other members of staff, in addition to the music lecturers, sought to encourage and enhance students' musical awareness. At Homerton, the vice principal, Miss Varley, was a frequent contributor to the meetings of the college's Musical Society. She introduced students to Elizabethan music (an advanced taste in 1915) and earlier that year she helped students' to select the songs for a programme of music by Grieg.[75] At Avery Hill, Miss Henley, a founder member of the college staff, gave the college Concert Club '50 season tickets to the Courtauld-Sargent concerts at the Queen's Hall', when she retired in 1930.[76] The college's cultural life at this period was greatly facilitated by the principal's connections in the artistic world (see Chapter 3). By the late 1920s,

Avery Hill students were enjoying a rich and varied musical life. In 1927, as part of the college's 21st birthday celebrations, Geoffrey Shaw, a leading contemporary composer, visited the college to talk about changes in the new edition of the hymnbook *Songs of Praise* and Jelly d'Aranyi, the well-known woman violinist, gave a recital.[77] Students were introduced to a wide variety of serious music ranging from the Elizabethans to the contemporary. An interesting comment on contemporary musical reputations was made in the college magazine: 'Rimsky-Korsakoff, Debussy and Ravel may now be of yesterday, almost classic, but Howells, Holst and York Bowen are in the van of the moderns.'[78]

Another college concert in 1931 included songs, piano and orchestral pieces ranging through Bach and Debussy to works by the contemporary composers George Dyson, Armstrong Gibbs, Thomas Dunhill and John Ireland.[79] In 1928 Avery Hill took advantage of its proximity to London and allowed some students to attend music lectures at Bedford College. The lecturers included two eminent musicologists – Percy Buck and Hugh Allen.[80] Meanwhile, at Bishop Otter, students' musical occasions often centred on the cathedral where students would join other singers for performances of oratorio. In 1921 they sung Mendelsohn's *St Paul* and in 1941, as part of War Weapons Week, Handel's *Messiah*.[81]

Musical life at Homerton was always greatly influenced by the presence of the university in Cambridge. A student in the 1920s recalled evensong at King's College as an unforgettable aesthetic experience:

> The great experience of the week to Kings College Chapel for Evensong . . . the choir singing the beautiful liturgical music, we half hidden in the ancient stalls, candles flickering in their glass shades, would share the solemnity of the moment.[82]

By the 1930s Homerton students were welcomed into the university's musical society (CUMS). Students saw this, however, primarily as 'a privilege' rather than a recognition of their own musical skills:

> Fifteen students have had the privilege of singing in the chorus of the C.U.M.S., and one student is a first violinist in the orchestra. They took part in the production of 'Jephtha', entering into it with the keenest enjoyment.[83]

By the late 1930s Homerton students were combining with individual colleges in the university to give joint concerts;[84] similarly, university students would also augment Homerton's own choir and orchestra on special occasions.[85] In 1941 the college appointed a new lecturer in music – Greta Lewis (née Tomlins). Lewis made an indelible impression on students both for her musical abilities and for her charismatic personality:

Dr Lewis. A slim little woman with a mass of curly (frizzy) hair who wore skirts that were too long for her and breathed music from her every pore. Her features were delicate and her enthusiasm boundless. She could have made the very stones sing. I remember her asking me to 'offer the voice' and specialize in music. I should so have loved to do so, but I hadn't the confidence (or dedication?) to tackle the necessary theory . . . (She was, I think, our only married lecturer married to a very handsome man).[86]

Lewis brought the flavour and practice of upper middle-class culture to the college. Educated at Roedean, Lady Margaret Hall and the Royal College of Music, she was also a composer of religious songs and carols.[87] Like Kay Melzi, the college's lecturer in Art, her positive and professional approach 'gave us immense competence and great all round confidence'. Lewis believed that 'everyone can sing, if only a nursery rhyme' and that 'music and art was in every child'. Choral singing was compulsory for every student on Friday evenings. Lewis would briskly divide students into the four singing parts and crying 'Right ladies, we'll begin' launch them into works which ranged from Hebridean love songs to the *Messiah*. Lewis' married status was also important to students. Unlike most of the lecturers, she was sympathetic to students' desire for relationships with the opposite sex. She readily signed every request for an exeat, giving the impression that 'to get a man when in Cambridge' was an understandable ambition.[88]

Literature and Drama

Literature

Reading and a love of literature were approved activities for middle-class girls. For some girls, like Virginia Woolf (née Stephen), access to their fathers' well-stocked private libraries provided them with the higher education which was still denied to all women but a privileged few.[89] In her diary for 1924, when she was in her early forties, Woolf describes the evolution of her literary taste which early exposure to great literature had made possible:

> When I was 20 . . . I could not for the life of me read Shakespeare for pleasure; now it lights me as I walk to think I have 2 acts of King John tonight, and shall next read Richard the 2nd. It is poetry that I want now – long poems . . . When I was 20 I liked 18th Century prose; I liked Hakluyt, Merimee. I read masses of Carlyle, Scott's life & letters, Gibbon, all sorts of two volume biographies, & Shelley.[90]

Other middle-class girls had access to literature at home or school, or could borrow books from the public library, but for many students at training college, who were from impoverished lower middle-class homes, such opportunities did not exist. As late as the mid-1930s for instance, one student at Homerton claimed that she 'had never been to the theatre or read Shakespeare'. She found the work at college 'hard' and paid tribute to the 'encouragement' of the staff and their 'inspired' teaching. The transmission of the literary canon of the liberal humanist tradition was the core purpose of those who taught literature to students, but in the training college culture, emphasis was always given to the moral and spiritual aspects of literature, as well as to its intellectual and aesthetic appeal. We have already seen in Chapter 3 how Homerton's principal Mary Allan encouraged students to share her own love of poetry. As well as optional Sunday afternoon sessions[91] second year students also received instruction from the principal as part of the curriculum:

> Miss Allan took Senior Year Students once a week for English Literature and poetry not covered by our syllabus (e.g. Browning, Meredith, Rossetti), and stimulated our interest in the subject, through which I was able to obtain a Distinction in English.[92]

Allan's purpose in devoting time to enhancing students' knowledge and appreciation of literature went beyond a desire to improve their academic achievement. She believed that the moral and spiritual values of great literature would guide students throughout their lives. Learning poetry by heart was a way to achieve this aim:

> She was very fond of poetry – especially Browning, and held Browning evenings each week to which all seniors were welcomed. Miss Allan encouraged us to learn poetry by heart, for which I am everlastingly grateful now that I am registered as blind and still have memories of some of the loveliest poems ever written.[93]

Browning seems to have held a particular resonance for students. Bishop Otter, for instance, formed its own Browning Society as early as 1908.[94] Not all students, of course, were receptive to what could be interpreted as cultural indoctrination. One Homerton student, for instance, rarely attended Allan's Sunday afternoon sessions because the principal's attitude and manner 'froze' her. She was so put off by Allan's insistence that students should recite, in front of fellow students, the poems they had learned by heart that she formed 'a long-standing dislike' for 'poems and poets'.[95]

A large well-stocked library was essential for the study of literature, and an inadequate college library always received a mark of censure from the inspectorate.[96] In the early days students usually ran the library themselves, 'under the general direction of a member of the academic staff'. This could lead to problems of administration and security, and in 1935 Avery Hill were in the vanguard of professionalization when they persuaded the LCC

Education Committee to appoint a librarian for the college, whose services they shared with Furzedown – a nearby training college.[97] At Homerton a professional librarian was not appointed until 1954.[98] Students were appreciative of the advantages of a good library and involvement in the day-to-day running of the library promoted the college's corporate ethic, as well as improving individual academic performance: 'I have pleasant memories of the library – I really enjoyed being there and helped as much as I could. I suppose it was because I took Advanced English.'[99]

Students also had their own fiction libraries for recreational reading, which they ran and administered themselves.[100] The fiction library at Homerton, which has only recently been dispersed, contained most of the nineteenth-century classics, as well as works by middlebrow twentieth-century novelists like Mary Renault and Daphne Du Maurier.[101]

Alice Skillicorn, Mary Allan's successor as principal of Homerton, continued her predecessor's policy of sharing her love of literature with students. Tastes were changing, and in the 1940s and 1950s modernist works by T. S. Eliot and James Joyce would be discussed, rather than works by Browning or Tennyson.[102] Students were usually asked at their initial interview 'what books they had read'[103] and one student remembered 'being told you must read *The Lighthouse* by Woolf'.[104] Life-long literary interests could be formed by the influence of the staff.

> At Homerton I was lucky enough to be introduced to the eighteenth century mainly through the literature of that time, as directed by Miss Haynes. (She lived until over a hundred incidentally, and I was in touch with her when she spent her last years in Oxford). It was through her that I met James Woodforde (1740–1803) whose diary has been my bedside book for years.[105]

Students were always influenced by the personality of lecturers and their individual personal rapport with them. Feminine values were important. Jennie Aberdein, lecturer in English at Avery Hill in the 1930s, had 'an incalculable and profound' influence on students not only because of her scholarly achievement and 'incisive mind' but for her 'charm and wit' and 'lively, gracious and gentle disposition'.[106] Similarly, at Homerton, Marjorie Baker, described as 'elegant' and the 'youngest and most intellectual' of a 'good English team' combined traditional feminine values with academic distinction.[107]

Students were also able to attend lectures when practising writers and poets visited college to speak about their work. At Avery Hill, in the 1920s, 'Walter de la Mare came on more than one occasion to read some of his poems and talk about poetry';[108] at Bishop Otter in the late 1940s the college was visited by the distinguished biographer, Robert Gittings.[109] At Homerton, students were fortunate in being able to attend special lectures at the university. One student's experience, with its concern for the lecturer's frailties, illustrates how traditional feminine values underlaid the cultural enhancement of college life:

> You went en masse. I can't remember whether it was all of us or some of us who went to the Clarke lectures at the University, and he (Middleton Murray) was lecturing on Keats, and he had just lost his wife, and he got mixed up, and he almost cried over it, and it was all acutely embarassing. But we were out at night – after dark![110]

Drama

Most students entering training college, especially in the earlier part of the century, had had little experience of live professional theatre, although they had enjoyed amateur 'theatricals' at home and at school. At college they were not only introduced to a wide variety of classical and modern drama as part of the curriculum, but were given the opportunity both to perform these plays themselves and to attend productions at the professional theatre. In-house performances formed part of the traditional Saturday evening entertainments, and as students' confidence grew, performances progressed from excerpts to full-scale productions. At Homerton, for instance, 'Scenes from Sheridan's "School for Scandal"' and 'Scenes from Shakespere [*sic*]' formed part of the entertainments in October 1914;[111] by 1927 the college's productions had become more ambitious:

> The Christmas item was Walter de la Mare's 'Crossings', very ably staged and performed. Among Saturday night performances, the outstanding ones were 'Becky Sharp', 'The Critic', Drinkwater's 'X=O' or 'A Night of the Trojan War', 'Riders to the Sea' by J. M. Synge, and the 'Golden Door', by Lord Dunsany.[112]

By the 1930s full-scale productions were staged at Christmas and Easter. The student Entertainments Committee were much encouraged by the reception of their production of Shaw's *You Never Can Tell*; next year they embarked on rehearsals for Goldsmith's *She Stoops to Conquer*. The following account shows not only how students enjoyed the excitement and liberation of dramatic performance, but that the occasion, with the participation of both academic and non-teaching staff (Miss Haynes, lecturer in English and Mr Cousins, head porter and chief engineer) involved the whole college community in the experience:

> After the marvellous effort of 'You Never Can Tell', we Juniors admittedly felt rather overwhelmed at the task confronting us when we settled down seriously to think of our item. A great consultation resulted in the final choice of 'She Stoops to Conquer', after much discussion of Shakespeare, Barrie, Sheridan and Goldsmith.

The casting was a co-operated [*sic*] effort of the committee, who spent a week in thinking and a few hours in talking about prospective players. You saw the result.

Rehearsals began shortly after half term, and several were the complaints when the strains of a noisy drinking song penetrated the ceiling of the gymnasium and entered the studio. Were we rising into Grand Opera or sliding into Revue?

Despite the nervous strain after a depressing dress rehearsal, the spirits of the cast were by no means damped, when on 18th March a host of betrousered females and four modest maidens waited for the curtain to rise.

Invaluable help was given by Miss Haynes in the production, and by Mr. Cousins in the scenery. We are extremely grateful to them.[113]

With the coming of Homerton's first lecturer in Speech and Drama in 1953, student productions became more professional. Through the good offices of John Barton, one of the college's external examiners, the college was allowed to hire the university's ADC Theatre for a week at the end of the Spring Term, giving students for the rest of the 1950s, the experience of performing in a professional theatre.[114]

There was no professional theatre at Chichester for Bishop Otter's students to attend but students were introduced to classical Greek drama as early as 1911, when Euripides *Orestes* was performed in English by the students[115] – in the principal's words 'the first time, as far as I know in any training college'.[116] The performance of a classical Greek play became an annual college tradition.[117] Homerton students were able to take advantage of the college's location in Cambridge and attend the Greek play (in Greek) put on triennially by the university. This introduction to high culture was carefully monitored by the principal:

The Greek play [*Oresteia of Aeschylus*] was performed and Miss Allan managed to get the Vice-Provost of Kings to explain the plot and background. She was very pleased and stressed that it was a great privilege. She remained on the platform – as she did with all visiting lecturers.[118]

A peak dramatic occasion for Bishop Otter was the young John Gielgud's visit in 1932. He arrived in 'an MG and wearing a jaunty beret'. On arrival he asked 'not for coffee, but a comb, a comb, my Kingdom for a comb'. Students were enthralled by his 'easy boyish manner' and the 'beauty of his verse speaking' and listened entranced to the 'death scene from Anthony' and 'Juliet and the nurse'.[119]

Avery Hill's proximity to London gave students, in theory at least, access to the wealth of the London stage. In the 1930s students were allowed two theatre permits to London a term – but although one student 'saw Laurence Olivier as Hamlet' another remembered that 'she could never afford to use more than one of her permits'.[120] The experience of top-quality professional theatre was also remembered by Homerton students as part of the cultural enrichment of college life. Saturday afternoon matinees at Cambridge's Festival Theatre in the 1920s were seen as 'very progressive'[121] – one student even saw Bernard Shaw coming out of the theatre and took a snapshot to memorialize the occasion.[122] Another Homerton student in the 1930s, captured the excitement for students of live professional theatre:

> When we could afford it we joined the queue for the Gods outside the Festival Theatre on a Saturday evening. I think Tyrone Guthrie was the director of it then. If the stalls were not full when the show was almost ready to begin he would walk along the queue and invite all of us students to fill up the stalls. I saw *Peer Gynt* and *1066 and All That* like this. The apron stage was so near the stalls that you felt you were part of the performance. They were magical evenings.[123]

Extra-curricular activities

I now want to examine some extra-curricular occasions in which the interaction between staff and students was integral to the cultural enrichment of college life. Debating topics of contemporary interest was an activity which was encouraged by the staff, but was taken up with less than enthusiasm by students. I would argue that students were not at home with the arguments, disagreements and even controversy of debating, and they felt that the essentially masculine adversarial nature of debate was not in accordance with their feminine culture. Staff, on the other hand, saw debating as a tool which would not only sharpen students' academic skills but make them more aware of the issues and controversies which would inevitably meet them in the world of the school. Religious discussions with members of staff, on the other hand, including expositions of difficult matters of belief and doctrine were very much appreciated by students, especially in the early part of the period. For training college students were still deeply embued with the tenets and practices of Victorian feminine piety – a piety which the higher education they received at college could sometimes cause them to question. Finally, I discuss students' participation in the peace movement of the 1920s and 1930s. Students' strong feelings about the threat to world peace at this time allowed them to overcome their usual reluctance to engage in 'political' activity. Interestingly, in the training college culture, involvement in the peace movement was structured as a religious, as well as a political activity.

Debating

Literary and Debating Society.

December 1914. The new plan of having a short discussion after each paper has proved to be a good one, but it is unfortunate that more people do not avail themselves of this opportunity for practice in debate.

November 1915. Why not come to the meetings, if it is only to get your mending done.[124]

Students' lack of enthusiasm for debating was also a reflection of the insularity of training college culture. There were, however, two political issues which did arouse interest − the Suffrage Movement in the years before the First World War, and the Peace Movement between the two world wars. Otherwise student debates tended to be either somewhat light-hearted (That palmistry is rubbish)[125] or suffering 'a little from a lack of practice and technique'.[126] At Avery Hill the 'Debating Society was very active in the early years' but it was only 'the suffrage question which brought their debates alive'. Moreover, it was not without significance that the lively debates on the suffrage question were stimulated and encouraged by Ethel Henley, lecturer in Nature Study, who was already closely involved in students' leisure activities.[127] In a debate in October 1908 'Miss Henley's Circle' carried by an 'overwhelming majority' the motion 'That the franchise should be extended to women'.[128] Only eight months later the Debating Society was reported to be 'languishing', although discussion on 'Women's Suffrage' remained 'eager'.[129] Interest in the suffrage also stimulated the formation of the short-lived Avery Hill Parliament in the years before the First World War.[130] At Bishop Otter student debates also owed much to the influence of a member of staff, the vice-principal, Stella Westaway. It was her idea, for instance, that in 1929, a General Election Year, students should hold their own election in college, when the Conservative candidate was elected. The student magazine reported that there was a 'lot of debate' and that 'our hazy ideas wanted a thorough shaking up of this kind'.[131]

Homerton's Literary and Debating Society was concerned far more with literary matters than debating until the mid-1930s.[132] It was only when the threat to international peace and the possibility of war became imminent that students became involved in political activity. I shall be discussing below students involvement in the peace movement by their support of such organizations as the League of Nations Union, but concern for peace now became central to students' concerns. Homerton's magazine reported in 1938 that 'the Literary and Debating Society had come to life' and that: 'There was a fiery debate on the subject "Communism and Fascism are founded on the same principles". No furniture was broken!'[133] With the actual advent of war, students' concerns had perforce to display 'consciousness of the outside world', and, again, it was the staff who mediated students' knowledge:

We have perhaps been almost too sheltered. However, our consciousness of the outside world has been recently displayed by requests for
information on Current Events and for a later lunch-bell to enable us
to listen to the One O'Clock News. Both have been granted, Miss
Skillicorn [the principal] and Miss Davies [lecturer in history] kindly
offering to answer questions on current problems.[134]

Religion

Religious education was not a part of the formal curriculum in training
colleges until after the Butler Act of 1944. However, religious observation,
church attendance and discussion of spiritual problems formed a central role
in the training college culture, even in Local Authority Colleges, like Avery
Hill, which had no statutory connections with the Church.[135] Bishop Otter,
as a Voluntary College of the Church of England, was deeply influenced by
its denominational foundation, more especially as the college was located
in the cathedral city of Chichester. Homerton College had been founded
by the Congregational Board of Education, but its Christian orientation was
undenominational rather than sectarian.

At Homerton, students were expected to attend church on Sundays, but
they were also encouraged to 'experiment' with different denominations. A
Congregationalist student, writing home in 1928, described her Sunday
adventures:

> 16 September. I've been to the Congregational chapel to hear Rev.
> Henry Carter. He was good.
> 2 October. Sunday morning I went to chapel with a crowd of
> Homertonians.
> 6 October. I went to the Anglo-Catholic church this morning with
> Howgie but I didn't really like it . . . there was too much bowing
> and ceremony for my liking.
> 16 October. On Sunday morning I went with Ellen to King's (College)
> Chapel.
> 9 November. Joss goes out to tea with people from the Baptist Church
> here nearly every Sunday.
> 30 November. Great news. I'm going to the Minister of Congreg: [*sic*]
> to tea next Sunday.
> December. Last Sunday I went to Baptist with Joss and was introduced
> to an undergrad. He said 'I'm Watson of Trinity' and I nearly laughed
> out loud.
> December. Oh. I went to the minister's to tea on Sunday. There were
> two undergrads there to tea also. They weren't too bad.[136]

These letters also bear witness to another vital function of church attendance; it was one of the few respectable venues for students to meet the

opposite sex. The Student Christian Movement (SCM) which I shall be discussing below, was frequently known as Student Christians Married, and evidence from the Homerton archive bears out the impression that churches and student religious societies were good places for the sexes to meet. Twelve students, for instance, whom I interviewed from the class of 1940, had all joined the Cambridge Inter-Collegiate Christian Union (CICCU) and were still in touch by round robin letters after fifty years. Out of the eight women who had married, three had met their husbands at CICCU, in spite of the fact that, in their day, the organization had separate sections for men and women![137]

Religious life at Bishop Otter centred on the cathedral and the college chapel. The Bishop of Chichester was ex officio chairman of governors and from 1897 to 1919, the college principal was a clerk in holy orders. In 1898 the College Guild was founded to provide a permanent link between former students and the cathedral.[138] Only students who joined the Guild were invited back to college for the annual reunion, and, after the Second World War, there was a move to found an Old Students' Association, which had no necessary connection with the cathedral. These dissenting students were firmly reminded of the college's ecclesiastical foundation: 'There is no place in the organization of a Church of England Training College for an Association of those who cannot identify themselves with the aims of the College as expressed in the Guild service.'[139]

The central focus for religious life in college was the chapel, and one of the purposes of the Guild was to raise money for its embellishment. In 1906 a stained glass window depicting St Hilda was erected in memory of the college's first principal Fanny Trevor.[140] The chapel remained central to college life throughout the period, and in 1953 the then principal, Elisabeth Murray, described its continuing influence: 'All the rich experience of two years here is of little lasting significance unless it bears fruit in life and the quality of the fruit depends upon the strength of the College as a worshipping community.'[141]

Most colleges formed branches of the Christian Union from their earliest days. These meetings were attended by both staff and students. Visiting lecturers or a member of staff would speak on a devotional topic. Edith Waterhouse was vice-principal at Avery Hill, before she returned to Homerton in 1911 (see Chapter 5). Her London students recorded her frequent 'helpful' addresses to the Christian Union and particularly her talks on prayer.[142] At Homerton, the principal Mary Allan, would often show 'her very practical sympathy' by presiding at the Union's meetings when students would be addressed by local clergy on 'Privilege and Responsibility of Prayer' or, more radically, 'about the the the spirit of hostile criticism of Christianity of the present age'.[143] By the time of the First World War, Homerton students had become involved in the world-wide Student Christian Movement and were holding inter-collegiate prayer meetings with other colleges in the university.[144] Waterhouse's spiritual influence on students continued throughout her long career at Homerton (she retired in 1937). Students were well aware of the beneficial effect which this sharing of religious experience had on the corporate life of the college:

> Miss Waterhouse discusses Bible study difficulties with the 'leaders' on Sunday evenings. Such informal meetings as these contribute enomously to the fullness of college life.[145]

> The nucleus of the SCM is always its study circles both religious, social and international, and here we would like to express our thanks to Miss Smith and to Miss Waterhouse for their help and guidance.[146]

The SCM was also very well supported at Avery Hill. More open-minded than the Christian Union, 'it encouraged open discussion' and provided students 'with a lively forum for exploration of the Christian faith'.[147] On the eve of the Second World War, students were allowed to travel to London to attend SCM services; student involvement in the SCM remained strong until the 1960s.[148] The highlight of the SCM calendar was the annual Swanwick Conference attended by hundreds of university and college students – male and female as the *Avery Hill Reporter* pointed out![149] – from all over the country. A predecessor of the Swanwick conference had been held at Haslemere in 1913 for London training colleges. After this experience, the two delegates from Avery Hill resolved to urge fellow students to pay attention to the religious aspects of their vocation for teaching: 'We aim to win the whole college for Christ and to try to make all students realize how great a work their vocation is.'[150] The Swanwick Conference further underlined the importance of spiritual and ethical values for training college students – certainly in the period up to and beyond the Second World War:

> Yesterday (for that is all it seems) a party of us returned from Swanwick, the great Student Conference, which is held every year at the 'Hayes' in Derbyshire. We came back full of enthusiasm, and eager to start on our special job in College. And, now, the year is nearly over and we have to turn and retrace the ground over which we have come – a ground not altogether smooth, but dotted with a good many pitfalls not all of which we have escaped, but at the same time not lacking in cheerful prospects as well.[151]

The peace movement

Student support for the peace movement of the 1920s and 1930s – and particularly for the League of Nations Union (LNU) – revealed a degree of political involvement which was highly unusual for women in teacher training colleges. Peace was, however, always a feminine, as well as a feminist issue, and women writers of the period, notably Vera Brittain[152] and Virginia Woolf[153] articulated forcibly women's hatred of war, and their construction of military aggression as an essentially masculine discourse entirely inimicable to the feminine doctrine of peace. During the First World War there were isolated individuals in training colleges whose interest in the women's peace movement prefigured the more general concern for peace which women students felt in the 1920s and 1930s. Beatrice Collins, lecturer in art at Homerton, was one of the British women refused permission to attend the Women's Peace Congress in The Hague in 1915, while a former Homerton student was given space in the college magazine in October 1915 for a long article on the International Peace Movement.[154]

The League of Nations Union (LNU) was founded in 1919 to mobilize public support for the newly-created League of Nations and it quickly received massive international support. Avery Hill students were early supporters of LNU; by 1926 over half the students had become members of the college branch. Nor was student involvement restricted to lectures and discussions in college. Students attended the LNU Summer School in Cambridge in 1927, and in 1930 six students joined the LNU delegation to Geneva to attend meetings of the League of Nations itself. Interestingly, and following the precedent of the Oxford University Union, students debated and carried by a large majority the motion 'That under no circumstances is war justifiable'.[155] Two years later the college magazine revealed students' need to know about the gathering threat to peace: 'The LNU talk on World Crisis and Disarmament helped us to see matters, at present so confused, from an international point of view.'[156]

By the 1930s, Homerton students were also enthusiastically involved 'in one of the most important movements in College'. Student participation was crucially guided by sympathetic members of staff: 'Miss Waterhouse very kindly spoke on the "Aims and Ideals of the League": those who went felt in some subtle way the spirit of the League and of Geneva, pervading the drawing-room.'[157] Two years later, the importance of LNU, and its integration with the college's religious life, was underlined at the end of term Christmas service:

> The Michaelmas Term ended with a most enjoyable service in Hall, on the last Sunday evening, given by the combined efforts of LNU, Musical and SCM Societies. The service took the form of appropriate readings, prayers and carols, followed by Laurence Housman's 'The Gate of Life'.[158]

By the mid-1930s some students were moving beyond the LNU to take up a specifically pacifist position. The developing connection between religion and politics, was shown in a heated debate on this controversial issue, in which both staff and students took part:

Another very interesting and wonderfully well-attended meeting was when the SCM and LNU combined and debated the motion that 'Every Christian should be a Conscientious Objector'. We are very much indebted to Miss Smith [lecturer in Biology] and P. Collis, who supported the motion, and to Mr Jones [lecturer in Geography] and F. Coates, who spoke in opposition. The motion was defeated by a very small majority.[159]

In 1935, 'the Peace Ballot was taken in College . . . : the result showed that Homerton is one hundred per cent, pro-League.' The pacifists, small in number but committed to their cause, had formed an Anti-War Group:

> This study-group began with about eight members who were vitally interested in peace. We wished to study the subjects of war and peace more deeply than we had done before.
>   We joined the Anti-War Movement in Cambridge and this enabled us to have excellent speakers to our Sunday afternoon meetings. The discussions at these meetings have been alive and interesting . . .
>   A great number of individuals are seeking out a means of producing peace by merely thinking about such a state. Active opposition against armaments, war propaganda and preparations is the only effective way.[160]

Another Homerton student's account of the 'Anti-War Society' was more analytical. Interestingly, she contrasted male students' 'revolutionary' ardour with her own more practical feminine approach:

> We were invited to join all the Cambridge University Societies, so I became a member of the League of Nations Union branch and later of an Anti-War Society, run by a very earnest group of young men. I felt very strongly about the cause until at one meeting they were discussing what should happen in the event of war: we must all immediately stand firm against war; we would naturally lose our jobs and be put in prison. They were so confident in their belief. I was horrified: my commitment went nowhere near such drastic acts; they were asking the impossible of me. I would not be able to give up my job; I could not let my parents down. They had banked on my security. I decided that I was no revolutionary.[161]

Nevertheless, even after the outbreak of the Second World War, fifteen Homerton pacifists reported to the college magazine that 'we still stand firmly in our faith'. The students' labelling of pacifism as a 'faith' is interesting showing that a religious rather than a political perspective was usually preferred by students. Moreover, as we have seen throughout this chapter, the involvement and support of a member of staff were crucial: 'We would like to thank Miss Smith for the support she has given us.'[162]

5 Sexuality

Heterosexuality

'He's not my young man, Kit,' protested Alison with a laugh. 'I don't know him at all really.'

Kit shook her head. 'Poor innocent,' she said. 'You underrate him. It's all perfectly clear to these old eyes. Jane will teach for a bit, I dare say, and then in three or four years she'll get married ... But you'll go quickly, Alison, mark my words. If not with this young man, then with another.'

Alison laughed aloud. 'And what about yourself, grandmamma?'

'I shall end up a headmistress I expect – one of the lean and stringy sort, and I look forward to receiving your children in my infant's department.'[1]

This dialogue, from a fictionalized account of life in a training college in the 1940s, paints an accurate picture of students' sexual destinations. The majority would 'teach for a bit' but then marry and retire from teaching;[2] only a minority would not marry and remain in the teaching profession until the retirement age. Most women teachers were both unmarried and celibate. In the 1920s and 1930s local authorities imposed a marriage bar which required women teachers to resign on marriage (see Chapter 1).[3] Furthermore, as I shall show below, contemporary mores obliged respectable women to restrict the expression of their sexuality to the marriage bed.

Sexuality, then, was bound to be a crucial issue in institutions where marriageable young middle-class girls were not only training for a profession which required them to be unmarried, but where they had been entrusted to the care of an unmarried female staff. In the first part of this chapter I shall show how attitudes to students' relationships with men friends changed over the period. In the early years of the century, both staff and students collectively shared an ethic which accepted that restrictions on sexual freedom were essential in order to maintain the respectability on which the credibility of their pioneering communities depended. But from the 1930s onwards, as sexual mores in society at large began to change, the perceptions of college staff became increasingly opposed to the needs of students. The ensuing tensions revolved around the central question of respectability. Could increased sexual freedom for students be reconciled with this ethic of respectability which lay at the heart of the colleges' culture of femininity? Moreover, although it was the students who pressed for greater sexual freedom and the staff who clung to the older ethic of strict sexual control, the issue of respectability cut across both sides of the argument.

Increasing employment opportunities for educated middle-class women had, from the later years of the nineteenth century onwards, allowed some women to lead economically independent lives and to remain unmarried. Foremost among those who took advantage of these new opportunities were the principals and staff of women's teacher training colleges. Recent feminist scholarship[4] has drawn attention to the link between feminism, women's independence and spinsterhood in the early years of the twentieth century. Spinsterhood was seen by feminists as a positive choice for women: 'They explicitly rejected, not only the patriarchal doctrine that women's primary vocation was marriage and motherhood, but the hetero-relational imperative, with its underlying assumption that a woman without a man was sexually incomplete.'[5]

In the second half of this chapter, I shall discuss the homoerotic friendships formed by some staff in women's colleges. But for Edwardian spinsters the strong moral and religious prohibitions on sexual relationships outside marriage made chastity obligatory. Respectability was a particularly crucial issue in the fledgling women's colleges who had to prove to the outside world that they were fit institutions to be entrusted with the care and training, *in loco parentis*, of young middle-class girls. Some staff in women's colleges were feminists and active in the suffrage movement, but such views were not considered appropriate by most students, let alone their parents.[6] However, staff at this period, whether or not they accepted the feminist critique, were confident in their spinsterhood and of their right to maintain strict control over students' behaviour and especially over their sexual behaviour. Students, by and large, were used to firm discipline, and accepted the restrictions of college life without complaint: 'We had been brought up by Victorian parents of firm ideas regarding those things a refined girl might or mostly might not do. Just think we were emancipated!'[7] Nevertheless Homerton's principal was taking no chances:

> Miss Allan gave us a lovely little lecture about the 5,000 youths who are coming up in three weeks' time. She says she's proud to say that Homerton girls have never behaved badly and she's sure that none of us will. She says if we've any friends (already) at the Varsity we can go out to tea with them but we mustn't make friends. It's not done.[8]

Sensitivity to the possibility of scandal was particularly acute at Homerton. For Cambridge was a town dominated by the male values of its university, which barely tolerated its own women students, let alone lower middle-class students at an obscure teacher training institution. Moreover, it had only been in the closing years of the nineteenth century that the university had lost its right to imprison women in the town – who could have included Homerton students – whom it suspected of being prostitutes.[9] Students' relationships with men were structured in terms of social class as well as respectability. Another student recalled the principal's annual homily:

> My most vivid memory is of the lecture we were given on our first morning in College – we were to remember that we were two hundred 'gels' among five thousand men, and must never stand giggling with a man at the gate like a servant 'gel', but bring him into the College. (One junior did so, amid great hilarity.)[10]

Relationships with men were not actually forbidden but they were hedged around with so many restrictions that only the most strongly motivated student persisted. To visit a man outside college it was necessary to obtain: 'Written permission from parents to the Principal in order to meet an undergraduate in his rooms or his college. Afternoons only and accompanied by a friend.'

No men, except relations, were allowed into students' rooms. Students were, however, allowed to host tea parties for men friends 'in a screened off corner of the students' drawing room'.[11] An interesting confirmation of the nature of these tea parties was received in response to a photograph of the drawing room (complete with its screen) published in the Homerton Centenary booklet.[12] A male graduate of Cambridge University wrote to the principal that he and three friends had regularly taken tea in Homerton's drawing room – but 'it was all strictly platonic'.[13] Boy friends at this earlier period were not the central pre-occupation with students that they were to become in the 1940s and 1950s. College life was an adventure and an all-absorbing experience; marriage, boy friends and the world outside could wait. A student writing home in 1928 revealed an attitude to potential men friends which was at once casual, almost off-hand, while still observing conventional middle-class proprieties:

> There were two undergrads there to tea. They weren't too bad ... I sat between them and I wasn't much impressed. The opposite sex hasn't much attraction for me.[14]

> I heard from Lew about 5 weeks ago. He said he was coming to Cambridge because he knew several of the boys up here and would I see him. Do you mind if I do see him if he ever comes. I don't suppose he ever will come but still – I'd better know.[15]

By the late 1920s society's attitude to female sexuality was undergoing a profound change. The self-confidence of spinsterhood as a political position and lifestyle was being undermined by the new 'science' of sexology. The sexologist's discourse was revolutionary in promoting women's needs for and right to physical sexual satisfaction; but it was retrogressive and anti-feminist in insisting that this satisfaction could only be obtained within the confines of heterosexual marriage. Extramarital and non-heterosexual sex remained taboo – particularly for respectable middle-class women.[16] This re-evaluation of female sexuality severely undermined the consensus which had hitherto prevailed in training colleges. If women 'needed' physical sexual satisfaction but could only obtain it through marriage, students' interest in boy friends and eventual marriage was inevitably quickened. The expression of their sexuality now increasingly became a central concern for students. As a consequence, some students began to chafe at the strict control over their sexuality which was still being exercised by staff. But the staff's authority over sexual matters – hitherto barely questioned – was being gradually eroded. For, by definition, the new sexologist's discourse put staff at a disadvantage. If sexual expression within marriage was now deemed essential – or at the very least highly desirable – for all women, how could staff who were necessarily celibate and spinsters, continue to maintain their customary authority over students in sexual matters? The staff's initial response to this new situation was to re-double vigilance rather than to relax any control.

The special circumstances of the First World War had seen some temporary relaxation in the rules. The *Homerton News Letter* recorded that 'several married old students have returned to teaching for the duration of the war'.[17] Although the marriage bar, as such, did not come into operation unil the 1920s, most middle-class women, including teachers, retired from paid employment when they married. An interesting exception, as Copelman has shown, was the case of women teachers in London, some 25 per cent of whom continued to teach after marriage.[18] At Avery Hill during the war, a student was, most unusually, allowed to entertain her fiancé in the principal's room – alone.[19] At Homerton, on the other hand, controls were tightened because the principal, Mary Allan, felt 'extra responsibility for 200 young women in war-time when Cambridge was full of officers'.[20] Allan continued her annual homily on sexual propriety until she retired in 1935. Restrictions on sexual freedom were generally accepted by students up to the Second World War, and some sympathy was still being expressed for the principal's stance: 'The warning was always (secretly) humorously received but it did show how concerned Miss Allan was about her role as [*sic*] "loco parentis"'[21]; and 'in the 1930s young people had a very healthy respect for those in authority'.[22]

Some students, however, were beginning to question the whole system of control. In the following anecdotes the intrusive over-fussy, even absurd, concern of staff is made clear:

> In those far off days males were all suspect. I was reported one Sunday morning for being seen walking with a young man. I had to see Miss

Allan and had to explain to her that my companion was a great friend from home. We went to the same Congregational Church at home. When we were seen together in Cambridge we were walking back from a Morning Service. Miss Allan listened to my explanation, but I had to write home for a permissive letter from my Mother.[23]

I was called to Miss Allan to be asked whether I thought it was a good idea to see my friend from Emmanuel so often. This interview shook me severely: what kind of an institution had I come to?[24]

I had to get a letter from my parents before being allowed to go for the first house at the Palladium [a London theatre] with a man friend from home. When I got back to college, a lecturer told me it would have taken her 'x' minutes to walk from the station. 'What have you done with the other 20 minutes?'[25]

The disruptions of the Second World War sharpened the tensions in the sexual debate. Many training colleges were evacuated to other sites for the duration of the war. Avery Hill students were evacuated from Eltham to Huddersfield early in 1941 to avoid the ravages of the London Blitz. Students were billeted in lodgings and it was only with difficulty that the academic and community life of the college was maintained.[26] Freedom from the strict controls of a residential community could, however, be advantageous for students. In September 1942, Bishop Otter was obliged to evacuate the college to Bromley. The 'very difficult conditions' for the principal and her staff were, on the other hand, welcomed by students because it gave them access to the facilities of London and allowed them to escape from the provincial confines of Chichester.[27] Homerton stayed put on its Cambridge site. In 1935 Mary Allan had been succeeded as principal by Alice Skillicorn. Skillicorn sought to modernize college regulations, including those on the entertainment of men friends, but always within the confines of an essentially conservative agenda. She now provided a special room for students to entertain men friends to tea. But although this 'at last eliminated the discomfort of crouching behind screens in the drawing room with visitors',[28] 'a lecturer popped in frequently to make sure you were behaving'.[29] Skillicorn also tried to lighten the control which was still being exercised by staff by the exercise of humour:

Miss Skillicorn was passing through the entrance hall where the various boy friends were waiting for the students. She turned to her guests and said, 'You can see that the RAF is in evidence today'.[30]

I understand that there are College Fathers and Uncles. I do not wish to see their washing hanging up in the drying room.[31]

The wartime blackout gave staff yet another reason for maintaining vigilance. This student drew attention to the tension – even animosity – between students and staff which was becoming increasingly apparent:

> I think most of the lecturers seemed to think in the first two years of the war – that we would all be raped if we were out after dark because of the black out. I somehow thought they didn't like us very much – especially if we wanted to enjoy ourselves.[32]

There was of course an actual as well as a cultural generation gap between staff and students. Many staff had been in post for twenty years and more. It is not surprising that they found it difficult to adjust to students' 'new' desire for increased sexual freedom, when they themselves had had their opinions formed in the entirely different sexual climate of the early years of the century. Students in their turn saw older members of staff as remote figures to whom they found it difficult to relate. Miss Glennie, for instance, had been on the Homerton staff since 1905: 'Poor Miss Glennie. She sat up waiting for students [to come in from exeat]. She was very ladylike but much too old for the job.'[33] 'I remember Miss Glennie. Her long old-fashioned clothes – her deadly lectures. She always seemed like Methusalah to me.'[34] Another student summed up the situation: 'It's incredible that at 18, 19 and 20 we were virtually imprisoned. Our morals like our laundry bags were open to inspection.'[35]

Some of the younger members of staff were seeking to understand and adjust to the students' point of view. One student was able to see her boy friend in private because a member of staff invited him to tea in her own room.[36] Other students were able to meet boy friends in a old hut used for games, thanks to the PE staff turning a blind eye.[37] Another staff member, appointed in 1943 straight from her first teaching post in a girls public school, remembered being highly critical of the old-fashioned regime she found at Homerton. She disliked having to check up on students and frequently found herself in embarrassing situations. One evening, while patrolling the grounds on fire watching duty 'a student suddenly popped out with a young man. "Oh, Miss . . . , I've been rather stupid." I shot him out to the station.' She felt a similar awkwardness when her tutees were obliged to introduce their boy friends in 'an attempt to keep tabs on them'.[38]

One member of staff whom I interviewed had also been a student at Homerton. Her recollections from 'both sides of the fence' throw interesting light on the sexual tensions in college. As a student, she resented the restrictive exeat system, although 'it was not so much the system as the attitude towards it'. By the late 1940s, the college was employing a porteress to mark in students after exeats. This woman was 'over-tough' on the students. Before granting exeats staff asked 'too many and too detailed questions where you were going'. This curiosity was motivated less by staff 'anxiety about students' whereabouts' than by a vicarious interest in students' sex lives. Staff of course were able to entertain men in their own rooms – but only younger staff had any personal relationships with men. Such was the feverish atmosphere by the early 1950s over the whole question of men friends that even when she herself became a member of staff and did her own entertaining 'she felt everyone was looking at her'.[39]

One of the older members of staff at Homerton – appropriately the Biology lecturer – was exceptional among her contemporaries in attempting to pursue a policy of sexual frankness with students. But although students acknowledged her sympathy and kindness and 'real interest in students' lives',[40] her attempts to give students 'very up-to-date sex instruction' exposed her to student ridicule rather than gaining their respect. Her warning that students should not 'wear french knickers when punting with boy friends'[41] was embarrassing, while her assertion that 'Anyone who's a virgin at thirty is a fool – and I'm no fool'[42] was simply not believed. Crucially hampered by their lack of actual heterosexual experience, older members of staff could have no credibility with students in sexual matters. Some staff were 'always discussing students' lives',[43] but sympathetic concern could shade into an undesirable prurience. Divisions over sexuality undermined the tightly knit feminine communities in training colleges and were a major factor in their eventual demise.

'Lovemaking is a lovely and beautiful thing but college provides neither the time nor place.'[44] This advice given to students by the deputy principal in the late 1940's was an attempt to hold back the floodgates. While acknowledging students' right to eventual sexual fulfilment, the staff still strove to banish the whole subject from college life. Miss Bradley was an attractive, well-dressed woman, popular with students, and, significantly, known to have her own 'private life in Cambridge'.[45] Wisely, the principal frequently delegated discussions with students on sexual matters to her deputy because she was felt to carry more authority (and knowledge) than her older colleagues.

Restrictions on sexual freedom

I now want to chart in some detail, using evidence from the minute book of the Homerton Union of Students,[46] the development of the sexual debate at Homerton in the 1940s and early 1950s. The students, in spite of considerable, sustained, and astute pressure, were unsuccessful in their attempts to obtain better facilities for entertaining men friends. The debate revealed, not only students' desire for more sexual freedom, and the staff's resistance to and fear of such freedom, but also issues of feminine respectability and feminine solidarity which cut across both sides of the argument. In October 1941 there was an early promise of victory for the students when the following proposition was passed:

Friends in Rooms

It was suggested that it should be allowed to entertain friends in rooms:

a)   Not enough tea-rooms
b)   Difficult to entertain or talk to friends outside college
c)   Suggested time 2–5 p.m.

College was in sympathy with the idea and it was passed by a two-thirds majority.[47]

It is interesting that this minute does not even mention that the friends under discussion were men – women friends could of course be entertained routinely. Moreover, the couching of the request in terms of administrative convenience (not enough tea-rooms) and social obligation (inability to entertain friends) rather than the desire to meet sexual partners in privacy, revealed students' firm adherence to notions of respectable middle-class femininity. Sex, as such, could not be openly discussed. Incredibly, however, in view of the prevailing staff attitude at the time, the principal granted the request. It could be that she considered the extraordinary conditions of wartime warranted it. Nevertheless this permission was almost immediately withdrawn:

> The Student Reps approached Miss Skillicorn, on behalf of all the students, to ask for permission to entertain our men friends in our rooms during certain hours each day. This was granted but within a few weeks it was withdrawn at the request of the students; it was disconcerting to find men upstairs when girls were dashing from PE or dance lectures, to wash or bath or scantily clad in 'pea-pods' [PE tunics] or dressing gowns![48]

For some students the presence of men in students' rooms was both an invasion of their own privacy and an impediment to the corporate life of a women's community. This tension between individual desire for sexual expression and the corporate needs of the feminine community remained. Resentment at intrusive male behaviour on college premises was recorded at a meeting of HUS in 1944: 'That members of the University should be discouraged from treating Homerton as a place of entertainment or public house and should refrain from creating a disturbance outside after "chucking out" at 10 p.m.'[49]

In July 1947 HUS returned to the attack:

Visitors in rooms

A request was made that permission should be granted by the staff to allow entertaining of male friends in the students' rooms between certain times. The point was made that no-one was able to return hospitality. It was pointed out that the bedrooms were not suitably furnished.

Voting	that men should be allowed in students' rooms	29
	that men should not be allowed in students' rooms	22

There were a number of abstentions.[50]

The closeness of the vote and the number of abstentions showed how divisive this issue had become. Again, the request was couched in terms of middle-class standards of femininity – the inability to return hospitality. The reference to bedroom furniture, i.e. beds, was a Victorian 'excuse', which by now had become risible in many middle-class homes. Its continued use in the training college context, and by students as well as staff, was an indication of the colleges' failure to adapt to changing standards of middle-class propriety.

The year 1948 saw the first mention in the minutes of the Back Drive. The Back Drive was a coded reference to students' behaviour when bidding farewell to their male escorts after an evening out. Forbidden to make these farewells in the privacy of their own rooms, students were obliged to express their sexuality in public, even if under the cover of darkness. Few respectable middle-class women at this period indulged in full sexual intercourse before marriage. Pregnancy outside marriage was still the proverbial fate worse than death. And yet it was acknowledged, however uneasily, that not only was it entirely desirable for women to be looking for marriage partners, but that before marriage some sexual outlet should be allowed. Heavy petting up to, but seldom beyond, mutual masturbation, became the norm.[51] In the collegiate setting this 'new' sexual discourse aroused acute anxiety and tensions – especially over the issue of feminine and corporate respectability:

Back Drive

The Senior Student urged the need for more lights in the drive when people are coming in after dark. The behaviour in the back-drive of students was dragging down the standards of college.[52]

The Senior Student again stressed the need for each individual to help pull up the standard of behaviour in the back drive, since further complaints had been made.[53]

The principal addressed the HUS early in 1951 on the whole question of 'entertaining in college'. Additional public rooms for entertaining had always been a central plank of the students' case. They were now suggesting that 'Macauley' – a common room furnished in memory of a previous student – be additionally allowed for entertaining outside visitors. Miss Skillicorn's reply was deeply ambivalent:

The meeting was opened by Miss Skillicorn who brought the question of entertaining in college to the notice of the students present. She stressed the limited accommodation for both staff and students. It was pointed out that Macauley was a room given by the parents of a student who died in college, and the terms of the endowment stated it was to be used as a student common room, as such Miss Skillicorn felt it was not suitable for entertaining outside friends as that meant that the rest of the student body was then excluded. She saw the difficulties of entertaining in college, and stated that it was not that she wished to prevent it but only to show that college as yet had not the facilities. After answering a few questions Miss Skillicorn proposed that the meeting should discuss more fully and send any proposal they had to herself. Miss Skillicorn then left the meeting.[54]

The principal was skating on thin ice and she knew it. Her attempt to couch her refusal in purely administrative terms was specious. Outside entertaining had always taken place in the students' other common room – the Drawing Room. Moreover, her vague reference to the possibility of suitable facilities being provided in the future (presumably in the Queen's Wing opened by the Queen Mother in 1956) was never to materialize. After Skillicorn's departure the meeting settled into 'heated discussion'. Demands were made that the 'exact wording' of the Macauley endowment be examined. Students also played on the principal's known concern with the college's reputation in the outside world – a concern which they also shared. 'Macauley was very rarely used purely as a common room and it presented a good impression to outsiders.' The debate then moved on to entertaining in students' own rooms. Again, student tactics were sensible. They first discussed an extension of visiting hours for family and women friends, and the abolition of the requirement that the Domestic Bursar be informed of all such visits. In the ensuing discussion on entertaining men friends, most of the old arguments were rehearsed yet again – with the addition of an appeal to class interests in the mention of the University:

> It was noted that many Homerton students received a great deal of hospitality from Members of the University, which, as things now stood with few entertaining rooms, could not be sufficiently repaid ... It should be brought to the notice of the staff that a revision of the entertainment rules would be appreciated and a tentative suggestion be forwarded that men friends could be entertained in student rooms between the hours of 3 p.m. and 6 p.m. on Saturday and Sunday afternoons. This was passed with only 6 voting against.

That this exceedingly modest suggestion was not accepted by the principal, even though it had overwhelming student support, bore witness to the social and sexual conservatism which continued to control the behaviour of women students throughout the 1950s. When I was a student at Exeter University in the early 1950s, no men were allowed in students' own rooms. Heavy petting in the 'Back Drive' was universal. We were not, however, as closely supervised as training college students. The usual entry in the 'signing out' book – OWL – (Out with lover!) was received by the authorities without comment.

Behaviour in the Back Drive remained a central concern at Homerton, In this impassioned plea from the Senior Student at the same 1951 meeting, sexual and class issues continued to intersect with the ethic of respectability which remained deeply embedded in the corporate culture:

> The Senior Student impressed upon the meeting that the question of discreet behaviour at the college gate had not been brought up by members of staff but by fellow students. It was felt very strongly that any behaviour at the gate could be noted by the residents in the district, and it was up to students to see that their behaviour was not a bad reflection on the College as a whole. She realised that Domestic staff were at times to blame, but that did not mean that students need be indiscreet as well.[55]

It was not, however, until the early 1960s that a new principal, intent on modernizing college procedures, bowed to the inevitable. This sanctioning of sexual freedom or at least the provision of the privacy which allowed it, seemed a daring move to contemporaries: 'After 1961 men were allowed in our rooms from 2.30 p.m. until 10 p.m., which was thought very daring when it was first introduced.'[56]

It seems curious that institutions which set such a store by respectability should have allowed semi-public displays of sexuality in their own grounds. I think the authorities in both training colleges, and to a lesser extent universities, were confused and, importantly, embarrassed by the whole question of students' sexual behaviour and needs. Older staff had never come to terms with the new sexual discourse, and because they had had no actual experience in a matter of such personal intimacy, they felt that their authority over student behaviour had been fatally undermined. Moreover, to have allowed men into student rooms, while it would have led to less public display of sexuality, would also have been seen to be granting a licence for full sexual intercourse in private. Better to hope that students would take heed of the exhortations for public discretion, than to be seen officially to condone sexual behaviour (including, of course, the possibility of pregnancy) which would offend against the perceived sexual mores of the period.

The rare pregnancies which did occur, in spite of all the colleges' precautions, were always hushed up. One student at Homerton was reported to have kept her condition secret until the very last minute, when she began to give birth in a lavatory! She was rushed to hospital and never returned to college. The principal showed her characteristic ambivalence in sexual matters when she offered to take another pregnant student back to college, after she had given birth. Staff considered that all that had concerned the principal in this case was that because the father was not an undergraduate, scandal and its ensuing damage to the college's reputation in Cambridge had been avoided. Another way of dealing with pregnancy was to pass the offending student onto another college with the title 'Mrs'. This was said to be necessary in order not 'to upset schools'.[57] Even when students were well aware of a pregnancy, staff would not admit it officially, but instead would announce that the pregnant student had gone home to visit a relative.[58] But however extreme – even absurd – this secrecy, in the teeth of the evidence, may seem in retrospect, it bears striking witness to the paramount importance of chastity before marriage – or at least the avoidance of pregnancy – for respectable middle-class girls at this period.

Students in the 1950s, in spite of the continuing restrictions on entertaining men friends in college, found plenty of opportunities to socialize with the opposite sex. Dances had always been traditional meeting places. Avery Hill was in the vanguard when it allowed its students, as early as 1929, to attend an NUT dance in the Woolwich Town Hall. The college's historian described an occasion which appears to have been more boisterous than romantic. The staff, as usual, were maintaining a strict watch over student behaviour:

> In 1929 students were allowed for the first time to attend an NUT dance in Woolwich Town Hall which was also attended by men from UCL (University College, London) and Marjons (the Training College of St Mark and St John in Chelsea). Coaches came to the College to collect the students but lecturers went too, not so much to enjoy the occasion but to keep an eye on their charges. When the dance ended students responded to the Marjons war cry by giving their own: – Animo et Fide, Avery, Avery, Avery Hill, Hurra, Hurra, Hurra, Hoo-Ha-Hoo.[59]

A student described the occasion more bluntly: 'Lecturers were strewn about so we did not go off the rails.'[60]

End-of-term dances at Avery Hill remained single sex until the end of the 1930s. A male band provided the music on these occasions, but the staff were taking no chances: 'The lecturers sat along the front of the band so that we could not speak to the men.'[61] It is interesting that when the 'final emancipation'[62] of a mixed dance in the college's Great Hall was instituted in 1939, middle-class standards of dress and deportment were heavily emphasized. Long evening dress for women and 'a black tie and dinner jacket were de rigeur for the young men who were prepared to travel considerable distances to attend these splendid occasions'.[63]

Bishop Otter's students were less fortunate. Chichester, unlike Avery Hill and Homerton, could not provide a ready supply of suitable dancing partners. Nor did the college have a Great Hall, like Avery Hill, which could provide a suitable venue for a Ball. Students were invited to attend dances outside college, e.g. a dance hosted by the city's mayor in 1954 for 'US midshipmen', but worry about the status and eligibility of the men they had been invited to meet, made student response lukewarm: 'Students grumble about the lack of eligible partners at our dances – but if they don't accept outside invitations, e.g. to local hospitals how can they expect others to partake of our hospitality?'[64]

By the early 1950s, Bishop Otter was using Chichester's Assembly Rooms, a local hotel and the County Hall for end-of-term Balls.[65] Homerton had also begun to hold an annual Ball at Cambridge's Dorothy Cafe, as well as informal dances in the college itself.[66] Homerton students' central social and sexual concerns at this period, however, centred on undergraduates at Cambridge University. Students had always had some contact with undergraduates – mainly through the social activities of local churches.[67] But fraternization had not been encouraged by either the University or by Homerton. From the late 1920s Homerton students began, in the principal's words, 'to receive a few crumbs which fall from the University table'[68] and, after the Second World War, changing economic and social conditions made fraternization between university and training college more acceptable. For elementary teaching had now become acceptable as a suitable career for middle-class as well as lower middle-class girls (see Chapter 1). However, in spite of their increased social acceptability, Homerton students were not accepted as equals by male undergraduates. This worked to Homerton students' advantage as far as social and sexual relationships were concerned. For 'men liked Homerton girls because they were not so highbrow' (as the women undergraduates)[69] and the tag 'Girton for Brawn, Newnham for Brains, Homerton for Beauty',[70] underlined Homerton students' status as social/sexual partners rather than intellectual equals:

Such feminist concerns, however, rarely concerned the 1950s Homerton generation:

> Students at Homerton could have a very full social life and we realised how very fortunate we were, compared to students in teacher training colleges which were not in a university town. It was wonderful to be in a place where girls were outnumbered by male undergraduates by 10–1. No shortage of partners at dances, and certainly no wallflowers! Many of us went to the Saturday informal dances at Houghton Hall and to be invited to a May Ball was wonderful.[71]

Houghton Hall was a local dance hall frequented by both town and gown. It was 'the place you went to get picked up. I can remember a guy who said "What are you reading?" and I said "Infants"'.[72] Each college at the university held an annual May Ball in June. These were all-night affairs, traditionally ending with a punt up the river in the early morning.

All Homerton students were 'desperate to go to May Balls'.[73] The principal was equally keen that her students should be seen to shine socially at this apex of the university's social calendar. But although an all-night exeat was granted for the Ball itself, students had to be back in time for college breakfast. There were to be no opportunities for private love-making (so she thought!) and no absence from morning lectures: 'Do you remember when we'd been to a May Ball? We had to go up and report and then sit and have breakfast. We couldn't punt down the river to Grantchester – we weren't allowed to stay.'[74]

Critics complained that because of students' hectic and glamorous social life, Homerton resembled a smart finishing school rather than a teacher training college. Special permission was even given in the late 1950s for students, who were also debutantes, to attend Queen Charlotte's Ball, the traditional opening of the London season.[75] While it is true that Homerton students had access to a more glamorous and high-status social life than many other training college students, concern with their 'sex appeal' was paramount among all students. For the conventional image of a teacher – in students' eyes at least – was not necessarily attractive to men. A student from Bishop Otter was anxious:

How to become a teacher

You must dress respectfully. . . . You chose teaching partially for its social status but have you ever noticed the way the man in the street looks at the unmistakable teacher?[76]

Some students found being 'pressurized by men in colleges' stressful and looked to their own colleges as 'a woman's haven'.[77] Friendship between women students was an important, if not the most important feature of college life (see Chapter 2), but students' relationships with the opposite sex could be competitive as well as romantic:

One day, as I was entering the college gate, I practically collided with a handsome young man in a red open MG sports car. I wondered which lucky female had managed to snare such a catch. He turned his large orbs on me and flashed his teeth in a dazzling smile. 'Yes, I'm looking for Miss "X".' I went weak at the knees. 'That's me', mentally furious that there wasn't a single soul in the lobby to see this gorgeous creature hand me an invitation.[78]

In the 1950s the status of older unmarried staff was further undermined by the appointment of married women as part-time lecturers. The marriage bar had been abolished in the Second World War and by the 1950s, far fewer professional women remained unmarried. Colleges therefore turned to married women to fill staff vacancies. Married women's higher social status (through their husbands) and their extra-collegiate allegiances to family and home 'were a constant reproach to the unmarried. They made the unmarried feel they had failed'.[79] Curiously, although many of the unmarried staff disliked married women and envied them their social and sexual status, they felt no such antipathy to the young married men who also began to be appointed to the staff at this time. Indeed, male staff were usually required to be 'young men with families'.[80] Presumably this was thought to be a safeguard against the possibility of male staff forming sexual relationships with students. The gulf in age between older women and younger men also allowed women staff to treat their younger male colleagues (who remained very much in the minority until the mid-1960s) as protégés rather than as rivals.

Homoerotic friendship

> Students accepted the lesbian relationships of some members of staff. They were used to it in girls' schools.[81]

> There were only 2 sets of lesbians, 1 girl was from G—, and she still lives with the woman she met there.[82]

> Of course one did suppose there were lesbians – but I didn't encounter any.[83]

Close friendships between women, which contained the possibility of a sexual relationship, remained a taboo subject for respectable middle-class girls throughout our period. Some students were nevertheless aware of the existence of lesbianism among both students and staff, as the quotations above show. Such friendships between members of staff were tacitly accepted within college communities, but they were never, at the time, given the taboo label of lesbian. Royal Holloway College's historian, writing in 1986, described the prevailing attitude of disapproval and denial:

> Close friendships . . . were common among women of this generation, but sexual relationships between them were probably far rarer than a more permissive generation imagines. Disapproval of lesbianism was so extreme as to render it completely unmentionable so that ignorance of its existence was not uncommon in the young. As late as the 1940s ignorance of homosexuality was still possible.[84]

As late as 1963, an American university teacher was still reluctant to use the taboo label 'lesbian', although she recognized that the practice had existed at her college some 60 years earlier:

> As might be expected, Dr Hamilton denied that there was any open lesbianism between Hull House residents but did agree that 'the close relationship involved an unconscious sexuality'. She hastened to interject

that because it was unconscious it was 'unimportant'. Then she added with a smile that the very fact that I would bring the subject up was an indication of the separation between my generation and hers.[85]

I have side-stepped the use of the term 'lesbian' to describe the friend-ships of college staff by using the term 'homoerotic', first employed by Martha Vicinus to describe close friendships between women in residential educational institutions in England during the late nineteenth and early twentieth centuries.[86] Vicinus used the term to signal an intermediate phase in the construction of women's relationships with each other, between the acceptable 'romantic' of the earlier nineteenth century and the condemna-tory 'lesbian' of the mid-twentieth. Faderman had argued that romantic friendship was accepted as appropriate feminine behaviour under certain circumstances – either as an apprenticeship to heterosexual love or as a consolation for women who could not find husbands. Romantic friendship was only acceptable because it did not challenge hegemonic discourses of gender and power. For not only did women at this period lack the economic resources to lead independent lives outside marriage, but they were also encouraged to believe that, unlike men, they had no innate sexuality which needed physical expression.[87] Faderman's assertion of Victorian women's lack of innate sexuality has been strongly challenged by historians.[88] For instance, the recently de-coded diary of Anne Lister, a prosperous Yorkshire spinster in the early nineteenth century, contains explicit genital details of her sexual conquests of women.[89]

By the last quarter of the nineteenth century changes in the social and economic position of women in England, coupled with developments in medical opinion, led to an increasingly ambivalent attitude towards women's close friendships. The increase in employment opportunities for middle-class women now allowed some women, who included staff in training colleges, to lead economically independent lives, and therefore to be in a position to reject marriage altogether. Furthermore, medical theorists, like Kraft-Ebing and Freud, had now problematized the whole area of sexuality, and, as part of a radical new sexual discourse, were declaring that women, as well as men, needed to express their sexuality by physical means. This expression was, of course, only available to women within heterosexual marriage.[90] This volte-face on women's sexuality was to have major consequences in teacher training colleges, as we have already seen. It undercut college staff's belief that their spinsterhood was a positive choice, which enabled them to lead valid and fulfilling lives, free of 'the patriar-chal doctrine ... with its underlying assumption that a woman without a man was sexually incomplete'.[91]

But ambivalence towards homoerotic friendship intensified as the sexo-logists' discourse took hold; and, as the twentieth century moved into its third decade, culminating in the *Well of Loneliness* trial in 1928, ambiva-lence turned to overt hostility. If sexual fulfilment for women was now mandatory within the confines of the marriage bed, all close relationships between women, which not only precluded marriage but included the possibility of the physical expression of sexuality, must be given the deviant label of 'lesbian' and outlawed.[92]

Jefferys has argued that single women in the 1920s and 30s 'though pilloried by the sexologists of the period', nevertheless 'retained some of the self-respect and status won for spinsters by a generation of feminist struggle'.[93] Oram has also drawn attention to the positive models at this period for single women and their friendships, including the possibility of the physical expression of sexuality, being promoted by feminist doctors, like Esther Harding and Laura Hutton.[94] Some college staff would have been familiar with this literature, as with the equally positive messages for spinsters being promoted by such well-known feminists as Maud Royden and Winifred Holtby. Royden was indeed a friend of Mary Allan, Homerton's principal, whose homoerotic partnership I shall be discussing below.[95] Nevertheless, the sexologists' discourse remained paramount, and women who lived together in close relationships were now forced to employ the utmost discretion if they wished to remain within the bounds of respectable behaviour. For staff in women's training colleges the issue of respectability was all important. As leaders in educational institutions, entrusted with the care of young unmarried women, they could not afford to endanger their professional authority nor forfeit public respect by any hint of private scandal.

The sensitivities surrounding the whole subject of homoerotic friendship make the interpretation of the evidence for it difficult. Although some respondents and interviewees are willing, recalling events forty or fifty years ago, to use the taboo word 'lesbian', most are not. My interpretations have been influnced by Rupp's argument on the nature of close friendships between women in the twentieth century:

> Since there was such a thing as a lesbian culture, we need to distinguish between women who identify as lesbians and/or are part of a lesbian culture, where one exists, and a broader category of women – committed women who would not identify as lesbians but whose primary commitment in emotional and practical terms was to other women.[96]

The close friendships between staff in women's colleges fit into this broader category. They themselves would not have used the word lesbian – let alone identify with a lesbian culture as such. It was their primary emotional commitment to another woman which constituted homoerotic friendship.

At Homerton there were some established homoerotic partnerships between members of staff. The couples are invariably described as 'great friends'.[97] Students also noticed 'odd masculine'[98] features in appearance – like an Eton crop – or drew attention to the pair's inseparability: 'Wherever Miss "X" was there was Miss "Y".'[99]

One member of staff drew an interesting comparison between two pairs of friends. The first relationship was described unequivocally as 'lesbian' with one partner being 'very masculine'. In the other relationship, although one partner was described as 'direct and masculine' the partnership was 'not unhealthy – just hearty women together not homoerotic'.[100] Another relationship was described by a mutual friend in sado-masochistic terms. Interestingly, this evidence made her 'think it was a lesbian attachment'.[101]

Some homoerotic partners set up home together outside the confines of the college. This replication of the domesticity of the middle-class home was an important social support to homoerotic friendship, as well as allowing the expression of traditional feminine values. One such home was described as 'lovely' and the couple as 'very domesticated': 'I remember a meal – the loving care and presentation, from the flowers on the table to the parsley by the butter.'[102]

The respectability of homoerotic friendships and the lack of suspicion they aroused in the outside world are strikingly illustrated by the adoption of children by some couples. Children, of course, made more real the replication of the family values of the middle-class home. This not uncommon practice at the time in Britain surprised an American visitor: 'I was surprised to find that two single women had adopted daughters, a practice unknown to me in the USA.'[103]

The ability of homoerotic partners to lead a middle-class family life, which had its focus outside the work of the college, allowed them to forge important bonds with their students. Students enjoyed helping to look after the children and participating in domestic life.[104]

I now want to examine the homoerotic relationships of three women principals. Like other members of college staff, their need to maintain respectability and professional authority was paramount. But principals were also women in positions of power, and the need to reconcile their emotional needs with the reality of this power could prove problematic.

Mary Miller Allan

In Chapter 3, I described Allan's professional partnership with her second vice-principal, Edith Waterhouse. The combining of this professional partnership with homoerotic friendship could have raised considerable problems. But both women were able to overcome any potential difficulties by personal compatability and flexible role reversal. For in the private sphere they were able to set aside the power inequalities of their public roles to form an equal partnership in which 'it was uncertain as to who dominated who'.[105]

Allan and Waterhouse's friendship was well known to Homerton students, whose descriptions throw interesting light on the partnership:

The only Staff friend, though how friendly one cannot judge, was Miss Waterhouse ('Soda'), who, I think was Deputy Head, and lived in the same block as Miss Allan if I remember rightly. 'Soda' was an odd character, used an ear trumpet, and would fly off at a tangent for the smallest fault, storming away. She could smile though.[106]

She was very friendly with the Vice-Principal Miss Waterhouse. They were nick-named 'Whisky and Soda' by the students.[107]

Waterhouse's effervescent personality gave rise to her nickname 'Soda', and the coupling together of Waterhouse as 'Soda' and Allan as 'Whisky' (referring to her Glaswegian origins) was emblematic of the successful blending together of the two women's personalities.

Allan's pursuit of homoerotic friendship was complicated and for many years involved a triangular relationship. Triangular relationships were not unusual in homoerotic friendship, as we shall see with our third principal, Winifred Mercier. In 1903, immediately after her own appointment, Allan appointed Margaret Glennie to the Homerton staff. Two years later she gave a temporary contract for one year to Edith Waterhouse, to cover another lecturer's leave of absence. Both these women enjoyed from the first an intimate personal companionship with Allan: 'I believe her closest friend was Miss Waterhouse, lecturer in Education and she had a great affection for Miss Glennie (Science).'[108] That Waterhouse eventually became Allan's closest friend (one former student declared that Glennie was actually 'pushed out'[109]) was due both to differences in the two women's personalities, and to Allan's ultimate preference for the woman who could best serve both her public and private needs. Glennie was described by her obituarist as a 'Christian woman, gifted, beauty-loving and humble', who gave 'forty years of incalculable service to the college'.[110] She was much loved by her students,[111] whose frequent labelling of her as a 'lady'[112] signalled her conformity with middle-class ideals of femininity. Waterhouse was quite different. Her obituarist drew attention not only to 'the brilliant clarity of her mind', which made her a 'great teacher', but also to her 'keen elfin wit' and 'quick effervescent tantrums'.[113] Students were frightened of Waterhouse, as they were of Allan, and dreaded her shouting at them 'Speak up, gel'.[114] Importantly, she could stand up to the principal and not be intimidated by her. Allan was quick to recognize her need to retain Waterhouse's services on a permanent basis. Long before Waterhouse's temporary contract had expired, Allan was exercising her considerable management skills. She wrote to the Chairman of the Congregational Board of her desire 'to secure her [Waterhouse's] services' which were of a 'thoroughly satisfactory kind'. She warned the trustees that Waterhouse was 'applying for another job'. So keen was Allan to keep Waterhouse that she went so far as to write to several members of the Board privately to secure their support.[115] Nevertheless, although Waterhouse's appointment was made permanent,[116] she left

Homerton in 1907 to take up the post of Mistress of Method at Avery Hill College. A year later she was appointed Avery Hill's vice-principal.[117] Allan revealed in coded official language the loss which she, as well as the college had sustained: 'I cannot adequately state my appreciation of Miss Waterhouse's work. Her post will be very hard to fill.'[118]

It was not without significance that in the same year that Waterhouse became vice-principal of Avery Hill, Allan, perhaps reckoning that she had 'lost' Waterhouse, appointed Ada Varley, who had been on the Homerton staff since 1902, as the college's vice-principal.[119] (Varley was to take on the post of acting principal when Allan was abroad in 1919–20.) Nevertheless, Allan was determined to lure Waterhouse back to Homerton, even if she could not offer her, as yet, the post of vice-principal. Four years later in 1912, she informed the governors that she was retaining Waterhouse's service on a part-time basis as a supervisor for school practice.[120] This proved the thin end of the wedge, and by the end of the year Waterhouse was back at Homerton with a full-time lectureship in education.[121] It is difficult to believe that Waterhouse would have taken such a seemingly backward step in her career unless she had a compelling personal reason to do so. Certainly the rivalry between her and Glennie now became visible in college,[122] and in 1914 Glennie was given leave of absence for unstated reasons.[123] The power struggle between the two women was finally resolved eight years later, a year after Allan had returned from abroad, when Varley was appointed principal of nearby Saffron Walden College.[124] Saffron Walden was a domestic science college, of inferior status to Homerton. We can only speculate if Allan had a hand in this appointment. But at last she was able to appoint Waterhouse as her vice-principal; Glennie was given the consolation prize of resident tutor. Allan showed great skill in managing a situation which could have caused considerable friction in the college. She ensured both women's continuing loyalty to herself personally and to the college, by bracketing their names together in a public appreciation of their services:

> Great care must be taken to secure the services of women of as fine calibre and earnestness of purpose as those who retire and who have done so much to maintain the reputation of the College. I am very fortunate in retaining the services of able and responsible members like Miss Waterhouse and Miss Glennie.[125]

A central and visible site for the expression of Allan and Waterhouse's intimacy was their concern for each other's health: 'The vice-principal Miss Waterhouse had indifferent health and Miss Allan – may I say – cherished her.'[126] In spite of her 'indifferent health' Waterhouse lived till she was over 90 years old.[127] She periodically took extended sick leave including a term spent in the south of France.[128] Allan was able to express her feminine and emotional side in this cherishing of her partner. But at times she could fall victim to that 'emotional overloading' which another principal,

Constance Maynard founder of Westfield College, had warned was an ever present danger in a relationship between a principal and a member of her own staff:[129] '[Miss Allan] was always very solicitous about the health of the Vice-Principal. She at times waited outside the lecture room to enquire after Miss Waterhouse's health.'[130]

Waterhouse had a lighter touch:

> Miss Waterhouse was vice-principal and was very close to Miss Allan. They were close friends. Miss Allan obviously admired Miss Waterhouse very much and praised her to students. Miss Waterhouse gave warmth to the relationship. I remember one evening when I was due to see Miss Allan in her apartment, I was met by Miss Waterhouse coming out of Miss Allan's bedroom, smiling and signalling me to go away quietly – evidently Miss Allan had gone to bed early and Miss Waterhouse was seeing she was not disturbed.[131]

Waterhouse's warmth and sense of humour made possible her intimacy with the dour and aloof Allan. These qualities, in alliance with the mutual respect which both women had for each other, allowed Waterhouse to take the initiative in the private sphere, and to, for example, encourage Allan to relax with her in their shared enjoyment of Gilbert and Sullivan opera.[132] Allan's successor as Homerton's principal, Alice Skillicorn, was to be equally successful in her choice of partner in homoerotic friendship.

Alice Havergal Skillicorn

> She found it hard to let herself go and yet those of us who knew her great friend Dorothy Sergeant realised that there must be depths of understanding and affection that she found difficult to bring to the surface.[133]

This tribute to Skillicorn, at her memorial meeting in 1979, bears witness not only to her notorious lack of social skills but to the deep emotional support she received from her homoerotic partner, Dorothy Sergeant. That Sergeant, an HMI, was a professional woman of equal status to Skillicorn, and not a subordinate member of Skillicorn's staff were important elements in the success of their relationship. Skillicorn and Sergeant had met in London in the early 1930s when they had been colleagues in the Inspectorate.[134] Sergeant was influential in the teacher training world and was to give crucial help to Avery Hill College when it was reconstructing its bomb-damaged site after the Second World War.[135] The partnership was based on shared interests and mutual professional respect but its success was based above all else on their complementary personalities. For Sergeant's 'relaxed personality did Skilly good'[136] and 'the relationship gave Skilly some warmth'.[137] Skillicorn was always known as 'Skilly' to her staff, but not of course to her face.

Glimpses of their private relationship can be seen in the memories of their contempories. One member of staff asked 'Skilly' if she and 'Dolly' would like to join a party of other members of staff to see the hit musical *My Fair Lady*: 'Skilly then ran up the corridor, as fast as she could waddle, and rung up "Dolly" ... She was thrilled to bits.'[138] Another member of staff characterized the relationship in conventional gender terms, with Skillicorn being 'incredibly masculine' and 'Dorothy very feminine'.[139] The two women's household standards could also be characterized in masculine and feminine terms. Skillicorn thought nothing of putting a bottle of milk straight onto the table; Sergeant would produce a mat![140] Skillicorn and Sergeant had the means to live in considerable style. They owned a house in Cambridge near the college, and they also had a flat in Homerton's London hostel, Millbrook House. They enjoyed a pre-war standard of personal service which was becoming rare in the 1950s. In the principal's flat in the college, where she lived during the week, Skillicorn had her own personal maid Esme, who looked after all her domestic needs, including bringing her breakfast in bed each morning. At the weekends in their Cambridge house, the college's domestic bursar 'would tell Chef to send over a meat pie when Dr Sergeant was coming'.[141] And in the holidays the two women could get right away from Homerton to Millbrook House, enjoy the London theatres, and relax in the comfort provided by Millbrook's resident housekeeper.[142]

The class dimension to homoerotic friendship in women's colleges is important. All the relationships examined in this chapter were between equals – educated middle-class women with professional salaries. The standard of living which Skillicorn enjoyed afforded her a level of comfort and access to personal service which had by then almost disappeared in the postwar world. This made it easier for her to conduct her homoerotic friendship with a discretion and tact that did much to forestall public criticism. At Homerton the relationship, far from being condemned, was welcomed even if it was not named as such. For it was seen to give Skillicorn the warmth and stability in private whch compensated for her isolated public persona: 'They were greatly in support of each other – a happy fulfilling relationship. Miss Skillicorn relied on her [Sergeant]. If she were troubled she talked freely to her.'[143]

Skillicorn was heartbroken when Sergeant died suddenly, and in her absence in 1969. She wrote to a former member of staff with unusual intimacy:

> My dears, I'm afraid my news is sad this year, though I am very thankful for many happy years in the past. Dorothy Sergeant died, suddenly and unexpectedly in her sleep on July 28. It has been a shock and a sorrow to me as I was away in the Isle of Man. She was lively and active with her friends until the last hour of her life.[144]

When Skillicorn herself died ten years later, the two women shared the same grave. The tombstone recorded 'the dear and devoted friendship' which they had enjoyed for nearly forty years. This public recognition was not only a tribute to the woman she had loved, but it was also a political statement celebrating the important role which homoerotic friendship could play in women's colleges.[145]

Winifred Mercier

> Winifred Mercier had the gift of putting her love for humanity into her love for individuals.[146]

> If most friendships are like silver threads in the fabric of life, Winifred's were like golden cords, so strong were they and so untarnishable.[147]

Of all the principals discussed so far, Winifred Mercier possessed the most charismatic personality. To all her many women friends she gave not only 'the magnetic quality and quickening force' of her personality but also some of the emotional commitment of homoerotic friendship. During her first teaching post in Edinburgh she formed an homoerotic partnership with two colleagues Jean Borland and Kay Scott Moncrieff, which was to be life-long.[148] Mercier had a distinguished career in women's teacher training. During the First World War she was vice-principal of Leeds Training College. She resigned from this post after only three years, over the issues of status and professional freedom, and thereafter she was always identified with the cause of liberalizing the curriculum in women's training colleges. She became principal of Whitelands College in 1918 where she remained until her early death in 1934.[149]

Mercier's old friend, Lynda Grier, principal of Lady Margaret Hall, Oxford, wrote Mercier's biography, which was published by the Oxford University Press in 1937. This biography bears witness to the constraints which faced even sympathetic writers in 1937, when writing of homoerotic friendship. Grier was torn between her desire to reveal the emotional intimacy of Mercier's friendships, and her fear lest by these revelations she would imply that the relationships were of a homoerotic or lesbian nature. This dilemma was particularly acute for a woman as well known and respected as Mercier. Jean Borland, who, with Kay Scott Moncrieff, formed a life-long homoerotic relationship with Mercier, provided Grier with much of the material for the biography, including Borland's own letters from Mercier. Grier's use of Mercier's letters epitomizes her difficulties in expressing the reality of Mercier's emotions, without exciting hostile comment. At the end of the biography she comments that 'it will be noticed that few of her [Mercier's] letters appear in this biography'.[150] For a woman who was a prolific letter writer this needed explanation. The letters were 'full of affection' and indeed 'it is almost true to say that affection dominated her letters to her friends so much as to leave room for little else'. One letter, which Grier does allow herself to quote in this section, gives an indication of Mercier's diffuse homoerotic affections: 'You are so good to me . . . that it is like having a sun-bath all over to be with you.'[151]

In another incident, recalled by Grier, Mercier is openly affectionate towards her friends:

> Now and again her affectionate demonstrativeness would embarrass her more conventional friends. . . . When two of them teased her about some trifle in a London restaurant, she quelled them by saying 'If you say that again, I'll kiss you both, at once.' They knew she would be as good as her word.[152]

Grier does in fact quote quite extensively from Mercier's letters to both Borland and Scott Moncrieff, but her comment on one letter to Borland that 'for the most part it is too intimate to quote'[153] is a coded reference to the homoerotic nature of their friendship. Throughout the biography she is at great pains to remove all possibility of lesbian taint from Mercier by portraying her as a practical idealist, uninterested in sexual feelings. Thus in dealing with student 'crushes': 'Like all fine people who have their eyes set on great things, she had no time to waste on infatuation and no vanity to be flattered by it.' Grier's long-winded account of such infatuations and her insistence that unlike other people, Mercier had no interest in them, point to a culture in which it was a common occurence:

> There were just a few, whose aspirations were wrapped up in passionate personal attachments, who took it as an insult and not as a compliment that their infatuation was ignored. In such cases silly adoration is apt to resolve itself into sillier resentment. Their victim [i.e. Mercier] was equally unconscious of both. Both were sufficiently rare not to force themselves on her attention, and always she had other things to think of.[154]

There is always a danger in writing about homoerotic/lesbian friendship to read back into the past the knowledge and preoccupations of the present.[155] I would argue that women like Winifred Mercier, who felt a warm emotion towards their many friends which was sometimes expressed in physical intimacy, nevertheless did not construct their relationships as sexual partnerships. This attitude had been commoner in the nineteenth century before the sexologists had provided a new vocabulary which allowed women for the first time to make and name the 'complex connections' in their friendships between 'sexuality and personal emotions'.[156] By the 1930s, however, the sexologist's discourse was common knowledge. But Mercier's seeming refusal of it was not necessarily an interpretation by Grier to allay public hostility:

Psychology was also something of a closed subject to her. Over-psychological novels did not hold her, though she was a great novel reader. Novels which talk for ever about sex did not shock her, but bored her profoundly; she thought it right that people should know what there is to know about sex, but found endless repetition of that knowledge insufferably tedious.[157]

In an earlier passage, Grier emphasizes not only the strength of Mercier's affection for women, but her lack of interest in the hegemonic heterosexual discourse: 'It has been said of her that she was essentially a nun. Many who knew the strength of her affections . . . would disagree. . . . However this may be, she certainly had no time for and no interest in young men as such.'[158] Mercier's emotions were committed to her women friends, and especially to Borland. Like Mary Allan, such emotional intimacy was inevitably bound up with concerns for her friend's body and anxiety about its health. This was the intimacy of homoerotic friendship:

Tell me, when you write, exactly how you are. In case you don't write to my satisfaction, I perpend a list of questions for your answers: 1. Do you sleep well? 2. Do you feel hungry? 3. Has any one remarked on your looks, if so, what did they say? 4. Are you any fatter? 5. Have you any black rings? . . . Now on your peril answer true.[159]

6 The last days of the women's college
The 1950s

This chapter examines the last days of the women's college. We have seen in earlier chapters evidence that, by the 1950s, the corporate ethic and practice of the colleges were being undermined by changing social, and particularly sexual, mores. There was also growing concern nationally that the two-year course was not long enough to equip trainee teachers with sufficient academic knowledge and vocational skill to meet the demands of the post-war world. This concern had been forcefully stated in the influential McNair Report, published in 1944:

> The course should be lengthened for three reasons. First, the schools need better educated men and women and this better education cannot be secured unless students are released from the strain and hurry which now conditions many of them. Secondly, students in general have not, by 20 years of age, reached a maturity equal to the responsibility of educating children and young people; and thirdly, we intend that a longer amount of time than at present should, during training, be devoted to contact with and teaching in schools.[1]

The three-year course was eventually introduced for training colleges in 1960. By this time the shortage of teachers in school was becoming acute. This was largely due to demographic factors. The number of unmarried women, who had been the mainstay of the teaching profession up to the Second World War – was in serious decline. An increasing surplus in the marriageable age groups of men over women – in sharp contrast to the surplus of women in the first half of the century – increased the pressure on women to marry. In 1911, 552 out of every 1000 women between the ages of 21 and 39 were married; by 1931 this number had risen to 572. By 1961 this number had leapt to 808; and in the mid-1960s 95 per cent of the female population had married by the age of 45. Moreover women were marrying at a younger age, and there had been a sharp rise in the birth-rate after the Second World War.[2] The marriage bar, which required women to leave teaching on marriage, had been lifted during the war, but most married women teachers, after only a few years in post, left teaching to start a family. The introduction of the three-year course would only exacerbate the situation.[3] In 1958 the government seemed suddenly to wake up to the crisis and the National Advisory Council for the Training and Supply of Teachers issued a memorandum outlining its plans for a rapid expansion in the numbers of trainee teachers. The criteria for this expansion crucially threatened women's training colleges. For only colleges with over 200 students and those 'ready to become mixed if they were not mixed already'[4] were to be chosen. Many women's colleges had less than 200 students and would therefore be sidelined. The real threat, however, was the introduction of men students into women's colleges. How could the culture of femininity be adapted, let alone maintained, under such circumstances?

The post-war period also saw a considerable debate on the whole question of the education of women. In the changed circumstances of the post-war world and particularly the rapid rise in the marriage rate for women, was it any longer appropriate for girls to receive the same education as boys, when, in contrast to the pre-war period, nearly all of them were destined to be wives and mothers? On the other hand, with the national shortage of labour, and the demise of the unmarried woman, married women provided the only possible reserve for the workforce. Could married women combine work outside the home with the demands of husband and family? In the first part of the chapter I shall examine this debate, with particular attention to its relevance for trainee teachers. Next I shall outline the condition of the training colleges in the 1950s. A discussion of students' subsequent teaching careers will follow in order to discover how far teachers succeeded in combining 'women's two roles' of home and work, as recommended by Myrdal and Klein.[5] Finally, in the Epilogue to this chapter, I shall examine what actually happened when men entered the world of the women's training college.

The 'Education of Women' debate

> Until we have a much clearer idea about what we expect of women and about our attitudes to married women working, we are bound to be at sea in deciding what is the best education for girls.[6]

The debate on 'what is the best education for girls', was prompted by the changed economic and social conditions of the post-war world. Two seemingly opposed ideals needed to be reconciled – married women's primary role as wives and mothers, and the state's need for married women's labour outside the home. Women as a percentage of the workforce, disregarding the exceptional circumstances of the war-time years, had only risen marginally between 1931 and 1951 – from 29.8 per cent to 30.8. However, the number of married women employed outside the home had risen from 10 per cent in 1931 to 22 per cent in 1951.[7]

Married women's traditional role had been firmly inscribed in the influential Beveridge Report, published in 1942:

> In the next thirty years housewives as Mothers have vital work to do in ensuring the adequate continuance of the British Race and of the British Ideal in the world.
>
> The great majority of married women must be regarded as occupied on work which is vital but unpaid, without which their husbands could not do their paid work and without which the nation could not continue.[8]

Other influential writers emphasized the unique importance of women's role as mothers (interestingly, not as wives) and the necessity of the mother's presence for the welfare of young children. An American doctor, Benjamin Spock, first published his *Baby and Child Care*, which was to become the bible of middle-class mothers, in 1947. Although this was a generally permissive work, it also declared that 'useful, well-adjusted citizens are the most valuable possession a country has, and good mother care during early childhood is the surest way to produce them'.[9] More sinister in its effect on mothers was John Bowlby's *Maternal Care and Mental Health*, first published in 1951. This defined good mother care as a 'warm, intimate' and importantly 'continuous' relationship between mother and child.[10] The book, which was largely based on disturbed children in institutions or on those who had been evacuated during the war, achieved great popularity (by 1969 it had run to nine impressions); regrettably, it could be, and was, used to make women feel guilty if they worked outside the home when their children were young.[11] This sentiment, which chimed in with conservative contemporary opinion, received little criticism at the time. An exception was Alva Myrdal and Viola Klein's seminal work *Women's Two Roles: Home and Work*, published in 1951.

A. Myrdal and V. Klein. Women's two roles: home and work

> We are convinced . . . that work and family are not in principle two irreconcilable alternatives; and it is not beyond the means and ingenuity of our society to devise techniques which would reduce the dilemma of working mothers to a tolerable minimum.[12]

Myrdal and Klein's book was the first to suggest, with extreme caution, that there might be a case for women 'having it all', albeit sequentially, becoming first workers, then wives and mothers, and finally re-entering the labour market to become workers again.[13] This bimodal pattern of work, motherhood and work again was already an established pattern for married women's lives by the time Myrdal and Klein's book was published in 1956. It was their achievement that their sociological analysis, written determinedly from the belief 'that the state needed women's contribution to the labour force' rather than 'from the view that women had a right to exercise their choice', gave legitimacy to what was already happening, and made 'women's two roles' socially acceptable. The view that a woman did have the right to choose had received, two years earlier, what with hindsight seems a surprising endorsement by a Mrs Margaret Thatcher later to become the notoriously conservative Prime Minister.[14]

Myrdal and Klein's thesis paid careful attention to the socio-economic climate of the period, with particular attention to its effects on children, and to the problems of employers. Interestingly, their book mounted one of the few challenges of the period to the Bowlby thesis, arguing that more finely tuned research on the subject was necessary:

> It is surprising that no research has yet been done to investigate more closely when such breaks [in a mother's constant care for her child] become possible, for what length of time they can safely be made, and whether they are equally injurious when they form part of an established regular routine. The studies which exist, and which are ably and conveniently summarized by J. Bowlby in *Maternal Care and Mental Health* refer to *total deprivation of maternal care* [my italics]. . . . Here is a field of research which is of great social importance, but has received remarkably little attention.[15]

Myrdal and Klein's sociological analysis was always more assured than the practicality, at the time, of their suggested reforms – like maternity leave and re-training of women over 40.[16] Their book was full of contradictions. Thus the authors chided women for not taking a more professional and realistic attitude towards their careers, and urged them 'to choose occupations which they will be able to continue after marriage or resume after an interval of a few years'.[17] On the other hand, they also urged 'girls with a special talent' to go ahead with their training, come what may. The following passage reveals not only a somewhat dismissive attitude to the teaching profession, on their own admission the most suited profession for women's two roles, but also a surprisingly candid statement on the real priorities in women's lives:

> Girls with special talent for, or an overriding interest in, any of the traditionally masculine professions should certainly not be discouraged from following their inclinations. It would be wrong, for instance, to persuade a woman who is eager to become a barrister to be trained as a Froebel nurse instead, simply because she hopes to marry if a suitable opportunity arises and also, if possible, to have children. In this way, a woman who might otherwise have become a competent, or even excellent, lawyer may be doomed for the rest of her life to be a moderate and inwardly dissatisfied kindergarten teacher if her hopes of eventual

escape into marriage are not fulfilled. And of the two possible failures it seems that to have pinned all hopes on marriage, and then not to be able to realize them, is a more cruel disappointment than having to throw up a promising career because of family demands.[18]

Myrdal and Klein's attitude to the teaching profession was both extra-ordinarily perfunctory (only one paragaraph in a book of 200 pages) and complacently ignorant of the reality of women's lives:

> There are jobs which are so easy to combine with marriage and mother-hood that, metaphorically speaking, a woman can practise them almost with one hand at the cradle. Teaching, for instance, particularly in nursery and primary grades, seems next to ideal, because the working hours of mother and child are more or less the same, they can go to school together, their vacations coincide, and a joint interest may help them mutually in their work.[19]

The authors were also unenthusiastic about part-time work for married women. Again, their reasoning was based not on the needs of married women themselves but on the adverse reactions of both employers and trade unions to part-time workers. Nevertheless, their compromise solution that 'part-time work seems a good temporary solution for the women who want to resume their careers later on'[20] was in fact the path eventually followed by many married women teachers, as we shall see later in this chapter.

J. Hubback. *Wives who went to college*

> When a girl is in her teens, it cannot be known whether she will marry, nor what kind of life she will lead. Consequently she should be educated as highly as her abilities will allow. I am not disregarding her absolute right to the highest possible education from which she personally can benefit: that I take as axiomatic.[21]

> There are many years ahead for the educated woman, after she has combined the satisfaction of her emotional and biological nature with society's need for intelligent children. Her education will then justify itself in the lives of her husband and her children, and also in some wider society than her own family.[22]

Judith Hubback's study of women who went to college betrays all the muddled thinking and attempts to reconcile the irreconcilable which char-acterized the whole debate on the education of women. As a married woman graduate herself, she was well aware of the problems. Her feminist belief that women were entitled to 'the highest possible education' as an axiomatic right was constantly at cross-purposes with the realities of her equally fervent belief that married women's primary duty was to their homes and families. Could higher education and specialized training be justified when in probability 'in our present society' it will be 'wasted'[23] or as one of her respondents graphically commented – 'I wonder if their [her children] careers, like my own, will end at the kitchen sink'. The post-war demise of domestic servants, who before the war would have done the housework and much of the child care in middle-class homes, was a crucial element in the debate.[24] The strength of Hubback's book lies in the evidence she obtained from the questionnaire which she sent to 2,000 'married women graduates' (1,165 of them replied) and to 420 'non-graduate wives'. As a married graduate herself she was well able to empathize with respondents' problems and discontent. Revealingly, the non-graduate wives were chosen for the similarity of their 'social background' to her graduate sample.[25] Hubback tied herself into her usual knots when justifying her decision to concentrate on graduates.

> I think that the desire to do some non-domestic work is felt most acutely by the university graduate because she is, in most cases, of more intellectual cast of mind than the woman with a certificate or diploma. Yet this is not always or necessarily so. Moreover, looking at the problem from society's point of view, the loss of the hospital nurse and the non-graduate teacher who give up their work when married is as serious as the loss of the graduate administrative Civil Servant or the grammar school mistress. It was not from lack of interest in the certificated and diploma-ed women that my research did not cover them: but, having to set myself limits . . .[26]

Women who had been to teacher training college accounted for 13 per cent of her non-graduate sample.[27] It is striking that, in spite of Hubback's concern with social class, the accounts of her graduates' lives share the same culture of middle-class femininity as the former training college students who will be discussed later in the chapter. A minority of her correspondents were happy to give up their careers on marriage: 'Personally I planned a career – with the completely silent reservation that I should give it up for marriage if I had the chance. I did not wish to go on working outside after marriage.'[28]

Some regarded 'running a house and caring for a husband and family' as a 'career and profession in itself'.[29] But the vast majority of her respondents took the opportunity to express some dissatisfaction with their lives. Hubback was clearly ambivalent about these replies. On the one hand, she wanted to reveal her respondents' dissatisfaction with their lives, but on the other hand she feared that if they complained too shrilly she and they would be seen to be 'letting the side down'. Her preferred option were those respondents who pointed out dispassionately that time spent in domestic work prevented educated women from being more socially useful:

Many of the correspondents were obviously being very careful not to complain. The general tone of their letters, time after time, was: 'Of course I'm very lucky to be so happily married, but . . .' They were trying to be reasonable; some were fatalistic; others, rueful; some, even bitter. 'I certainly think it is a pity that so many women, because they want a family, are more or less forced to spend a large part of their time in domestic work, when they might be doing something more socially useful and satisfying' sums up what was said at greater length in many of the letters[30]

Hubback's attitude to the teaching profession was less dismissive and more realistic than Myrdal and Klein's. She drew attention to the difficulties schools encountered when part-time (her preferred option for married women) teachers were unable, because of their domestic commitments, to take part in schools' extra curricular activities.[31] Again Hubback tied herself into knots. She first proposed a 'solution' to the difficulty; then objected to this proposal because it contravened the middle-class service ethic for women; finally she declared that some (unspecified) way must be found around the problem:

> Governing bodies and local authorities may have to face another increase in salaries in the form of overtime to be paid to those mistresses who work, at school, out of teaching hours. . . . Admittedly, many people feel that the extra work . . . would lose much of its valuable quality if the time thus spent had to be computed, checked and paid for. Devotion, loyalty, enthusiasm, can in fact never be bought. But at the same time, some practical way will have to be found for carrying these activities on if the supply of full-time mistresses continues to fall off owing to marriage.[32]

K. Ollerenshaw. *Education for girls*

> Too few girls go on to higher education. We need more well-educated women to help in building happy and cultured homes, to work in the professions, particularly teaching, and to make the best contribution generally to the community.[33]

Kathleen Ollerenshaw's critique of girls' education was published in 1961. As the headmistress of a Manchester girls' grammar school, she was well qualified to enter the debate. Her bibliography included both Hubback and Myrdal and Klein and the book assumed that 'the developing pattern of work-marriage-work'[34] would continue. Ollerenshaw's approach was brisk and realistic. While acknowledging that marriage and motherhood would remain women's primary goal, and that schools 'tread the tightrope' in trying to prepare girls adequately for their two roles, she neverthless adopted a solidly feminist approach on women's right to an academic education: 'The chance of able girls to acquire real mental discipline and real knowledge leading to professional careers in the hard world of strict competition on equal terms with men has to be safeguarded.'[35]

As a teacher herself, Ollerenshaw was concerned to maintain and improve the status of her profession. 'The high esteem in which education should and must be held in society will only be sustained in so far as we hold the teaching profession itself in high esteem.'[36]

Unlike her predecessors in the education debate, she devoted a thoughtful section of the book to women's training colleges. Although many teachers were graduates, there were also many intending teachers who, even if they were qualified for university entrance, preferred to attend training college where 'the child and the school are never far out of the mind'. Moreover, with the introduction of the three-year course, Ollerenshaw looked forward to an increased participation by training colleges in degree programmes.[37] She was concerned that the 'desperate shortage of teachers' and particularly of primary school teachers (largely trained at the colleges rather than at university) would not be solved unless more girls at school stayed on into the sixth form.[38] She was also critical of the 'rigorously controlled'[39] lecture programme at training colleges, and agreed with the government that large mixed colleges were preferable to smaller single-sex ones:

> There can be no doubt that the large college is preferable to the small, if only to provide a broad social life and a wide variety of interests. The larger the college, the stronger the case for it to be mixed. In general, again, I would favour the mixed college when it is large, particularly when so high a proportion of grammar and direct-grant schools (from which the majority of students come) are single sex.[40]

Ollerenshaw drew attention to the difficulties training colleges faced in recruiting staff of 'the right calibre and experience'. Staff, in her opinion, should be graduates, but few graduates had the experience of 'modern and primary' schools which was essential to the vocational aspect of college teaching. In advocating greater opportunities for staff interchanges between schools and training colleges, 'on lines advocated in the McNair Report', but admitting that such a development would need 'courage, imagination, faith and considerable goodwill',[41] Ollerenshaw was expressing a realism which was based on her own experience.

In her conclusion Ollerenshaw admitted that, as a result of studying the current situation, she had now modified her previously feminist position on the education of girls:

> I used to think that the essential purity of basic education implied that in all the really important aspects there should be no question of differentiation between the education of girls and that of boys. Now it seems

to me clear that the differences are so great, that we would do well to develop a new and distinctive philosophy of education and educational practice with the needs of girls in mind as distinct from the needs of boys.[42]

In her final paragraph, however, Ollerenshaw, seems to have changed her mind again. Her previous advocacy of a new educational philosophy for girls has now become just 'a different slant'. Moreover, in her call for a full intellectual and aesthetic education for girls which would equip them to be of service to the community, she was re-inscribing just those values which had always been the hallmark of the best women's training colleges:

If women are to be the mainstay in setting standards of family life; if they are to uphold traditions of decent conduct in the community; if they are to play their full part in the economic, social and spiritual development of society . . ., they require an education which stimulates their imaginations, develops their intellectual, artistic and practical talents, and leads them to greater awareness of the world around them and a lasting sense of service.[43]

Women's Group on Public Welfare. *The education and training of girls*

Are we making the best use of our intelligent women? The answer is, regretfully, 'No'.[44]

This report, drawn up by a working party of the Women's Group on Public Welfare, was published in 1962. The Women's Group on Public Welfare consisted of representatives of 'widely varied and representative women's organisations' and this working party did in fact reflect a wide-spread of women's interests. Importantly, a quarter of the working party were members of the teaching profession (three headmistresses and a representative of the National Union of Teachers). Moreover, eleven of its seventeen members, and all six of its assessors, were single professional women. A membership dominated by professional women influenced a report which, although it addressed all the other issues in the debate, was chiefly concerned to uphold and protect a feminist belief in women's right to higher education. Unusually, for instance, it gave women's role as wives and mother only third place in its terms of reference:

To consider and report whether, in the group's view, the education of girls today adequately fits them to play their part (a) as members of the community (local, national and international), (b) in industry, commerce, the arts and the professions, (c) as wives and mothers.[45]

The Working Party examined in detail a lively debate on the education of women question, which had taken place in the letter columns of both *The Times* and the *Guardian* early in 1960. This correspondence had been prompted by an article by M. L. Jacks, a former Director of the Oxford University Department of Education, who called for a 'fundamental re-thinking' on the subject. Jacks had drawn attention to the 'powerful vested interest' maintaining the status quo, i.e. that girls should have the same education as boys.[46] The ensuing correspondence[47] mirrored the attitudes of Hubback's respondents[48] in the early 1950s, but the Working Party gave most space to those who endorsed traditional feminist thinking, among them Elizabeth Pakenham, later, as Lady Longford, to become a distinguished biographer as well as the mother of eight children:

> One fact emerges from this enthralling correspondence which appals me. The battle has not been won. The pendulum shows signs of swinging back to pre-emancipation days. All agree that boys should be educated as people. . . . Girls, however, are regarded as 'little women' before they are human beings.[49]

Nevertheless, in spite of the evidence to the contrary revealed by this correspondence, the Working Party, all of whose members had forged successful professional lives outside the home, dismissed the frustrations of their contemporaries: 'We strongly disagree with those who have claimed that higher education is a cause of frustration to married women who are for the time being bound to the home.'[50] The elitist perspective of the Working Party was further revealed in their suggestions for ways in which schools might prepare girls for 'marriage and home life'. Thus for girls 'in the general sixth of a grammar school for girls who are not intending to go on to further education, or in the final year or two years in the secondary modern school', they suggested a detailed syllabus to be chosen from no less than twelve subjects devoted to all aspects of marriage and home life. Clever girls, on the other hand, would only need to attend a few 'special lectures' on the subject.[51]

In its discussion on teacher training, the Working Party seemed to have been influenced by the somewhat exaggerated scenario told to them by the 'principal of a women's training college':

> We were told that most of the students complete their courses and that, although most are engaged to be married when they leave the college, they usually teach for a year or two before marrying and sometimes continue for a few more years before the arrival of their families.

With this information in mind the Working Party even went as far as to suggest, somewhat cryptically, that colleges might even consider making their courses: 'More generally educational and less vocational in character in view of the fact that for most women teachers the greater part of their professional life may take place ten or more years after their education for teaching.'[52] A more sensible suggestion was that 'earnest consideration' be given to ways of helping 'the older woman who wants to take up or return to teaching by means of special short training or refresher courses'.[53]

Summary of the 'Education of Women' debate

In the event, the debate on the education of women led to no changes in the status quo. Girls and boys continued to receive the same education in school. Married women returned to work after their youngest child was of school-age, usually, at least at first, on a part-time basis. The debate had been conducted almost entirely in terms of the needs of the state and of society as a whole, rather than focusing on the needs of individual women themselves. With the coming of Second-Wave Feminism in the 1970s, the issue of women's subordination to men, and the structural difficulties which women, and especially mothers, faced in entering the workforce began at last to be analysed as well as discussed. However, it was the achievement of those who took part in the 1950s' Education of Women debate, that, women's right 'to the highest possible education from which she can benefit',[54] although challenged, was never in serious jeopardy.

It is now time to turn to the actual experience of women in training colleges in the 1950s.

Women in training colleges in the 1950s

Bishop Otter

In 1950, two years after her appointment, Elisabeth Murray, Bishop Otter's new principal, was congratulated by Bishop Bell, chairman of the college's governors, for her wise guidance of the college community. In stressing the importance of 'resident members of a corporate society' supplying 'the fellow-ship of belonging to a large family' and the need for 'consideration of one another's personalities',[55] Bell was re-inscribing the traditional familial and domestic values of the college's culture of femininity. Murray herself, as we have seen in Chapter 3, was well equipped by temperament and experience, to uphold these values. Such innovations as she did introduce were also entirely in keeping with the college's traditional way of life:

> After Council meetings there was tea, in Miss Murray's sitting-room, to which staff were invited and able to meet and talk with the members of Council. A further innovation was the weekly Open Lecture: this brought to the College men and women active in many spheres. . . . For a brief period sabbatical years were allowed to staff to pursue some

study entirely remote from their own – Miss Jenkin (Education lecturer) studied Church embroidery, evidence of which lies among the chapel vestments, and a music lecturer acquired a Cordon Bleu in cookery! [*sic*][56]

Bishop Otter's students in the 1950s were, on the whole, content with college life, acknowledging that they were treated 'more or less' as adults.[57] Some old customs, like inviting lecturers to dine on students' own tables on Friday nights, were even revived.[58] We have seen in Chapter 5 that students chaffed at the restrictions on entertaining men friends and regretted the limited opportunities for meeting suitable men in the Chichester environment. Irritation at the intrusion of staff into students' privacy could also occasionally became overt, with the wish expressed that 'students would appreciate it if lecturers would knock loudly before entering their rooms'.[59] The college magazine contained many literary pieces by students but attendance at college clubs and societies was deemed to be 'poor'.[60] Financial pressures on students were also increasing and many students took paid jobs in the vacations. Working for money in the vacations rather than further equipping themselves for their vocation as teachers was not, however, in accordance with the culture of femininity and the principal voiced her disquiet: 'I hope the necessity for vacation work especially in shorter vacations will no longer exist [with the standardization of Local Authority grants]. I would rather see cheap adventurously planned holidays.' She further underlined the social and financial gulf between herself and students by stating that for many students 'the problem of vacation reading is lack of quiet and the pressure of domestic duties at home'.[61] A portent of the seismic changes that lay ahead was the waiving by the Ministry of Education in 1956 of the pledge that on leaving college 'all students in receipt of grants must teach in a state school'. The pledge was never legally binding and had for some time been a dead letter, but its abolition was official recognition that many students on leaving college now taught for only a short time, if at all, before getting married and starting a family. The principal nevertheless emphasized students' continuing moral duty to be of service to the community: 'Students trained at government expense should realise that they must in return be prepared to follow the profession for which they are equipped and go to schools where they are needed.'[62] The following year Sir Edward Boyle, Parliamentary Secretary to the Minister of Education, paid an 'informal' visit to the college. He 'saw everyone' and drew attention to the grave national shortage of teachers, citing as one of the main reasons the 'unexpectedly high marriage rate among women teachers'.[63] The purpose behind Boyle's visit became clear the following year when the government announced that with the introduction of the three-year course in 1960, it was proposed not only to double Bishop Otter's student numbers to 400, but to make the college co-educational. In recognition of the changed composition of the college it was further agreed that the office of vice-principal should become a permanent appointment and be offered to a man.[64] Twelve more 'hostel units' as well as a new chapel would be needed.[65] The speed with which these changes occurred was deeply disturbing to the whole college community. The principal and her staff put a brave face on the situation, but the threat to traditional college values was immediately recognized:

> It will no longer be possible for every student to live in a hostel over which a resident lecturer presides. In future most students will spend one year in the three in lodgings and the majority of lecturers will be non-resident. Students will have full responsibility for the use of their leisure time.[66]

The co-residence of staff and students had been the foundation of the corporate life of the college, as had been the monitoring by staff of student activities. The college magazine might optimistically declare that the changes did not 'mean any changes in standards or fundamental relationships'[67] but others viewed the situation with instant nostalgia for a college where 'the pony now grazes' on a field soon to be disfigured with unwelcome new hostel units.[68]

Avery Hill

'All knew their place and few kicked against the system.'[69] Avery Hill's historian described the college in the 1950s as a society in which dissent was unusual. Even when students resented 'petty and restrictive regulations', and being 'gated for two or three weeks for some minor peccadillo', they nevertheless 'laughed at the indignities imposed on them'.[70] In the absence of oral evidence from former students it is difficult to discover how widespread was such consensual conservatism. Certainly the magazine continued to reflect traditional college values. Tributes to 'the experience of living together as the aspect of college life which we shall remember with greatest pleasure',[71] and acknowledgement that 'relationships are at the heart of college society'[72] show students' appreciation of the basic tenets of the corporate culture. There were signs, however, that sentiments and practice within the college community were becoming out of date. It is difficult, for instance, to imagine young women in a university environment at the same date referring to 'the death of a noble king' (King George VI died in February 1952) as a moment when 'life was suddenly dulled and college numbly accepted the tragic event'.[73]

The principal, Frances Consitt, had held office since 1938. She had taken the college through the difficult war-time period, when the college was evacuated to Huddersfield. On the return to Eltham in 1946 she was faced with the necessity for a massive re-building programme of the war-damaged site. This 'battle for the buildings' had still not been won by the mid-1950s.[74] As the 1950s progressed she became increasingly irritated at the petty financial restrictions imposed on her by County Hall. These included car travel expenses[75] and the requirement to hand over to the LCC the stubs of the tickets when she had taken students to the theatre.[76] More important were criticisms of the college's academic work and governance. London University's Institute of Education, who examined students, continued to press for more staff representation on the governing body.[77] An 'excellent'[78] report from HMI in 1954 nevertheless criticized the library provision and catering arrangements at the college and urged the setting up of tutorial groups for teaching. Consitt reported to the governors that such groups were 'best left to the lecturers' and admitted that the art and craft department was 'weak' owing to 'personal difficulties' and 'lack of leadership'[79] In 1957 the college celebrated its Jubilee. Although the occasion was marked by the attendance of Lord Hailsham, Minister of Education, whose speech reflected traditional training college values in its urging students 'to keep up high standards' and 'to shoulder responsibilities', the celebrations lacked the confidence and the presence of the outside world which had marked the college's 21st birthday in 1928. The Minister also confirmed that the three-year course would start in 1960.[80]

A year later the LCC received a commmunication from the Ministry of Education announcing that, because of its size and location, Avery Hill College had been 'selected for rapid expansion in the next three or four years'. It was envisaged that student places might rise to 500 – of which 140 would be reserved for men. The government would be prepared to expedite and expand the outstanding building work on the site. The college also received a visit from Geoffrey Lloyd, now Minister of Education.[81] The principal, who would retire in 1960, wrote in the college magazine of 'the end of an epoch for college as a place of solely women's education'. Men students would at first be housed in Westminister College in London, which would serve as an annexe to Avery Hill until the building work was completed. Although the principal wrote positively of a 'stimulating new "beginning" as a large mixed college' and that 'our *future* is full of hope', the fact that she put inverted commas around beginning and italicized future showed her awareness of the difficulties which would inevitably lie ahead. The senior student also viewed the changes in a positive light, drawing attention to the need for a wider context and outlook in training colleges.

> There will be a considerable number of changes with the coming of men; many of them necessary for education to be fulfilled in its widest sense and not merely corrupted into qualification. The art of living together will be advantageous to all students.[82]

Homerton

> I loved every minute of my 2 years at Homerton. For the particular period,
> I think it was one of the best colleges and that we received sound training.
> We were encouraged to develop our own potential – no undue stress was
> created. A discipline was maintained regarding free time – system of exeats
> and a limited number of nights out did no harm! The encouragement to join
> in University clubs and activities too was an excellent thing.[83]

In spite of the agitation within the Homerton Union of Students for a more
liberal attitude to entertaining men friends (see Chapter 5), Homerton
students in the 1950s, like their counterparts at Bishop Otter and Avery
Hill, were generally satisfied with their college experience. Most students
accepted the provisions of the corporate culture and welcomed a 'formality
which gave stability to college life and gave one a sense of community '.
Interestingly, these same students recalled that college restrictions were
'not seen as such'; that the exeat system was seen as 'quite fair'; and 'that
there was no resentment at strictness because they didn't stay out late at
home'.[84] An added attraction for Homerton students had always been the
presence of the university in Cambridge. By the 1950s Homerton students
were playing a full part in the university's cultural and social activities.
The 'strictness' of Homerton's regulations, however, could still impede
students' full participation in university activities. One student, who was
unable to accept an invitation because she did not have an exeat, received
the following put down from her undergraduate host: 'Oh! I didn't realise
that Homerton had hours more in keeping with a factory than an educational establishment.'[85] The principal, Alice Skillicorn, was well aware
that excessive socializing by Homerton students could damage the college's
academic reputation:

> I remember her talking to us on our first night: we sat on the floor
> mainly in what was then the 'Drawing Room' and she told us what
> was expected etc. and ended by saying 'Please remember, ladies, that
> this is a college of learning and not a finishing school'.[86]

Although Homerton's flagship status in the training college world was
acknowledged – 'My school disapproved of anyone who didn't go to university – but if you didn't go to university the only place was Homerton,'[87]
by the later 1950s students were becoming increasingly critical of college
life. Moreover, critics were not confined to the 'bolshie students who had
pushed for extended (exeat) hours to 10.30'.[88] Academic work was considered 'not intellectually stimulating'[89]; 'patchy'[90]; 'some lectures were good,
others very poor indeed',[91]; 'the work was not difficult for clever girls'.[92]
Criticisms of the staff reflected an increasing gulf between staff and students
within the college community; importantly, there was also a lack of confidence in the staff's vocational expertise: 'The staff were out of touch with

what was going on in schools – they were not good role models'[93]; or 'The staff appeared rather old! and some were rather peculiar to put it mildly. Many seemed out of touch with the classroom.'[94]

An American professor, on an exchange visit to Homerton in the mid-1950s, contrasted the dynamic international atmosphere of his own college with the staid, even parochial regime at Homerton:

> I come to Homerton from a large municipally owned college in one of the boroughs of New York City. . . . There is the hustle and bustle of thousands of students, diverse in color, race, religion, national background, belief, interest and aim. There is excitement, exhiliration, determination, boredom, tension, and trouble. Anything can happen and nobody is surprised when it does.
>
> Thus my first impression of Homerton focuses on the Combination Room and the High Table. Here reign peace and dignity. When I tell Homerton students that I like the graceful living of the College, they look at me somewhat blankly. Whatever the adjectives they attach to life at Homerton, evidently graceful is not one of them. For them the 'elevenses', the tea at four, the serving of the staff at lunch are prosaic and hardly worthy of notice.[95]

The recollections of staff, who were appointed to Homerton in the 1950s and stayed on until the 1960s and beyond, throw interesting light on the college at the end of the two-year era. One member of staff, who had also been a student at Homerton, was able to see the situation from both perspectives. In her view, students were given no opportunity to 'grow up'. The restrictive regime and the constant monitoring of student behaviour by staff prevented students from learning to manage the freedom of adult life. Interestingly, the 'lack of mechanism for complaint' and the fact that there 'was no such thing as democracy' applied to younger members of staff as well as to students. Such members of staff were warned to 'keep a low profile and not speak out at meetings' and they were even obliged to tell the housekeeper if they were going out in the evening.[96] Another member of staff, while acknowledging that the small staff community could seem 'claustrophobic almost closed' nevertheless praised its commitment and worth.[97] The values of the residential community, however, lived on at Homerton – more especially as, although men were appointed to the staff in the 1960s (see Epilogue) no male students were admitted until the end of the 1970s. At the end of the 1950s, new members of staff were still being encouraged to reside in college.[98] One reckoned that 'she couldn't have done her job without being resident in college', for as well as her teaching responsibilities, she provided 'a safety valve for students to talk to'. As 'virtually the last resident' she lived in college for the next 22 years.[99]

Homerton's principal, Alice Skillicorn, was nearing the end of a long principalship, and like her contemporary at Avery Hill, Frances Consitt, she retired in 1960. The 1950s were a busy time for Skillicorn. At the end of 1952 she went on a five-month tour of the United States. In 1956 she celebrated 21 years service as principal of Homerton and former students presented the college with a magnificent pair of wrought iron entrance gates to commemorate the occasion. Finally on 29 May 1957 she had the privilege of welcoming the Queen Mother to the college to open the newly erected Queen's Wing.[100] In spite of her lively intelligence and shrewdness, Skillicorn did not see the necessity to adapt college procedures to conform to contemporary mores. Comments from younger staff that when Skillicorn retired the college went 'from the medieval age to the present day'[101] and that she was 'living in 1958 as if all the clocks had stopped in 1939 or even earlier'[102] underlined the college's failure to meet changing expectations. Skillicorn did, however, realize that the coming of the three-year course, even without the requirement to become co-educational, would necessarily involve the college in changes in most aspects of its life: 'A good deal of planning and preparation has been done for the three year course which is to begin in 1960 and which will make a great difference to the life and work of students at Homerton.'[103]

Teaching careers: women's 'two roles' after leaving college

How far were married women teachers able to combine their primary role as wives and mothers with the exercise of the profession for which they had been trained? Myrdal and Klein had cited teaching as 'next to ideal' for the performance of women's two roles, although their airy assumption that teaching was a job 'which [is] so easy to combine with marriage and motherhood that, metaphorically speaking a women can practise [it] almost with one hand at the cradle'[104] was hardly realistic. In September 1955 the Ministry of Education appealed to married women teachers to continue teaching after marriage.[105] One ex-Homerton student 'read the appeal in the paper' and when her eldest child was five went back to teaching.[106] This pattern became the norm for married teachers. Most taught for a few years after leaving college, usually until the birth of their first child. After a break of perhaps ten years, or until their youngest child was at school, they would return to teaching. Subsequent career patterns were diverse, but were characterized by part-time work (at least at first), 'starting again from the bottom',[107] i.e. they lost any seniority they have may have achieved in their pre-marriage careers; a lack of any planned career development; and a complete subordination of their own professional life to the needs of their husbands and children. These themes re-echo in students' oral testimonies. A student from the mid-1940s taught for five years and then stayed at home for ten years to bring up her children. She 'fell into into her career again' in 1960, becoming a supply teacher.[108] She obtained a full-time post in 1968, where she stayed for three years. In 1971 she 'fell into the job' of deputy head of a primary school. Thirteen years later she became head of this school until her retirement two years later in 1986.[109]

Married women's teaching careers were fragmentary and opportunistic. The teaching experience of two students from the mid-1950s show not only how subordinated women's working lives were to the needs of their families, but that their confidence in their abilities could be eroded by long disuse. One student taught for three years before taking a 'career break'[110] of twelve years. She then taught part-time in a private school and after four years became full-time. Her husband then moved jobs and she ended her teaching life by 'doing supply in five different schools.' Her companion also taught for three years before a career break of nine. She eventually obtained a full-time post in a primary school; subsequently, encouraged by the local adviser, she applied for and obtained the headship of a small village school where she remained for fourteen years until she retired. On her own admission without external encouragement she would never have thought of applying for the headship.[111]

Returning to teaching could also have financial implications, and for those whose husbands were high earners it could also involve additional taxation.[112]

> Six years teaching. 1964–7 years out for family. Back part time. Had home help – thought it worth going back but took a lot of her salary. Eventually full-time. Took Open University degree 1986–90. Moved round with husband – meant that she hadn't had scaled post since 1981.[113]

Some students went to university in preference to returning to teaching when family responsiblities allowed them to do so.

> Two years London primary. Huge classes. Then to Buenos Aires for a year in private school. Then married. Moved round with husband a banker. At 42 to Sussex University. 'Difficult to get job outside teaching'. MA at Institute of Education, London. Now studying for M.Phil. at Wolfson College, Cambridge.[114]

This reflected the high academic potential of some training college students, who at later periods, when there were more university places for women, would have gone to university rather than training college. Some students would indeed have preferred to go to university rather than training college after leaving school, but were prevented either because their 'school didn't encourage it'[115] or because their families could not afford it.[116]

Participants in the 'Education of Women' debate had commended teaching for women's 'two roles' largely on grounds of convenience (fitting in with family needs) and previous vocational training. Little mention was made of the advantage which the actual experience of mothering gave to teachers. Mothers who themselves had returned to teaching spoke out of that experience:

> I once heard a well-known educationalist and broadcaster advise a student teacher to marry, have her family and then, when she was old enough, to return to her job. He added that she would then be of much greater value to the teaching profession. My experience since leaving college in 1947 has convinced me that he was right. . . . I hope to return when my two children are old enough. I feel quite sure that motherhood is the best training a teacher can have. A teacher who is a mother has more support from parents and is more confident with children.[117]

A Homerton student in the early 1950s also drew attention to the valuable lessons of mothering. Her account reveals not only how she was able to put her vocational expertise to the test with her own children, but that their needs and those of her husband always remained uppermost in her mind:

> I suppose you might call me 'semi-wastage', though my husband courteously offers to punch anyone caring to do so. What I mean is that I taught for only four terms before getting married and 'resting', as the acting profession would put it for five years. At the end of this time, having found resting to be the most exhaustive occupation known to woman, I returned last April, as a part-time teacher in a local Sec. Mod. Here, though in a rather drab establishment, I am slowly recuperating, if that's the word.
>
> My five years' rest has been spent in bringing up a husband and two sons to the stage when they can be safely left in other hands. . . . Five years is a long time. It has been an interesting time too. Putting into practice you-know-who's ideas on child psychology on one's own children (and husband) is rather different from trying them on someone else's. . . . I cannot help feeling that I have had many valuable experiences here which would not otherwise have come my way. . . . Just as interesting has been watching them learn . . .
>
> I was going to write about my feelings on getting back to teaching, but I seemed to have strayed off the point. Maybe that too proves something. I don't know.[118]

The semi-facetious tone adopted by this writer was typical of former students' accounts of their domestic lives. Like Hubback's respondents,[119] they were anxious to put the best face possible on the frustrations and tedium they experienced at home looking after their homes and children. In keeping with the cultural attitudes which they had imbibed at college, former students tried always to put a positive gloss on their experiences, rather than indulge in straightforward moaning or complaining. Importantly, even if they eventually abandoned teaching, they still sought to be of service to the community outside the home.

> To be immured for ever in a city suburb, with apparently only the role of wife and mother to justify (my) existence. 'Only' is indeed the wrong word! The world of housework and shopping, the endless washing and cooking, however dull it seems to the eyes of the busy professional woman, can be an absorbing and complete job in itself. But so often it is a *lonely* [writer's italics] job.
>
> When I got married three years ago, I did some part-time teaching for a little while, as I felt it was too soon to become one of those lonely housewives. I had a long journey to my school and the pay (it was a small private school) was low, so it became both physically and economically a very unrewarding post. My house was fairly large and I found it was difficult to cope efficiently with the house and the job . . . so I gave up teaching. It was then that the local Community Centre stepped into the gap in my life . . . I am chairman of the Drama Section this year, so that at home we always seem to be discussing Committee meetings and agendas. . . . When my son Nicholas was born, I was inundated with bootees and mittens and committee meetings had to take place here so that everyone could meet the new arrival. It won't be long before he will be able to go to the Nursery School held in the Hall.[120]

Homerton's principal had already recognized the inevitable when she told her students that 'even if you don't teach you have been given something you can give back to the community'.[121] Another student, immured in the chaos of domestic life, saw her present situation analytically as 'one of the greatest challenges to your self-confidence and intelligence' and interestingly cited the sustenance she was able to obtain from the values that she had imbibed during her college life:

> Can you combine marriage with such an exacting job (teaching). You compromise and hope that perhaps the deep happiness and greater sympathy you bring to your class will make up for those lessons you didn't always prepare. But comes the day when you resign and quick-witted third-formers hand you tiny white garments. . . . Abruptly your life changes irrevocably. You are house-bound, you wash, cook and are the Eternal Comforter. . . . You forget your narrow-minded Head, the dinner-duties, the wet 'breaks' and teaching is 'Mecca'.
>
> Now is one of the greatest challenges to your self-confidence and to your intelligence. You have to plan your days without a time-table, and learn to grin cheekily when your husband sees a chaotic household at the end of your hard day's labour, instead of a neat pay-cheque. . . . You have to nourish your cravings for stimulating discussion and

creative activity and you fight to tunnel your way out of the mounds
of dirty clothes and washing-up to look around at what's new in politics, fashion and the adult world. . . . You wonder why they selected
you for Homerton. But they did. And gave you that rich experience
and those values which strengthen you to cope with changing and chal-
lenging situations.[122]

Epilogue

Bishop Otter

> Deeper voices in chapel, larger appetites in the dining hall our first gentlemen
> were within and Orchard had become the haunt of jazz band players, foot-
> ball and rugger enthusiasts.[123]

Within the first year of their admission to the college, Bishop Otter's male
students were making their presence felt. Their numbers rose from 42 for
the year 1960–1, to 103 in 1961–2 and 213 in 1967–8.[124] In the early
years of co-education, male students briefly formed around two-thirds of
the student population, but later this proportion dropped considerably.[125]
The rise in the number of male staff was swift. There were only two men
on the staff on the eve of co-education. In successive years the numbers
rose to twelve and then fifteen. By 1964, four years into the three-year
course, there were 20 men on the staff (1 of whom was part-time) and 29
women (4 of whom were part-time).[126] By weight of numbers, if for nothing
else, the conversion of a female-only college into one in which women
formed only just over half of the corporate body was bound to have a considerable effect on the institution.

The new Bishop of Chichester (Bishop Bell had resigned from the
governors in 1957),[127] showed, in his annual reports as chairman of
the governors, that he was well aware of the threat which the new situation imposed to the college's corporate ethic. He admitted, after the first
year of co-education, that the changes amounted to a 'revolution' and that
the revolution had only remained 'bloodless' because of the leadership of
the principal 'who can scarcely have had any easy moments'.[128] The following
year while welcoming 'the greater maturity' of students in a 'mixed college'
he nevertheless expressed his concern that the growing number of non-
resident students made 'progress in community building slow'.[129]

The principal, in her public utterances, remained confident that the values
of the women's community could still be maintained. In 1961, she wrote
that the college was 'no longer feeling its way' that 'mixing' has happened
and we like its results' and that 'of course the place of worship remains at
the heart of the college'. Furthermore: 'Opinions are voiced now with less
restraint than when the Union was all female, this proving to be one of

the many advantages of living in a mixed community.' She admitted, though, that other changes like allowing 'trousers to be worn in Chichester' had been 'forced on' the college.[130] In 1962 the senior student (still a woman) echoed the principal's confidence: '"It will not be the same with the men" has proved correct but it has not been so in a detrimental sense.'[131]

In the early days of the new era the principal represented men students as a minority in need of protection:

> Men lecturers led by a man Vice-Principal have seen that the interests of men although in a minority are not neglected
>
> Proportional representation of the sexes on the SRC [Students Representative Council] was by no means unanimous but many felt there should be some basis on which to elect for a few years at least until College is established in its mixed capacity.[132]

This last quotation could of course be taken both ways. But in reality the principal was worried that men rather than women would come to dominate the college community. In a private letter to a sister woman principal dated May 1961 and headed 'Going Educational', she included the advice to take 'a firm line on Pin Ups'. More crucially she admitted that: 'I insisted on proportional representation because the men were openly saying "In 2 years time we shall run this college."'[133] Murray's fears proved accurate. In May 1963, less than three years after men had arrived in college, one of their number was elected Senior Student.[134] The principal contented herself with the somewhat barbed comment that although men formed half of the student body, 'they seem to have the direction of many affairs firmly in their hands'. The male Senior Student gave an accurate if patronizing analysis of the situation: 'Men, inevitably perhaps, have taken the positions of greater prominence but the women are by no means eclipsed. They occupy many of the more essential (if less prominent) positions.'[135]

The 'inevitable eclipse' of women students in positions of authority in the college was perhaps a consequence of the culture of femininity. Middle-class mores, even as late as 1960, still required women to regard themselves as subordinate to men, and therefore to cede political and administrative authority to them. In a women's community this ideology was not of course relevant, but it is interesting that in the absence of men, the principal and to a lesser extent the staff, took on these 'male' characteristics. In the women's college students had accepted the 'male' authority of the principal and staff. Now with the increasing freedom in the co-educational college for students to manage their own affairs, it seemed equally 'natural' to allow male students to take the lead. However, not all the traditional values of the women's college vanished overnight. A male student in the 1960s attributed the relatively easy assimilation of men into the college community to the principal's skill in maintaining traditional female practice:

The incorporation of such young men as ourselves, hairy, noisy, and vulgar, was Betty Murray's crowning achievement. What had been a quiet, conventional orthodox college for young ladies, or so it seemed to us, managed to assimilate, nay convert, males from many different backgrounds, notably those with experience elsewhere of industry and commerce, and an appropriate veneer of 'done it'.

There was always the possibility that such individuals would subvert the institution; instead, such was the Principal's alchemy that, confronted by the soothing regime of one's own room 'bedder', together with morning cocoa (inclusive of sticky buns), the reverse occurred, and we became committed educationalists and discovered ourselves.

Interestingly, this student attributed Murray's success not to the female attribute of nurturing individuals in the private sphere, but, on the contrary, to her public masculine authority over the college as a whole:

The Vice-Principal, it was asserted, 'dealt' with the men. There are those who can speak of individual acts of kindness on Miss Murray's part, but, paradoxically, it was the aloofness and austerity of her demeanour which ensured that her will and her regime prevailed.[136]

Avery Hill

The college has developed from an academy for young ladies outwardly formal and very correct to a lively, sometimes boisterous community of men and women.[137]

The 'boisterous' young men who joined Avery Hill's women students on the Eltham site in the autumn of 1962, had, since 1959 formed an annexe to the college in central London at a site recently vacated by Westminster Training College. The men students, many of whom had already completed their period of National Service,[138] quickly developed a culture of their own. The college's historian was treading delicately when he wrote:

It took a little time to adjust to the new situation. Changes came gradually and for most of the time the two establishments, Eltham and Westminister, went their separate ways. . . . Mixed social occasions had been a marked success and the Eltham lecturers were giving 'considerable guidance' to the Westminister staff . . . some women at Eltham felt it a little strange when they came across men wearing 'their' scarf, and the Westminster men had to bear with the taunts of other students who asked 'What are you doing at a girls' college?'[139]

Articles in the college magazine show that during these years of separation both sides of the 'divide' were aware of the adjustments that would have to be made. Until the merger, the *Avery Hill Reporter* carried a men's section entitled 'Life at the Annexe'. This was largely devoted to sporting activities but did record men students' musical pleasure at 'blending with the "silvery sounds" of the Eltham ladies' and expressed the hope 'for present friendships and many new alliances to be made with our sister college at Eltham'.[140] Both male and female students, of course, welcomed the increased opportunities for social and sexual activity which co-education would bring. One former student indeed lamented in verse that she had attended Avery Hill 'twelve years too early':

> My beloved Avery Hill
> Is open to Tom, Jack and Bill.
> Men, yes, two hundred men, to share,
> The lives and studies of students fair.
> I think, I frown, in hurly burly;
> Alas, I was twelve years too early.[141]

On the eve of the merger, Eltham and Westminster addressed each other. Eltham students emphasized the college's existing reputation – 'They looked forward with interest to the merger with men' and to the 'renewed vigours for high standards'. Westminster were more aware of the difficulties. Students 'must remember that Avery Hill had been for many years a training college for women' and that they must 'do all in their power to fit into existing patterns'. Reference was also made to some male students' dismay at having to leave the centre of London and abandon their separate collegiate traditions. Neverthless Westminster's 'ultimate aim' was 'with the least delay to create a mixed training college on grounds of mutual respect and trust'.[142]

Frances Consitt retired as principal in 1960. The college appointed as her successor a married woman – Kathleen Jones. It was interesting that the authorities chose by six votes to three to 'update' the principal's image by choosing a married rather than a single woman (but still a woman as befitted the head of what was still a women's college) rather than opt for Jones' rival – a man.[143] The new principal was well aware of the difficulties of her task: 'It could not be an easy period as new patterns are being battered out, but it is a vastly interesting one.'[144]

The problem of residential accommodation was acute at Avery Hill, for both women and men students. The college was only able to provide residence in college for about one-third of its students and this inevitably had deleterious effects on the practices and standards of collegiate life. Equally central to the attack on the values of the woman's college was the take-over by men of most of the leadership roles of student life. Even more rapidly than at Bishop Otter, and within one year of the merger on the Eltham site, a man was elected president of the Students Union. Men were also elected to the posts of secretary and treasurer of the Union; the only post held by a woman student was deputy social secretary. Women still retained their posts in some college societies, like the Catholic Society, but the loss of control of the Union – the central focus of student life – was critical. Male pressure also led to changes in the college magazine – the *Avery Hill Reporter*. Within a year of the merger the magazine 'after 50 years of feminine isolation' was redesigned 'to satisfy the critical tastes of students'. The comment that 'more humour' was necessary along with the reference to '50 years of feminine isolation' revealed that men students were aiming to fashion a periodical more in keeping with their interests than those of female readers.[145] This impression was confirmed the following year when it was stated that 'this could be the last issue' of the AHR. Although it was emphasized that the journal was 'not a student newspaper or Rag Mag' male interests would predominate. It was admitted that the 'new magazine was controversial among old girls', who had reluctantly conceded that 'we suppose we must move with the times'.[146]

The transformation of the magazine was yet another threat to corporate feminine tradition. For college magazines had always played a vital role in linking together members of the colleges' extended family. Here the principal could communicate with her former students. These 'grandmothers' could read about the activities of their 'granddaughters' (current students). Importantly former students could also keep up with the activities of their contemporaries at college and experience once more the feeling not only of being a member of an educational institution but also of belonging to its extended family.

Homerton

At Homerton, in contrast to Bishop Otter and Avery Hill, men were not introduced as students with the advent of the three-year course. Alice Skillicorn retired from the principalship in 1961 and was succeeded by Miss (later Dame) Beryl Paston Brown, who had been principal of the City of Leicester Training College since 1952. Leicester Training College had been a women's institution until 1958, when under Paston Brown's enthusiastic leadership it had become co-educational. Paston Brown's positive experience of a 'mixed college' led her as a matter of policy to appoint men to the Homerton staff.[147] But her personal enthusiasm for co-education, in marked contrast to her predecessors, was not the only reason why 'the numbers of male members of the College Staff went 'up and up'.[148] It was necessary with the advent of the three-year course to enhance the academic teaching in college. Single women with the necessary qualifications were in short supply; and married women, unless they lived locally, were not applying for posts because of their family commitments. This left the field open for men whose qualifications were in any case generally considered 'superior'.[149] Many of the men appointed to the Homerton staff had held senior teaching posts at grammar schools.[150] The rise in the number of men on the Homerton staff was swift and spectacular. In 1961 there were 22 women on the staff and 4 men; by 1964 the numbers were respectively 23 and 14, and in 1967, 26 and 21; by 1969 virtual parity had been achieved with the numbers standing at 29 and 26.[151] Thus in less than ten years a staff which had been almost entirely female had become one in which the numbers of men and women were equal. Most of these male staff were in junior positions rather than heads of department so that, for the time being at least, they did not occupy the posts of most influence and power in the college.

The new principal moved swiftly to modernize the college's culture and practice. Most students remained resident in college – although it was less common for either men or women staff to be so. The reforms of the principal's 'glorious bloodless revolution' included the modification of the system of exeats; the establishment of a democratic Academic Board; and a general relaxation of hierarchical formalities between principal and staff, and staff and students.[152] Most importantly for students, the principal showed her support for relationships between the sexes by breaking an old college taboo: 'After 1961 men were allowed in our rooms from 2.30pm until 10 pm. which was thought very daring when it was first introduced.'[153]

The domestic standards of the female college were, however, closely maintained and guarded by the college's formidable domestic bursar, Dorothy Westall (see Chapter 4). Westall, who had joined the college staff in 1958, remained in post until her retirement in 1980; and it was largely due to her vigilance that the college's traditional domestic and social standards lingered on.[154] It was not without significance that, for many of the young men appointed to the staff in the 1960s, it was just these values and standards which attracted them to the college in the first place.[155] Young men, who had previously been subject to the rough and tumble of school life, welcomed the 'collegiate feel'; the 'caring attention' to the decor; and the 'little extra touches' – like flowers in guest rooms – all hallmarks of the culture of femininity.[156]

Nevertheless, in spite of this appreciation of the college's middle-class domestic standards by some new male members of staff, the advent of men to the staff had a crucial effect on the whole ethos of the college. Male staff, most of whom were 'family' men,[157] did not live in college, and many women staff also now chose not to be resident. The co-residence of staff and students was, as we have seen, essential to the corporate life of the women's college. Interestingly, this crucial change was not at first appreciated by older members of staff. The 'endless' changes of the 1960s were seen as 'being dictated from outside' rather than emanating from within.[158] Older women staff generally welcomed, in the principal's words 'the leavening of married men staff'.[159] New men staff felt 'no patronising responses from the older women' and no awareness that they were seen as a threat. As one male member of staff perceptively commented 'the family model was too strong'.[160]

The invocation of the central metaphor of the women's college – the family – lies at the heart of the eventual take-over by men staff of the authority and power once wielded by women. Men staff were welcomed as younger members of the college family – sons perhaps or younger brothers. This was made additionally interesting by a certain hostility which was felt towards the married women, who were now being appointed in increasing numbers as part-time members of staff. Married women could be seen as a reproach to the unmarried who had failed to achieve women's central role – marriage and a family. Married men, on the other hand were welcomed, both because they were thought to be less likely to form sexual relationships with the students, and also because their married status and youth enabled them to relate to women staff in a civilized rather than predatory fashion.

For the time being, power remained with women heads of department (and crucially with the principal)[161] but the advent of the Academic Board – a 'democratic community of equals'[162] rather than a forum for heads of department – opened the way to power for male members of staff. This new democratic forum was in sharp contrast to the autocratic rule of the college's previous principals, and was therefore quite contrary to older staff's experience. 'A lot of the old hands didn't want the responsibility of being involved in the Academic Board'.[163] In keeping with the family model of college life, women staff saw their role as giving young men a chance: 'Women staff would say "I think I shall resign from the Academic Board to let younger staff in".'

The first secretary of the Academic Board was a man and male members of staff could expect election to the Board within a few years of their appointment.[164] A woman member of staff noticed this shift of power at the time but 'couldn't quite put her finger on it'. Better qualified women seemed to be giving way to 'comparative whippersnapers'. She commented that women were not used to dealing with issues of power and were bad at it. Later, with the advent of men students, she noticed the same thing when men would, e.g. monopolize discussion at student seminars.[165] The culture of femininity in women's colleges had been structured by the autocratic masculine rule of a woman principal. It was therefore, perhaps, only to be expected that women in training colleges – staff as well as students – all of whom had been conditioned to accept the natural authority of men – should, with the advent of men to their institutions, willingly cede power to them.

7 Conclusion

This study has sought to bring back into the historical record an area of women's experience which has heretofore remained largely hidden. Previously women in teacher training colleges have been glimpsed but rarely, buried in the dim shadows of larger surveys of the history of education. Conventional accounts of training colleges have largely failed to pay any separate attention to women's experience, or characterized it as narrow, restricted and illiberal. In this concluding chapter I want to draw attention to three themes in my study which are of particular importance to feminist history: the training colleges' provision of higher education for women; their role in the social mobility of the elementary school teacher; and the experience of women, and its legacy, within a particular type of residential educational community.

Without the existence of training colleges, opportunities for the higher education of women in the first half of the twentieth century would have been largely confined to the few, largely middle-class, women who were admitted to the universities. The inadequate education available to women had been central to feminist pressure for reform in the nineteenth century. Unlike the campaign for the suffrage, the right to an education and more particularly a higher education, previously only available to men was ceded to women with comparatively little resistance. Changing social and economic conditions in the second half of the nineteenth century had increased the state's need for a well-educated and skilled workforce. The role of the teacher, a profession dominated by women, was crucial to this process. It was the training colleges' achievement that they transformed the narrow vocational training of the nineteenth century into the wider educational and cultural attainments of the twentieth. This gave clever girls from lower middle-class homes, who wished to train as elementary school teachers, access to a higher education which would otherwise have been denied them. Moreover, after the Second World War and until the expansion of the university sector in the late 1960s, many middle-class girls also received their higher education at a training college.

The social mobility of the elementary school teacher was the result of the training colleges' culture of femininity. This culture translated the family organization of the middle-class home, and some of its social practices, from the home into a new institutional setting. In this residential setting the staff played the crucial role in transmitting to students the cultural, aesthetic, intellectual and spiritual values of the liberal humanist traditions of the middle class. This provision of an education, which went far beyond the narrower requirements of vocational training, was acknowledged and actively encouraged by the Board of Education and its Inspectorate. That it was not similarly welcomed and encouraged by middle-class society, let alone middle-class parents, throws interesting light on the rigidities of the English class system, particularly within the middle class itself. By the end of the nineteenth century middle-class parents were beginning to accept that it was appropriate for their daughters to receive secondary education at boarding school. The crucial factor was that at such schools girls would associate only with members of their own class. Similarly, a few middle-class girls were allowed to attend residential university colleges because here too they would only associate with their own kind. It was also becoming acceptable for middle-class girls to train for the teaching profession – but not at a residential training college. For although at training college they would receive instruction from members of their own class, they would also be obliged to live with fellow students who were their social inferiors. The fear of such social contamination was very real and lingered onto until the middle of the twentieth century. Middle-class girls wishing to train as teachers attended day training colleges or taught in school on the strength of their university degree.

The middle-class boycott of residential training colleges was deeply to affect the colleges' development. Colleges were already being encouraged by the Inspectorate to widen students' cultural opportunities beyond the narrow confines of a strictly vocational training but the development of a full culture of femininity peculiar to the colleges themselves was the creation of their principals and staff. Their primary aim was to improve the status of the teaching profession by introducing students to the wider culture which would enable them to become, like themselves, full members of the middle class. Staff also knew that the achievement of middle-class status was as bound up with domestic and social mores as it was with educational and cultural attainment. Values and customs that could have been assumed to be shared, if students had come from middle-class rather than lower middle-class homes, would need to be learned. The co-residence of staff and students made this transformation possible by the careful attention which principals and staff were able to pay to every aspect of students' lives. The family organization of training colleges, for instance, facilitated students' adjustment to an institutional life. Within such a secure framework, girls, who might never have been away from home before, were able quickly to benefit from the opportunities of college life. The close watch that was kept on students' social and sexual activities was also prompted by the need for students to achieve a secure middle-class status.

Staff were also concerned with their own quality of life. They wished their educational work to be accomplished within an environment which re-created the civilized domestic and social arrangments of their own homes. The commitment and dedication of principals and staff gave the corporate life of the colleges its particular resonance. For, importantly, staff not only transmitted to students their own knowledge of the liberal humanist tradition and their appreciation of the social values of the middle class, but they actively sought to share their own pursuit of these values and ideas with students in the shared activities of the colleges' corporate life. Social hierarchies were always strictly observed within college, and the acceptance by students of the authority of the staff was unquestioned. But the joint participation of both staff and students in the cultural, aesthetic, spiritual and social activites, which formed an integral part of corporate life, transformed the colleges from narrowly focused educational institutions into cultural communities of mutual encouragement and enrichment.

The role of woman principal was always difficult. The reputation of a college crucially depended on the abilities and authority of its principal. Each of the principals in my survey achieved within her college the public masculine role of a strong, authoritative and powerful father. They were less successful in integrating this masculine role with the private needs of their own femininity. Most principals, in practice, chose to 'sacrifice' some of their private emotional needs in the interests of their public role. Some principals were able to temper their private isolation with the warmth of homoerotic friendship. But this was always a hidden discourse, unsanctioned and unnamed. Moreover, although principals were successful in establishing authority and power over their own colleagues and within their own institutions, they encountered many difficulties in establishing this authority in their relationships with the world outside the college. Difficulties ranged from the purely domestic to serious educational matters. Principals were also constantly vulnerable to society's perception of training colleges, and more particularly to any adverse criticisms of their students' behaviour. This fear lay behind the anxious, even obsessive, control which was kept over all aspects of students' lives. Moreover, criticism, or the fear of it, encouraged college principals to' keep a low profile' in their relationships with the outside world. This defensive attitude encouraged public ignorance; instead of the colleges enjoying the reputation for innovative educational and cultural achievement which they deserved, they were dismissed as narrow institutions, insular and illiberal.

The negative reputation of training colleges was a contributory factor in their decline and eventual demise. But more importantly, the colleges were fatally undermined by events outside their control: first, in the inter-war period, by changing attitudes to women's sexuality, and then, after the Second World War, by the changing educational needs of the post-war world. Changing attitudes to women's sexuality had been sweeping though society since the end of the First World War, although they were slow to reach the insular world of the training college. In the early years of the century, both staff and students had collectively shared an ethic which accepted that restrictions on sexual freedom were essential in order to maintain the respectability on which the credibility of their pioneering communities depended. Under the wider influence of the suffrage movement, spinsterhood and chastity were seen by many educated women, including the staff in training colleges, as a positive choice. But the 'new' discourse began to chip away at the consensus within colleges on sexual behaviour. Crucially, the discourse's assertion that all women had the right to physical sexual satisfaction, but only within heterosexual marriage, had a crippling effect on college staff for whom marriage was not an option. Students, on the other hand, increasingly welcomed the new orthodoxy and began to chafe at the restrictions in college preventing their access to it. Staff, because of their lack of experience in this central area of life, began to lose confidence in their own authority; students in turn began to lose respect for this authority. Although the breakdown of consensus was at first confined to sexual conduct only, the shared values of the college community had been crucially undermined.

The death knell of the women's training colleges and their culture was sounded by the influential McNair Report, published in 1944. By this time middle-class girls were beginning to attend training colleges, and the importance of the colleges' role in training teachers for the post-war world was recognized. The colleges were extensively consulted by the McNair Committee; their work was praised but it was also subjected to the same criticisms of narrow outlook and illiberal attitudes which had long been current. Importantly, students, who were by now better educated and increasingly from middle-class homes, now also began to add criticisms of the colleges' educational and vocational teaching to their long-standing complaints about the restrictions on their social and sexual lives. Younger staff too began to share the perception of the outside world that the whole training college culture was old-fashioned, inward-looking and out of touch with the realities of the post-war world.

The McNair Report's recommendations therefore fell on receptive ears both within the colleges and outside them. But two of its main recommendations struck at the very heart of the colleges' culture and practice. For the report not only declared that it was highly desirable that colleges be co-educational but that staff residence in college was not an essential requirement for college life. The training colleges' culture would not have been possible without the co-residence of staff and students. Moreover, the advent of men, both staff and students, led to their swift take-over of most of the positions of influence and power which had previously been held by women. The fact that this take-over was accomplished with only token resistance points to the continuing acceptance by even highly educated women of men's right to authority over them.

By the 1960s the era of the women's training college was over. Its transitory existence in no way lessens its important role in the wider feminist struggle to provide women with an adequate education. For students, the lasting legacy of their training college experience was the opportunities it had given them for individual development and fulfilment. Even when the traditions and practices of corporate life began to fall victim to changing cultural and social expectations, students as individuals continued to value and profit from the education in the widest sense of the word which they had received. Not the least important result of this individual enrichment was the personal confidence which students could now exercise in both the professional and private spheres. Moreover, although in the long run most of the customs and practices of college life came to be regarded as means to an end rather than an end in themselves, the friendship networks which students developed at college, many of which continued throughout life, were a direct result of living in a community.

Nevertheless the training college experience in no way promoted a feminist consciousness. On the contrary, and in spite of the feminist aspirations of some early members of staff, the defensive and increasingly insular corporate culture encouraged rather than challenged hegemonic conservative attitudes towards femininity. Individual enrichment and personal confidence equipped students to take their place in middle-class society. It did not equip them to challenge this society's patriarchal values. Indeed, social conformism was an additional proof of students' achievement of middle-class status.

The story for the staff is less progressive. Unlike that of the students, the commitment of principals and staff to their colleges was long-term, even lifelong. The college provided clever middle-class women, who remained unmarried either through choice or necessity, not only with an interesting profession but a comfortable home. In addition, these single women were part of a community which gave them both a sense of purpose and congenial companionship. It also protected them from the patronage and boredom which, as unmarried women, they might have endured in the middle-class home. The homoerotic friendships which some principals and staff formed during their college service are an important part of lesbian history. Staff's failure to adapt to the changing social and sexual expectations of students was an inevitable consequence of their life-long commitment to older models of chastity and respectability. After the Second World War, when heterosexuality and marriage became not only hegemonic but virtually obligatory, the unmarried spinster seemed old-fashioned and an anachronism.

The women's training college and its culture of femininity fell victim to the changing educational and social expectations of the post-war world. Its transitory role in no way diminishes its importance in the evolving history of women's education. Training colleges were institutions which served the needs of their time. College staff had been able to valorize their celibacy in purposeful service within a nurturing feminine community. Generations of women students had not only had the opportunity for professional training but had received an education which equipped them to enter the middle-class world. It was on this firm basis that they and their successors were later able to develop a feminist analysis of patriarchal society which was eventually to lead them to empowerment. I am glad to have had the opportunity of recovering these women and their communities for the historical record.

Notes

Introduction

1 J. Purvis, 'A national library for women in Britain', *Women's History Review* 7 (3), 1998, p. 293.
2 P. Summerfield, 'Cultural reproduction in the education of girls: a study of girls' secondary schooling in two Lancashire towns', in F. Hunt (ed.) *Lessons for life: the schooling of girls and women 1850–1950* (Oxford: Blackwell, 1987), p. 161.
3 F. Widdowson, *Going up into the next class: women and elementary teacher training 1840–1914* (London: Hutchinson, 1983), p. 7. Foreword by A. V. John.
4 L. G. E. Jones, *The training of teachers in England and Wales: a critical study* (Oxford: Clarendon, 1923).
5 H. C. Dent, *The training of teachers in England and Wales 1800–1975* (London: Hodder and Stoughton, 1977).
6 M. Vicinus, *Independent women: work and community for single women 1850–1920* (London: Virago, 1985), pp. 121–62.
7 Ibid., pp. 163–210.
8 C. Dyhouse, *No distinction of sex? Women in British universities 1870–1939* (London: UCL Press, 1995).
9 See e.g. D. H. J. Zebedee, *Lincoln Diocesan Training College 1862–1962* (Lincoln: The College, 1962); A. M. Wilkinson, *Ripon Training College 1862–1962* (Ripon: The College, 1963); C. More, *The training of teachers 1847–1947: a history of the Church Colleges at Cheltenham* (London: Hambledon, 1992); R. Smart, *On others' shoulders: an illustrated history of the Polhill and Lansdowne Colleges, now De Montfort University, Bedford* (Bedford: De Montfort University, 1994); F. A. Montgomery, *Edge Hill College: a history 1885–1985* (Liverpool: Edge Hill College, 1985).
10 See e.g. Montgomery, *Edge Hill*, p. 37. Montgomery's study is unusual in being written from a feminist perspective.
11 See e.g. Zebedee, *Lincoln Training College*, p. 80; Wilkinson, *Ripon Training College*, p. 70; Smart, *On others' shoulders*, p. 58.
12 More, *Training of teachers*, pp. 75–6.
13 D. Shorney, *Teachers in training 1906–1985: a history of Avery Hill College* (London: Thames Polytechnic, 1989).
14 G. P. McGregor, *Bishop Otter College and policy for teacher education 1839–1980* (London: Pembridge, 1981).
15 T. H. Simms, *Homerton College 1695–1978* (Cambridge: Homerton College, 1979).
16 D. W. Hackman, *First year up* (London: Dent, 1951). Doris Hackman was a lecturer in education at Homerton from 1943–5.
17 I was librarian and archivist at Homerton from 1984–93.

18 See E. Edwards, 'Revisiting Miss Skillicorn: a journey in auto/biography', *Auto/Biography*, 1, 2 and 3, 1997, pp. 95–103 for a discussion of this project.
19 Ibid.
20 Summerfield, 'Cultural reproduction in the education of girls', pp. 158–61.
21 A. Oram, *Women teachers and feminist politics 1900–1939* (Manchester: Manchester University Press, 1996), p. 17.
22 D. Copelman, *London's women teachers: gender, class and feminism 1870–1930* (London: Routledge, 1996), pp. 136–44. See e.g. L. C. Knights, 'Will training colleges bear scrutiny', *Scrutiny*, 1, 1932–3, pp. 247–63 for a typically dismissive account of the training college regime.
23 Dyhouse, *No distinction of sex?*, pp. 91–3.
24 Ibid., p. 112.
25 Widdowson, *Going up into the next class*.

1 The historical context

1 The information on which this account is based is largely taken from H. C. Dent, *The training of teachers in England and Wales, 1800–1975* (London: Hodder and Stoughton, 1977) and F. Widdowson, *Going up into the next class*. (London: Hutchinson, 1983). Notes for this chapter will therefore be confined to direct quotation from these two works or for information from other sources.
2 L. G. E. Jones, *The training of teachers in England and Wales* (Oxford: Clarendon, 1923) p. 401.
3 Ibid., pp. 400–1.
4 Dent, *The training of teachers*, p. 19.
5 T. H. Simms, *Homerton College 1695–1978* (Cambridge: Homerton College, 1979) p. 15.
6 Ibid., p. 41.
7 Dent, *The training of teachers*, p. 26.
8 G. P. McGregor, *Bishop Otter College and policy for teacher education 1839–1980* [London: Pembridge, 1981) pp. 37–79.
9 Dent, *The training of teachers*, p. 33.
10 See below. Middle-class women would not be obliged in day colleges to be co-residential with members of the lower middle class.
11 Jones, *The training of teachers*, p. 400.
12 D. Shorney, *Teachers in training 1906–1985: a history of Avery Hill College* (London: Thames Polytechnic, 1989), p. 16.
13 Dent, *The training of teachers*, p. 61.
14 Ibid., p. 54.
15 Widdowson, *Going up into the next class*, p. 95.
16 Jones, *The training of teachers*, p. 8/.
17 Simms, *Homerton College*, pp. 47–9.
18 Ibid., p. 49.
19 Shorney, *Teachers in training*, pp. 47–8.
20 Ibid., pp. 87–8.
21 Ibid., p. 122.
22 Ibid., pp. 166–7.
23 Simms, *Homerton College*, pp. 45–50 and 55.
24 N. Collecott, *Peggles and primroses: a country childhood* (Lavenham, Terence Dalton, 1989), pp. 109–10.
25 L. C. Knights, 'Will training colleges bear scrutiny?', *Scrutiny*, 1, pp. 247–62.
26 Homerton College Archive (hereafter HCA) Acc. no. ACc 15k. College register of staff.
27 Knights, 'Will training colleges', p. 261.

28 Ibid., pp. 261–2.
29 Ibid., p. 262.
30 Ibid., p. 247.
31 Ibid., p. 258.
32 C. Dyhouse, 'Signing the pledge? Women's investment in university education and teacher training before 1939', *History of Education*, 26 (2), 1997, p. 222.
33 A. Oram, *Women teachers and feminist politics 1900–1939* (Manchester: Manchester Univesity Press, 1996), p. 26.
34 D. M. Copelman, *London's women teachers: gender, class and feminism 1870–1930* (London: Routledge, 1996), p. 180.
35 Dent, *The training of teachers*, p. 98.
36 Ibid.
37 Shorney, *Teachers in training*, pp. 119–20.
38 Dent, *The training of teachers*, p. 105.
39 Ibid., p. 107.
40 Shorney, *Teachers in training*, p. 107.
41 see e.g. F. M. Montgomery, *Edge Hill College: a history 1885–1985* (Liverpool: Edge Hill College, 1985), pp. 49–52; L. Grier, *The life of Winifred Mercier* (London: Oxford University Press, 1937), p. 171–2, 214–20. Whitelands College moved from London to Putney in 1930 to magnificent new buildings designed by Sir Giles Gilbert Scott.
42 R. Smart, *On others' shoulders: an illustrated history of the Polhill and Lansdowne Colleges, now De Montfort University, Bedford* (Bedford: De Montfort University, 1994), p. 84.
43 Grier, *Winifred Mercier,* p. 214.
44 Shorney, *Teachers in training*, pp. 140–8.
45 Bishop Otter Archive (hereafter BOA) L1/2/15. Annual Reports, 1941–2, 1942–3.
46 *Homerton News Letter,* April 1940, March 1942.
47 P. Addison, *The road to 1945* (London: Pimlico, 1994), p. 171.
48 See Chapter 3 for the President of the Board of Education's visit to Homerton in 1941.
49 Board of Education, *Teachers and youth leaders* (London: HMSO, 1944) – the McNair Report.
50 Ibid., p. 73.
51 Ibid., pp. 12–14, 17.
52 Ibid., pp. 13–14.
53 Ibid., p. 14.
54 Ibid, p. 65.
55 Ibid., pp. 71–2.
56 Ibid., p. 73.
57 Ibid., p. 76.
58 Ibid., p. 75.
59 Ibid., p. 73.
60 Ibid., p. 76.
61 Ibid, pp. 48–9.
62 Ibid., p. 51.
63 Dent, *The training of teachers*, pp. 113–15.
64 Widdowson, *Going up into the next class*, p. 11.
65 Ibid., p. 14.
66 Ibid., p. 18 quoting, A. Tropp, *The school teachers* (London: Heinemann, 1957), pp. 40 and 60.
67 Ibid., p. 19.
68 Ibid., 27.

69 MacGregor, *Bishop Otter College*, p. 90.
70 Widdowson, *Going up into the next class*, p. 35 quoting from the Cross Commission. This Commission was set up to enquire into the working of the 1870 Education Act. See Chapter 3 for further evidence by Miss Trevor to the Commission.
71 Copelman, *London's women teachers*, p. 71.
72 Ibid., p. 33.
73 Shorney, *Teachers in training*, pp. 58–9.
74 Copelman, *London's women teachers*.
75 Widdowson, *Going up into the next class*, p. 77.
76 F. Hunt (ed.) *Lessons for life: the schooling of girls and women 1850–1950* (Oxford: Basil Blackwell, 1987), pp. xvi–xvii.
77 P. Summerfield, 'Cultural reproduction in the education of girls: a study of girls' secondary schooling in two Lancashire towns, 1900–1950' in Hunt, *Lessons for life*, p. 158.
78 Ibid., p. 159.
79 N. Collecott, *Peggles and primroses*, pp. 99–100.
80 Public schools, in the British context, charge expensive fees and are often residential. Consequently they are only available to middle-class girls whose fathers can afford the fees.
81 BOA L1/2/15. Annual Report 1925–6.
82 HCA College registers, 1914, 1929, 1939, 1949, 1959.
83 Simms, *Homerton College*, p. 62.

2 The culture of femininity

1   Homerton College Archive (hereafter HCA) Acc. no. 4. Letter from prospective student to her college mother, 1899.
2   D. J. Zebedee, *Lincoln Diocesan Training College 1862–1962* (Lincoln: Lincoln Training College, 1962), p. 17.
3   *Homertonian*, 1915.
4   HCA Acc. no. 807. Reminiscences of a student, 1922–5.
5   HCA Acc. no. 889–95. Letters home from a student, 1928.
6   *Homertonian,* January 1904.
7   *Homertonian,* May 1904.
8   *Homertonian,* Sept.–Oct. 1904.
9   Bishop Otter Archive (hereafter BOA) G78. Reminiscences of a student, 1920–2.
10 *Bishop Otter College Magazine*, June 1926.
11 D. W. Hackman, *First year up* (London: Dent, 1951), pp. 10–12.
12 HCA Acc. no. 1708, no. 21. Reply to centenary questionnaire from a student, 1970–4.
13 *Bishop Otter College Magazine*, June 1957.
14 BOA Box 35. Archivist's notes.
15 HCA Acc. no. 417. Annotated snapshots belonging to a student, 1925–7.
16 HCA Acc. no. 807. Reminiscences of a student, 1922–5.
17 HCA Acc. no. 1420, no. 9. Reminiscences of a student, 1944–6.
18 *Schoolmistress,* 27 February 1890, quoted in D. Copelman, *London's women teachers: gender, class and feminism 1870–1930* (London: Routledge, 1996), p. 139.
19 *Homertonian*, June 1906.
20 *Homerton Association News*, 1950.
21 HCA Acc. no. 630. *50 years of the Homerton Association.*
22 R. Smart, *On others' shoulders: an illustrated history of the Polhill and Lansdowne Colleges, now De Montfort University* (Bedford: De Montfort University, 1994), p. 61.

23 F. Young, *Margaret Stansfeld* (Bedford: Bedford Physical Training College, 1956), p. 14.
24 *Avery Hill Reporter*, 1952.
25 HCA Acc. no. 1189, no. 7. Reply to questionnaire on Miss Allan from a student, 1918–20.
26 HCA Acc. no. 945. Reminiscences of a student, 1940–2.
27 HCA Acc. no. 1708, no. 3. Reply to centenary questionnaire from a student, 1960–3.
28 A. Dixon, 'Ruskin's romantic fantasies', *Country Life*, 183, 1989, pp. 130–3.
29 *Avery Hill Reporter*, 1910.
30 *Avery Hill Reporter*, 1911.
31 *Avery Hill Reporter*, 1909.
32 *Avery Hill Reporter*, March 1916.
33 *Homerton Roll News*, 1987–8. Reminiscences of a student, 1906–8.
34 HCA Acc. no. 1404, no. 1. Reply to questionnaire on Miss Skillicorn from a student, 1935–7.
35 N. Collecott, *Peggles and primroses: a country childhood* (Lavenham, Terence Dalton, 1989), pp. 110–11.
36 HCA Acc. no. 1191, no. 23. Reply to questionnaire on Miss Allan from a student, 1931–3.
37 R. Strachey, *The cause* (London: Bell, 1928), p. 399.
38 Otter Memorial Paper no. 12. *Flints, ports, otters and threads: a tribute to K. M. Elisabeth Murray 1909–1998* (Chichester: Chichester Institute of Higher Education, 1998), p. 39.
39 Avery Hill Archive (hereafter AHA) E.2.10. Reminiscences of a student, 1927–9.
40 E. Edwards, 'Educational institutions or extended families? The reconstruction of gender in women's colleges in the late nineteenth and early twentieth centuries', *Gender and Education*, 2, 1990, pp. 21–2.
41 *Homerton Association News*, 1978–9.
42 HCA Acc. no. 888. Letter home from a student, 1928.
43 *Bishop Otter College Magazine*, 1952.
44 Otter Memorial Paper no. 12, pp. 45–6.
45 HCA Acc. no. 1190, no. 44. Reply to questionnaire on Miss Allan from a student, 1927–9.
46 HCA Acc. no. 43. Reply to questionnaire on Miss Allan from a student, 1922–4.
47 HCA Acc. no. 1189, no. 8. Reply to questionnaire on Miss Allan from a student, 1916–18.
48 HCA Acc. no. 1026. Reminiscences of a student, 1920–2.
49 Otter Memorial Paper no. 12, p. 45.
50 Smart, *On others' shoulders*, p. 62.
51 AHA E.2.1. Reminiscences of a student, 1912–14.
52 Otter Memorial Paper no. 12, p. 49.
53 *Avery Hill Reporter*, July 1949.
54 *Homerton Association News*, 1955.
55 HCA Acc. no. 1419, no. 3. Reminiscences of a student, 1935–7.
56 F. Montgomery, *Edge Hill College: a history 1885–1985* (Liverpool: Edge Hill College, 1985), p. 37, quoting two students 1907–10 and 1904–6.
57 BOA MSA 7. Council minutes, 19 October 1936.
58 *Homerton Association News*, 1988–9.
59 Collecott, *Peggles and primroses*, p. 113.
60 HCA Acc. no. 1420, no. 11. 'Mother's' letter to 'daughter', 1945.
61 *Avery Hill Reporter*, 1949.
62 *Homerton Association News*, 1962.
63 *Avery Hill Reporter*, 1948.

64 Otter Memorial Paper no. 12, p. 45.
65 D. Shorney, *Teachers in training 1906–1985: a history of Avery Hill College* (London: Thames Polytechnic, 1989), p. 63.
66 HCA Acc. no. 807. Reminiscences of a student, 1922–5.
67 *Homerton Association News*, 1962.
68 Hackman, *First year up*, p. 17.
69 HCA Acc. no. 1241. Minute and record book of Homerton Union of Students, 1940–54, 16 May 1941.
70 Copelman, *London's women teachers*, p. 137 quoting *Schoolmistress*, 1890.
71 HCA Acc. no. 1403, no. 4. Reply to questionnaire on Miss Skillicorn from a student, 1935–7.
72 F. A. Montgomery, *Edge Hill College*, p. 57.
73 HCA Acc. no. 1229. Reminiscences of a student, 1947–9.
74 *Homerton Association News*, 1944.
75 HCA Acc. no. 1241. HUS minute book, Michaelmas Term, 1943.
76 Ibid., October 1952.
77 HCA Acc. no. 967. Record of discussion with four students, 1946–8.
78 HCA Acc. no. 1241, HUS Minute book, October 1952.
79 V. Woolf, *A room of one's own* (London: Hogarth, 1929).
80 *Avery Hill Reporter*, 1913.
81 AHA E.2.2. Reminiscences of a student, 1912–14.
82 *Homerton Association News,* 1957.
83 *Homerton Association News*, 1962. Reminiscences of a student, 1902.
84 BOA Box 35. Memorandum from principal, December 1924.
85 Zebedee, *Lincoln Training College*, p. 76.
86 BOA G78 Reminiscences of a student, 1920–2.
87 Bishop Otter Annual Report, 1935–6.
88 *Bishop Otter College Magazine*, 1949.
89 Otter Memorial Paper no. 12, p. 37.
90 *Bishop Otter College Magazine*, 1956.
91 *Bishop Otter College Magazine,* 1958.
92 M. Cadogan and P. Craig, *You're a brick, Angela* (London: Gollancz, 1976).
93 T. H. Simms, *Homerton College 1695–1978* (Cambridge: Homerton College, 1979), p. 39.
94 *Homerton Association News*, 1967.
95 HCA Acc. no. 1403, no. 4. Reply to questionnaire on Miss Skillicorn from a student, 1935–7.
96 *Homerton Roll News*, 1988–9.
97 G. Freeman, *Alma Mater: memories of Girton College, 1926–1929* (Cambridge: Pevensey Press, 1990), p. 42.
98 HCA Acc. no. 888. Letter home from a student, 1928.
99 Hackman, *First year up*, pp. 19–20.
100 Collecott, *Peggles and primroses*, p. 107.
101 Shorney, *Teachers in training*, p. 60.
102 Smart, *On others' shoulders*, p. 62.
103 HCA Acc. no. 1241. HUS Minute book, October 1950.
104 Ibid.
105 BOA E.2.8. Reminiscences of a student, 1927–9.
106 HCA Acc. no. 1191, no. 14. Reply to questionnaire on Miss Allan from a student, 1932–4.
107 HCA Acc. no. 1241. HUS Minute book, 1943.
108 HCA Acc. no. 894. Letter home from a student, 1928.
109 Hackman, *First year up*, p. 74.
110 *Homerton Roll News,* 1987–8.

111 HCA Acc, no. 808. Reminiscences of a student, 1925–7.
112 *Avery Hill Reporter,* 1910.
113 *Bishop Otter College Magazine,* 1926.
114 *Avery Hill Reporter,* 1934.
115 Bishop Otter Annual Report 1907–8.
116 HCA Acc. no. 1190, no. 44. Reply to questionnaire on Miss Allan from a student, 1927–9.
117 HCA Acc. no. 1191, no. 6. Reply to questionnaire on Miss Allan from a student, 1932–4.
118 *Homerton Association News,* 1938.
119 *Homerton Association News,* 1937.
120 *Homerton Association News,* 1933.
121 *Homerton Association News,* 1935.
122 *Homerton Association News,* 1934.
123 Shorney, *Teachers in training,* p. 15. See also e.g. Smart, *On others' shoulders,* p. 123; *Homerton Roll News,* 1989–90.
124 Shorney, *Teachers in training,* p. 321.
125 See e.g. HCA Acc. no. 888–95. Letters home from a student, 1928.
126 *Homertonian,* June 1916.
127 Ibid.
128 *Avery Hill Reporter,* October 1936. Reminiscences of a student, 1906–8.
129 HCA Acc. no. 1404, no. 10. Reply to questionnaire on Miss Skillicorn from a student, 1939–41.
130 HCA Acc. no. 1592. Interview October 1991 with four students, 1949–51.
131 HCA Acc. no. 1441. Interview with twelve students from 1940–2.
132 Hackman, *First year up,* p. 41.
133 Ibid., pp. 69, 125, 132.
134 Ibid., pp. 181–3.
135 Ibid., p. 190.
136 HCA Acc. no. 1404. no. 3. Reply to questionnaire on Miss Skillicorn from a student, 1935–7.

3 The role of woman principal

1 Homerton College Archive (hereafter HCA) Acc. no. 1190, no. 28. Reply to questionnaire on Miss Allan from a student, 1923–5.
2 C. Heward, 'Men and women and the rise of professional society: the intriguing history of teacher educators', *History of Education* 22 (1) (1993), p. 17.
3 Ibid., p. 19 quoting BPP, Board of Education Report for 1908, XVIII (1909), p. 75.
4 C. Steedman, Lecture at Homerton College, 6 May 1994.
5 R. Smart, *On others' shoulders: an illustrated history of the Polhill and Lansdowne Colleges, now De Montfort University, Bedford* (Bedford: De Montfort University, 1994), pp. 48–9.
6 G. P. McGregor, *Bishop Otter College* (London: Pembridge, 1981), pp. 92–7. Bishop Otter had originally been founded in 1839 as a training college for men. It was closed down in 1867. McGregor, pp. 28–78.
7 Ibid., p. 101.
8 Ibid., p. 103.
9 Ibid., p. 108.
10 Ibid., pp. 112–13.
11 Ibid., p. 111.
12 Ibid., p. 114.
13 Bishop Otter Archive (hereafter BOA) L1/2/15, Annual Report, 1894.

14 Heward, *Men and women*, p. 19.
15 McGregor, *Bishop Otter College*, p. 151.
16 *Bishop Otter Guild Chronicle*, 1971.
17 Ibid.
18 BOA L1/2/15 Annual Report, 1925–6.
19 BOA L/1/2/15 Annual Report, 1919–20.
20 *Bishop Otter Guild Chronicle*, 1971.
21 BOA L/1/2/15 Annual Report, 1920–1.
22 *Bishop Otter Guild Chronicle*, 1971.
23 Ibid.
24 *Bishop Otter College Magazine*, 1930.
25 *Bishop Otter College Magazine*, 1927.
26 *Bishop Otter College Magazine*, 1929.
27 *Bishop Otter College Magazine*, 1921.
28 *Bishop Otter College Magazine*, 1923.
29 *Bishop Otter Guild Chronicle*, 1971.
30 Ibid.
31 Ibid.
32 *Bishop Otter College Magazine*, 1930.
33 *Bishop Otter College Magazine*, 1919.
34 *Bishop Otter College Magazine*, 1922.
35 *Bishop Otter Guild Chronicle*, 1971.
36 *Bishop Otter Guild Chronicle*, 1968.
37 *Bishop Otter Guild Chronicle*, 1951.
38 BOAL/1/2/15 Annual Report, 1930.
39 McGregor, *Bishop Otter College*, 1981, p. 159; BOA MSA 7 Council minutes, June 1930.
40 BOA MSA 7 Council minutes, July 1930.
41 McGregor, *Bishop Otter College*, p. 159.
42 Ibid., p. 160.
43 *Bishop Otter College Magazine*, 1933.
44 *Bishop Otter College Magazine*, 1932.
45 BOA A75, Finance Committee minutes, October 1935.
46 BOA A42, Council minutes, 1935.
47 McGregor, *Bishop Otter College*, p. 167.
48 BOA A75, Finance Committee minutes, October 1935.
49 *Bishop Otter College Magazine*, 1935.
50 McGregor, *Bishop Otter College* p. 167.
51 BOA A42, Council minutes, May 1936.
52 McGregor, *Bishop Otter College*, pp. 157–9.
53 *Bishop Otter College Magazine*, 1939.
54 *Bishop Otter Guild Chronicle*, 1960.
55 BOA G94 Interview with domestic bursar, 1945–60.
56 *Bishop Otter Guild Chronicle*, 1969.
57 McGregor, *Bishop Otter College*, pp. 172–3.
58 Ibid., p. 173.
59 BOA L/1/2/15 Annual Report, 1941–2.
60 BOA L/1/2/15 Annual Report, 1943–4.
61 *Bishop Otter College Magazine*, 1944.
62 BOA A44 Council minutes, 1943.
63 BOA L 1/2/15 Annual Reports, 1943–4, 1944–5.
64 BOA L/1/2/15 Annual Report, 1944–5.
65 *Bishop Otter College Magazine*, 1946.
66 BOA A46 Council minutes, 1947.

67 *Bishop Otter College Magazine*, 1947.
68 *Bishop Otter College Magazine*, 1959.
69 *Bishop Otter Guild Chronicle*, 1960.
70 McGregor, *Bishop Otter College*, p. 180.
71 Otter Memorial Paper no. 12. *Flints, ports, otters and threads: a tribute to K. M. Elisabeth Murray* (Chichester: Chichester Institute of Higher Education, 1998), pp. 9–20.
72 Ibid., p. 21. The McNair Report on ' The supply, recruitment and training of teachers and Youth Leaders' had been published in 1944 (see Chapter 1). Murray had bought her green outfit during the war when she was at Girton to wear when on a trip to London to buy equipment for the college kitchens.
73 Ibid., p. 15.
74 Ibid., p. 22.
75 Ibid., p. 37.
76 Ibid., p. 41.
77 Ibid., p. 41.
78 Ibid., p. 39.
79 Ibid., p. 45.
80 Ibid., p. 42.
81 Ibid., p. 44.
82 Ibid., p. 50.
83 Ibid., p. 41.
84 Ibid., p. 62.
85 BOA Box 35. Archivist's notes.
86 Otter Memorial Paper, no. 12, pp. 39–40.
87 Ibid., p. 40.
88 Ibid., p. 48.
89 *Bishop Otter College Magazine,* June 1953.
90 Otter Memorial Paper no. 12, pp. 25–34.
91 *The Times*, 17 February 1998.
92 Otter Memorial Paper, no. 12, p. 33, quoting from letter to editor of Girton Register.
93 D. Shorney, *Teachers in training 1906–1985: a history of Avery Hill College* (London: Thames Polytechnic, 1989), p. 53.
94 Ibid., pp. 53–71.
95 Ibid., p. 53.
96 *Avery Hill Reporter*, 1907.
97 *Avery Hill Reporter,* 1909.
98 Shorney, *Teachers in training*, pp. 77–8, 325.
99 Ibid., p. 86.
100 *Avery Hill Reporter*, 1909.
101 Avery Hill Archive (hereafter AHA) E.2.1. Reminiscences of a student, 1912–14.
102 AHA E.2.2. Reminiscences of a student, 1912–14.
103 Green and purple were the suffrage colours.
104 *Avery Hill Reporter*, 1936. See also A. Oram, *Women teachers and feminist politics 1900–1939* (Manchester: Manchester University Press, 1996) for women teachers' widespread support of the suffrage movement.
105 Shorney, *Teachers in training*, p. 96.
106 Ibid., p. 84.
107 Ibid., pp. 102–3.
108 Ibid., p. 105.
109 AHA E.2.3. Reminiscences of a student, 1918–20.
110 Shorney, *Teachers in training,* pp. 106, 109–10.
111 AHA E.2.10. Reminiscences of a student, 1927–9.

112 *Avery Hill Reporter*, 1929.
113 Shorney, *Teachers in training*, pp. 108, 119.
114 Ibid., p. 109.
115 AHA E.2.6. Reminiscences of a student, 1926–8.
116 *Avery Hill Reporter*, 1964.
117 *Avery Hill Reporter*, 1938.
118 Shorney, *Teachers in training*, p. 110.
119 Ibid., p. 109.
120 Ibid., pp. 110–11.
121 Ibid., pp. 109, 120, 123.
122 AHA E.2.8. Reminiscences of a student, 1927–9.
123 AHA E.2.5. Reminiscences of a student, 1925–7.
124 *Avery Hill Reporter*, 1964.
125 Shorney, *Teachers in training*, p. 131.
126 AHA E.2.8. Reminiscences of a student, 1927–9.
127 Shorney, *Teachers in training,* p. 109.
128 Ibid., pp. 108–9.
129 *Avery Hill Reporter,* 1964.
130 Shorney, *Teachers in training,* p. 109.
131 Ibid., p. 137.
132 Ibid., pp. 328–9.
133 *Avery Hill Reporter,* 1960.
134 Shorney, *Teachers in training*, pp. 140–4.
135 *Avery Hill Reporter,* 1960.
136 Shorney, *Teachers in training,* pp. 144–7. The McNair Committee on the training of teachers in the post-war era, reported in 1944. It was highly influential (see Chapter 1).
137 Ibid., p. 148.
138 Ibid., pp. 149–53.
139 Ibid., p. 153.
140 AHA L.1.1. Governing Body minutes, 20 October 1947.
141 *Avery Hill Reporter,* 1952.
142 AHA L.1.1. Governing Body minutes, 1951–6.
143 Shorney, *Teachers in training,* p. 187.
144 *Avery Hill Reporter,* 1960.
145 T. H. Simms, *Homerton College 1695–1978* (Cambridge, Homerton College, 1979), pp. 37–41.
146 Ibid., pp. 37–8.
147 Ibid., pp. 43–4.
148 Ibid., p. 38.
149 Ibid.
150 Ibid., pp. 45–6.
151 Ibid., p. 46.
152 C. Dyhouse, *No distinction of sex? Women in British universities 1870–1939* (London: UCL Press, 1995), p. 171.
153 Simms, *Homerton College*, p. 46.
154 Ibid., p. 47.
155 Homerton College Archive (hereafter HCA) Acc. no. 1190, no. 35. Reply to questionnaire on Miss Allan from a student, 1927–9.
156 HCA Acc. no. 1189, no. 7. Reply to questionnaire on Miss Allan from a student, 1918–20.
157 Simms, *Homerton College*, p. 48.
158 HCA Acc. no. 1189, no. 7. Reply to questionnaire on Miss Allan from a student, 1918–20.

159 Ibid.
160 HCA Acc. no. 1190, no. 28. Reply to questionnaire on Miss Allan from a student, 1923–5.
161 HCA Acc. no. ACa 58. Principal's Reports, 1903–1933 *passim.*
162 Ibid., December 1924.
163 Ibid., 11 and 14 March 1905.
164 Ibid., March 1926.
165 Ibid., June 1927.
166 *Homerton News Letter,* May 1928.
167 HCA Acc. no. ACa 58. Principal's Reports, 1903–33, October 1930.
168 HCA Acc. no. 1190, no. 23. Reply to questionnaire on Miss Allan from a student, 1927–9.
169 HCA Acc. no. 807. Reminiscences of a student, 1922–5.
170 *Homerton Newsletter,* 1923.
171 *Homerton Newsletter,* 1948.
172 HCA Acc. no. 898. Letter home from a student, 1928–30.
173 E. Edwards, The friendly societies and the ethic of respectability in nineteenth century Cambridge (PhD thesis, CNAA, 1987), p. 36.
174 HCA Acc. no. 1190, no. 39. Reply to questionnaire on Miss Allan from a student, 1925.
175 HCA Acc. no. 1190, no. 44. Reply to questionnaire on Miss Allan from a student, 1927–9.
176 HCA Acc. no. 1190, no. 24. Reply to questionnaire on Miss Allan from student, 1922–4.
177 HCA Acc. no. 1189, no. 5. Reply to questionnaire on Miss Allan from a student, 1906–8.
178 HCA Acc. no. 1190, no. 13. Reply to questionnaire on Miss Allan from a student, 1929–31.
179 HCA Acc. no. 1190, no. 45. Reply to questionnaire on Miss Allan from a student, 1924–6.
180 HCA Acc. no. 1190, nos 3 and 13. Replies to questionnaire on Miss Allan from students, 1927–9 and 1929–31.
181 HCA Acc. no. 1190, no. 10. Reply to questionnaire on Miss Allan from a student, 1926–8.
182 HCA Acc. no. 1190, no. 28. Reply to questionnaire on Miss Allan from a student, 1923–5.
183 HCA Acc. no. 1190, no. 22. Reply to questionnaire on Miss Allan from a student, 1925–7.
184 *Homerton Newsletter,* 1913.
185 M. Vicinus, *Independent women: work and community for single women, 1850–1920* (London: Virago, 1985), p. 201.
186 HCA Acc. no. ACa 58, Principal's Reports, 1903–33, June 1929 and March 1922.
187 HCA Acc. no. 1028. Reminiscences of a student, 1932–4.
188 *Homertonian,* 1935.
189 *Homerton Newsletter,* 1920.
190 *Homerton Newsletter,* 1948.
191 HCA Acc. no. 1533. Papers concerning Miss Skillicorn's early life and background from Manx Museum, Isle of Man.
192 HCA Acc. no. 1405. Interview with member of staff, 1952–64.
193 HCA Acc. no. 1533. Papers concerning Miss Skillicorn's background.
194 HCA Acc. no. 1404, nos 3 and 39. Reply to questionnaire on Miss Skillicorn from student, 1935–7 and member of staff, 1957–9.
195 HCA Acc. no. 1404, no. 10. Reply to questionnaire on Miss Skillicorn from a student, 1939–41.

196   HCA Acc. no. 1403, no. 8. Reply to questionnaire on Miss Skillicorn from a student, 1939–41.
197   HCA Acc. no. 1404, no. 45. Reply to questionnaire on Miss Skillicorn from a student, 1947–9.
198   HCA Acc. no. 1403, no. 19. Reply to questionnaire on Miss Skillicorn from a student, 1942–4.
199   HCA Acc. no. 1403, no. 4. Reply to questionnaire on Miss Skillicorn from a student, 1935–7.
200   HCA Acc. no. 1214. Reminiscences of a member of staff, 1949–74.
201   HCA Acc. no. ACa 61, Reports of Trustees Finance and General Purposes Committee, 1936, 1939 and 1940.
202   Simms, *Homerton College*, p. 65.
203   HCA Acc. no. ACa 1320. Principal's Reports to Trustees 1933–60, December 1938.
204   HCA Acc. no. ACa 61, Reports of Trustees Finance and General Purposes Committee, 9 March 1939, 24 April 1939, 11 July 1939, 24 October 1939, 15 May 1940. HCA Acc. no. ACa 1320. Principal's Reports to Trustees, March 1941.
205   HCA Acc. no. 1403, no. 36. Reply to questionnaire on Miss Skillicorn from a student, 1954–6; HCA Acc. no. 1410. Interviews with former members of staff, 1943–74 and 1952–74; HCA Acc. no. ACa1320. Principal's Reports, to Trustees, March 1941.
206   HCA Acc. no. 1411. Interview with member of staff, 1937–45.
207   HCA Ac. no. Aca 1320. Principal's Reports, 1933–60, December 1941.
208   HCA Acc. no. 1504. Interview with member of staff.
209   HCA Acc. no. 1412. Interview with member of staff, 1942–6.
210   HCA Acc. no. 1405. Interview with member of staff, 1952–64.
211   HCA Acc. nos. 1405, 1411 and 1488. Interviews with members of staff, 1952–64, 1937–45, and 1946–51.
212   HCA Acc. no. 1412. Interview with member of staff, 1942–6.
213   HCA Acc. no. 1404, no. 39. Reply to questionnaire on Miss Skillicorn from a member of staff, 1957–9.
214   HCA Acc. no. 1508. Tributes at Miss Skillicorn's memorial meeting, 2 June 1979.
215   Shorney, *Teachers in training*, p. 153.
216   HCA Acc. no. 1214. Reminiscences of a member of staff, 1949–74.
217   HCA Acc. no. 1404, no. 20. Reply to questionnaire on Miss Skillicorn from a student, 1944–6.
218   HCA Acc. no. 1403, no. 36. Reply to questionnaire on Miss Skillicorn from a student, 1954–6.
219   HCA Acc. no. 1422. Letter from Miss Skillicorn to member of staff, 1949–51.
220   HCA Acc. no. 444. Notes towards an obituary of Miss Skillicorn from Chairman of Trustees.
221   HCA Acc. no. 1403, nos 6 and 36. Replies to questionnaire on Miss Skillicorn from students, 1937–9 and 1954–6.

4 The staff

1   T. H. Simms, *Homerton College 1695–1978* (Cambridge: Homerton College, 1979), p. 60.
2   *Homerton Rolls News*, 1987–8. Reminiscences of a student, 1906–8.
3   C. Heward., 'Men and women and the rise of professional society: the intriguing history of teacher educators', *History of Education* 22 (1), pp. 17–19.
4   Homerton College Archive (hereafter HCA) Acc. no. ACc. Staff register 1846–1974.

5 Simms, *Homerton College*, p. 58.
6 C. More, *The training of teachers 1847–1947: a history of the Church Colleges at Cheltenham* (London: Hambledon, 1992), pp. 55–6.
7 D. Shorney, *Teachers in training 1906–1985: a history of Avery Hill College* (London: Thames Polytechnic, 1989), p. 137.
8 Ibid., p. 120.
9 C. Dyhouse, *No distinction of sex? Women in British universities 1870–1939* (London: UCL Press, 1995), p. 112.
10 HCA Acc. no. 1406. Interview with member of staff, 1955–1980.
11 HCA Acc. no. 1504. Interview with member of staff.
12 HCA Acc. no. 1408. Interview with member of staff, 1953–75.
13 HCA Acc. no. 1406. Interview with member of staff, 1955–1980.
14 HCA Acc. no. 1488. Interview with member of staff, 1946–51.
15 HCA Acc. no. 1421. Interview with member of staff, 1951–7.
16 Board of Education. *Teachers and youth leaders: report of the Committee appointed by the President of the Board of Education to consider the supply, recruitment and training of teachers and youth leaders* (The McNair Report) (London: HMSO, 1944), p. 73.
17 HCA Acc. no. 1408. Interview with member of staff, 1953–75.
18 HCA Acc. no. 1410. Interview with members of staff, 1943–74.
19 HCA Acc. no. 1422. Interview with member of staff, 1948–51.
20 HCA Acc. no. 1488. Interview with member of staff, 1946–51.
21 HCA Acc. no. 1408. Interview with member of staff, 1953–75.
22 HCA Acc. no. 1504. Interview with member of staff.
23 HCA Acc. no. 1411. Interview with member of staff, 1939–45.
24 HCA Acc. no. 1488. Interview with member of staff, 1946–51.
25 HCA Acc. no. 1408. Interview with member of staff, 1953–75.
26 HCA Acc. no. 1410. Interview with members of staff, 1943–74.
27 HCA Acc. no. 1488. Interview with member of staff, 1946–51.
28 Shorney, *Teachers in training*, p. 86.
29 *Avery Hill Reporter,* January 1929.
30 G. P. McGregor, *Bishop Otter College and policy for teacher education 1839–1980* (London: Pembridge Press, 1981), p. 270, note 2.
31 *Bishop Otter Guild Chronicle,* July 1956.
32 HCA Acc. no. 1592. Interview with four students, 1949–51.
33 *Man in a Club Window*, The habits of good society (1859), p. 230 quoted in P. G. Nunn, *Victorian women artists* (London: Women's Press, 1987), pp. 5 and 8.
34 *Avery Hill Reporter*, January 1929, Reminiscences of a student, 1909–11.
35 *Avery Hill Reporter*, December 1909.
36 A. Robinson, J. Purkis, and A. Massing, *A Florentine procession* (Cambridge: Homestead Press, 1997).
37 D. Hackman, *First year up* (London: Dent, 1951). This novel is a fictionalized account of life at Homerton immediately after the Second World War. The author was a member of staff at the time.
38 Ibid., pp. 54–6.
39 *Avery Hill Reporter*, February 1932.
40 HCA Acc. no. ACc 1511. Staff register.
41 HCA Acc. no. 1441. Interview with students, 1940–2.
42 HCA Acc. no. 1404, no. 13. Reply to questionnaire on Miss Skillicorn from a student, 1940–2.
43 HCA Acc. no. 1441. Interview with students, 1940–2.
44 HCA Acc. no. 1687. Interview with students, 1936–8 and 1937–9.
45 HCA Acc. no. 1404, no. 1. Reply to questionnaire on Miss Skillicorn from a student, 1935–7.

46 HCA Acc. no. 1663. Kay Melzi's 80th birthday tribute book. Students, 1937–9.
47 Ibid., students, 1944–6.
48 HCA Acc. no. 1441. Interview with students, 1940–2.
49 HCA Acc. no. 1420, no. 4. Reminiscences of a student, 1940–2.
50 HCA Acc. no. 1441. Interview with students, 1940–2.
51 HCA Acc. no. 1663. Kay Melzi's 80th birthday tribute book. Student, 1947–9.
52 HCA Acc. no. 1892. Correspondence from Henry Lamb concerning Miss Skillicorn's portrait 1953.
53 Ten decades: exhibition of ten women artists born 1897–1906. *Catalogue* (Norwich: Norwich Institute of Art and Design, 1992).
54 HCA Acc. no. ACc 1551. College register.
55 HCA Acc. no. 1628. Reminiscences of Nan Youngman, 1992.
56 HCA Acc. no. 1554. Interview with class of 1951.
57 HCA Acc. no. 1629. Memoir of Kay Melzi by Nan Youngman.
58 HCA Acc. no. 1628. Reminiscences of Nan Youngman, 1992.
59 BOA *The Bishop Otter College Permanent Art Collection* (Chichester, West Sussex Institute of Higher Education, 1989).
60 BOA G94 Interview with domestic bursar, 1945–60.
61 Shorney, *Teachers in training*, p. 166.
62 HCA Acc. no. 1404, no. 26. Reply to questionnaire on Miss Skillicorn from a student, 1947–9.
63 *Bishop Otter College Magazine*, February 1903.
64 *Homertonian*, December 1909.
65 HCA Acc. no. 807. Reminiscences of a student, 1922–5.
66 HCA Acc. no. 1030. College song. *c.* 1920.
67 HCA Acc. no. 1420, no. 12. Reminiscences of student, 1945–7.
68 *Bishop Otter College Magazine,* vol. 3, no. 1, March 1912.
69 *Avery Hill Reporter*, 1918–19.
70 *Avery Hill Reporter*, July 1932. Reminiscences of a student, 1907–9.
71 *Bishop Otter College Magazine*, May 1910.
72 *Bishop Otter College Magazine*, 1910.
73 HCA Acc. no. 1404, 20. Reply to questionnaire on Miss Skillicorn from a student, 1944–6.
74 HCA Acc. no. 1404, no. 28. Reply to questionnaire on Miss Skillicorn from a student, 1949–51.
75 *Homertonian*, June and March 1915.
76 *Avery Hill Reporter*, January 1930.
77 *Avery Hill Reporter*, December 1927.
78 *Avery Hill Reporter*, April 1927.
79 *Avery Hill Reporter,* July 1931.
80 *Avery Hill Reporter,* July 1928.
81 Bishop Otter Annual Reports, 1920–1 and 1940–1.
82 *Homerton Roll News*, 1988–9. Reminiscences of a student, 1924–6.
83 *Homerton News Letter*, May 1934.
84 HCA Acc. no. 1403, no. 9. Reply to questionnaire on Miss Skillicorn from a student, 1938–40.
85 HCA Acc. no. 1574. Interview with member of staff, 1948–51.
86 HCA Acc. no. 1404, no. 15. Reply to questionnaire on Miss Skillicorn from a student, 1942–4.
87 HCA acc. no. ACc 1511. College register.
88 HCA Acc. no. 1979. Interview with class of 1943.
89 H. Lee, *Virginia Woolf* (London: Chatto & Windus, 1996), pp. 142–3.
90 A. O. Bell (ed.), *The diary of Virginia Woolf, Volume II: 1920–24* (London: Penguin, 1981), p. 310.

91 HCA Acc. no. 1189, no. 7. Reply to questionnire on Miss Allan from a student, 1918–20.
92 HCA Acc. no. 1190, no. 35. Reply to questionnaire on Miss Allan from a student, 1927–9.
93 HCA Acc. no. 1189, no. 4. Reply to questionnaire on Miss Allan from a student, 1915–1917.
94 *Bishop Otter College Magazine*, February 1908.
95 HCA Acc. no. 1189, no. 8. Reply to questionnaire on Miss Allan from a student, 1916–18.
96 See e.g. A. M. Wilkinson, *Ripon Training College 1862–1962* (Ripon: The College, 1963), p. 81.
97 Shorney, *Teachers in training*, pp. 125–6.
98 HCA Acc. no. 1230. Papers concerning librarian.
99 HCA Acc. no. 808. Reminiscences of a student, 1925–7.
100 HCA Acc. no. 1419, no. 9. Reminiscences of a student, 1937–9; Shorney, *Teachers in training*, p. 125.
101 Author's personal recollection.
102 HCA Acc. no. 1420, no. 19. Reminiscences of a student, 1949–51.
103 HCA Acc. no. 1592. Interview with four students, 1949–51.
104 HCA Acc. no. 1245. Interview with class of 1949.
105 *Homerton Roll News,* 1988–9. Reminiscences of a student, 1931–3.
106 Shorney, *Teachers in training,* pp. 173–4.
107 HCA Acc. no. 1270. Interview with student, 1951–3.
108 Shorney, *Teachers in training,* p. 133.
109 McGregor, *Bishop Otter College,* p. 183.
110 HCA Acc. no. 1465. Reminiscences of students from 1920s and 1930s.
111 *Homertonian,* October 1914.
112 *Homerton News Letter,* 1927.
113 *Homertonian,* 1932.
114 HCA Acc. no. 1408. Interview with member of staff, 1953–75.
115 Bishop Otter Annual Report, 1911–12.
116 *Bishop Otter College Magazine,* March 1912.
117 *Bishop Otter College Magazine,* March 1914.
118 HCA Acc. no. 1191, no. 5. Reply to questionnaire on Miss Allan from a student, 1932–4.
119 *Bishop Otter College Magazine,* June 1932.
120 AHA E.2.13. and E.2.14. Reminiscences of students in the 1930s.
121 HCA Acc. no. 810. Reminiscences of a student, 1927–9.
122 HCA Acc. no. 808. Reminiscences of a student, 1925–7.
123 N. Collecott, *Peggles and primroses* (Lavenham: Terence Dalton, 1989), pp. 113–14.
124 *Homertonian,* December 1914, November 1915.
125 Shorney, *Teachers in training,* p. 73.
126 *Homertonian,* 1934.
127 Shorney, *Teachers in training,* pp. 71–3.
128 *Avery Hill Reporter,* December 1908.
129 *Avery Hill Reporter,* June 1909.
130 *Avery Hill Reporter* June 1910; Shorney, *Teachers in training* pp. 99–100.
131 *Bishop Otter College Magazine,* June 1929.
132 See e.g. *Homertonian,* 1933.
133 *Homerton News Letter,* 1938.
134 *Homerton News Letter,* 1942.
135 Shorney, *Teachers in training,* p. 125.
136 HCA Acc. nos. 887–900. Letters home from a student, 1928–30.

137 HCA Acc. no. 1441. Interview in 1990 with twelve students from the class of 1940.
138 BOA Annual Report, 1898–9.
139 *Bishop Otter College Magazine,* June 1947.
140 *Bishop Otter College Magazine,* February 1906.
141 *Bishop Otter College Magazine,* June 1953.
142 *Avery Hill Reporter,* June 1910, December 1911.
143 *Homertonian,* December 1909, January 1910.
144 *Homertonian,* December 1914.
145 *Homerton News Letter,* May 1923.
146 *Homertonian,* 1933.
147 Shorney, *Teachers in training,* p. 132.
148 Ibid., pp. 137, 177, 256.
149 *Avery Hill Reporter,* October 1936.
150 *Avery Hill Reporter,* June 1913.
151 *Homertonian,* 1933.
152 V. Brittain, *Testament of Youth* (London: Gollancz, 1933).
153 V. Woolf, *Three guineas* (London: Hogarth, 1938).
154 *Homertonian,* October 1915.
155 Shorney, *Teachers in training,* p. 132; *Avery Hill Reporter,* April 1927.
156 *Avery Hill Reporter,* February 1932.
157 *Homertonian, 1933.*
158 *Homertonian,* 1935.
159 *Homertonian,* 1934.
160 *Homertonian,* 1935.
161 Collecott, *Peggles and primroses,* p. 111.
162 *Homertonian,* 1940.

5 Sexuality

1 D. Hackman, *First year up* (London: Dent, 1951), p. 96.
2 Bishop Otter Archive (hereafter BOA) College register, 1939.
3 A. Oram, *Women teachers and feminist politics 1900- 39* (Manchester: Manchester University Press, 1996), p. 26 See also Chapter 1 for discussion of the marriage bar.
4 L. Bland, *Banishing the beast: English feminism and sexuality 1880–1930* (London: Pandora, 1995); M. Jackson, *The real facts of life: feminism and the politics of sexuality c. 1850–1940* (London: Taylor and Francis, 1994); S. Jeffreys, *The spinster and her enemies: feminism and sexuality 1880–1930* (London: Pandora, 1985).
5 Jackson, *The real facts of life,* pp. 14–15.
6 *Avery Hill Reporter, 1936.* Green and purple were the suffrage colours.
7 *Avery Hill Reporter, 1935.*
8 Homerton College Archive (hereafter HCA) Acc. no. 888. Letter home from a student, 1928.
9 E. Edwards, 'The friendly societies and the ethic of respectability in nineteenth century Cambridge' (PhD thesis, CNAA, 1987), p. 36.
10 HCA Acc. no. 1191, no. 17. Reply to questionnaire on Miss Skillicorn from student, 1931–3.
11 HCA Acc. no. 810. Reminiscences of a student, 1927–9.
12 E. Edwards (ed.). *Homerton 1894–1994: 100 years in Cambridge* (Cambridge: Homerton College, 1993).
13 Personal communication from principal to author, 1994.
14 HCA Acc. no. 900. Letter home from a student, 1928.

15 HCA Acc. no. 896. Letter home from a student, 1928.
16 Jackson, *The real facts of life*; J. Weeks, *Sex, politics and society* (London: Longman, 1981).
17 *Homerton News Letter*, 1916.
18 D. Copelman, *London's women teachers: gender, class and feminism 1870–1930* (London: Routledge, 1996), pp. 136–44.
19 Avery Hill Archive (hereafter AHA) Acc. no. E.2.3. Reminiscences of a student, 1918–20.
20 HCA Acc. no. 1189, no. 8. Reply to questionnaire on Miss Allan from a student, 1916–18.
21 HCA Acc. no. 1191, no. 8. Reply to questionnaire on Miss Allan from a student, 1932–4.
22 HCA Acc. no. 1191, no. 21. Reply to questionnaire on Miss Allan from a student, 1933–5.
23 HCA Acc. no. 1190, no. 19. Reply to questionnaire on Miss Allan from a student, 1920–2.
24 HCA Acc. no. 1191, no. 1. Reply to questionnaire on Miss Allan from a student, 1932–4.
25 AHA Acc. no. E.2.12. Reminiscences of a student, 1928–30.
26 D. Shorney, *Teachers in training 1906–1985: a history of Avery Hill College* (London: Thames Polytechnic, 1989), pp. 143–4.
27 Bishop Otter Annual Report, 1942–3; *Bishop Otter College Magazine*, 1944.
28 *Homerton News Letter*, 1938.
29 HCA Acc. no. 1404, no. 13. Reply to questionnaire on Miss Skillicorn from a student, 1940–2.
30 HCA Acc. no. 1404, no. 14. Reply to questionnaire on Miss Skillicorn from a student, 1940–2.
31 HCA Acc. no. 1441. Interview with students, 1940–2.
32 HCA Acc. no. 1404, no. 9. Reply to questionnaire on Miss Skillicorn from a student, 1939–41.
33 HCA Acc. no. 1441. Interview with students, 1940–2.
34 HCA Acc. no. 1404, no. 9. Reply to questionnaire on Miss Skillicorn from a student, 1939–41.
35 HCA Acc. no. 1419, no. 5. Reminiscences of a student, 1937–9.
36 HCA Acc. no. 1441. Interview with students, 1940–2.
37 HCA Acc. no. 1410. Interview with member of staff, 1943–74.
38 HCA Acc. no. 1412. Interview with member of staff. 1942–6.
39 HCA Acc. no. 1421. Interview with member of staff, 1951–7 (former student, 1947–9).
40 HCA Acc. no. 1441. Interview with students, 1940–2.
41 HCA Acc. no. 1404, no. 1. Reply to questionnaire on Miss Skillicorn from a stdent 1935–7.
42 HCA Acc. no. 1419, no. 5. Remniscences of a student, 1937–9.
43 HCA Acc. no. 1421, Interview with member of staff, 1951–7.
44 HCA Acc. no. 1245. Interview with students, 1949–51. Quotation attributed to Miss Bradley, deputy principal.
45 HCA Acc. no, 1421. Interview with member of staff, 1951–7.
46 HCA Acc. no. 1241. Homerton Union of Students (hereafter HUS) Minute book, 1940–1957.
47 Ibid. October 1941.
48 HCA Acc. no. 1420, no. 8. Reminiscences of a student, 1941–3.
49 HCA Acc. no. 1241. HUS Minute book, 13 November 1944.
50 Ibid., 1 July 1947.

51 Birmingham Feminist History Group, 'Feminism as femininity in the 1950s', *Feminist Review*, 3, 1979.
52 HCA Acc. no. 1241. HUS Minute book, 28 June 1948.
53 Ibid. 16 February 1949.
54 Ibid. 23 February 1951.
55 Ibid.
56 HCA Acc. no. 1708, no. 3. Reply to centenary questionnaire from student, 1960–3.
57 HCA Acc. no. 1412, Interview with member of staff, 1942–6; HCA Acc. no. 1421. Interview with member of staff, 1951–7.
58 HCA Acc. no. 1592. Interview with students, 1949–51.
59 Shorney, *Teachers in training*, pp. 134–5.
60 AHA Acc. no. E.2.12. Reminiscences of a student, 1928–30.
61 Ibid.
62 *Avery Hill Reporter,* 1948.
63 Shorney, *Teachers in training*, p. 135.
64 *Bishop Otter College Magazine*, 1959.
65 *Bishop Otter College Magazine*, 1951; Bishop Otter Annual Report, 1954–5.
66 *Homerton Association News*, 1953.
67 HCA Acc. no. 1190, no. 19. Reply to questionnaire on Miss Allan from a student, 1920–2.
68 HCA Acc. no. 1190, no. 3. Reply to questionnaire on Miss Allan from a student, 1927–9.
69 HCA Acc. no. 1675, Interview with students, 1954–6.
70 HCA Acc. no. 1708, no. 3. Reply to centenary questionnaire from a student, 1960–3.
71 HCA Acc. no. 1420, no. 13. Reminiscences of a student, 1945–7.
72 HCA Acc. no. 1245. Interview with students, 1949–51.
73 HCA Acc. no. 1204. Interview with a student, 1959–61.
74 HCA Acc. no. 1245. Interview with students, 1949–51.
75 HCA Acc. no. 1576. Interview with a student, 1956–8.
76 *Bishop Otter College Magazine*, 1952.
77 HCA Acc, no. 1576. Interview with a student, 1956–8.
78 HCA Acc. no. 1520. Reminiscences of a student, 1953–5.
79 HCA Acc. no. 1504. Interview with a member of staff.
80 HCA Acc. no. 1406. Interview with member of staff, 1955–80.
81 HCA Acc. no. 1204. Interview with a student, 1959–61.
82 AHA Acc. no. E.12. Reminiscences of a student, 1928–30.
83 HCA Acc. no. 1404, no. 9. Reply to questionnaire on Miss Skillicorn from a student, 1939–41.
84 C. Bingham, *The history of Royal Holloway College* (London: Constable, 1986), p. 135.
85 L. Faderman, *Odd girls and twilight lovers: a history of lesbian life in 20th century America* (London: Penguin, 1991), p. 27.
86 M. Vicinus, *Independent women: work and community for single women 1850–1920* (London: Virago, 1985).
87 L. Faderman, *Surpassing the love of men* (London: Junction Books, 1981), pp. 17–19.
88 See e.g. E. Donoghue, *Passions between women: British lesbian culture 1688–1801* (London: Scarlet Press, 1993); L. Stanley, 'Romantic friendship: some issues in researching lesbian history and biography', *Women's History Review*, 1 (2), 1992, pp. 193–216.
89 Stanley, *Romantic friendship,* pp. 196–7.
90 Faderman, *Surpassing the love of men*, pp. 178 and 241.

91 Jackson, *The real facts of life*, p. 14.

92 Jefferys, *The spinster and her enemies*, pp. 105–27.

93 S. Jefferys, *Anticlimax: a feminist perspective on the sexual revolution* (London: Women's Press, 1990), p. 39.

94 A. Oram, 'Repressed and thwarted or bearer of the new world? The spinster in inter-war feminist discourses', *Women's History Review*, 1, 1992, pp. 413–34.

95 HCA Acc. no. 1190, no. 18. Reply to questionnaire on Miss Allan from a student, 1920–2.

96 L. J. Rupp, 'Imagine my surprise: women's relationships in mid-20th century America', in H. B. Duberman and others (eds), *Hidden from history: reclaiming the gay and lesbian past* (London: Penguin, 1991), p. 408.

97 See e.g. HCA Acc. no. 1403, nos 3 and 15. Replies to questionnaire on Miss Skillicorn from students, 1935–7 nd 1942–4.

98 HCA Acc. no. 1305 Reminiscences of a student, 1958–60.

99 HCA Acc. no. 1653. Interview with students, 1942–4.

100 HCA Acc. no. 1421. Interview with member of staff, 1951–7.

101 HCA Acc. no. 1636. Interview with student, 1924–6.

102 HCA Acc. no. 1663. Tribute book.

103 Ibid.

104 Ibid.

105 HCA Acc. no. 1028. Reminiscences of a student, 1932–4.

106 HCA Acc. no. 1190, no. 24. Reply to questionnaire on Miss Allan from a student, 1922–4.

107 HCA Acc. no. 1191, no. 18. Reply to questionnaire on Miss Allan from a student, 1932–4; Acc, no. 1028 Reminiscences of a student, 1932–4.

108 HCA Acc. no. 1190, no. 42. Reply to questionnaire on Miss Allan from a student, 1922–5.

109 HCA Acc. no. 1192. Interview with student, 1915–17.

110 *Homertonian*, 1950, p. 7.

111 HCA Acc. no. 1026. Reminiscences of student, 1920–2.

112 see. e.g. HCA Acc. no. 1028. Reminiscences of a student, 1932–4.

113 *Homerton Association News*, 1952, p. 11.

114 HCA Acc. no. 1191, no. 2. Reply to questionnaire on Miss Allan from student, 1932–4.

115 HCA Acc. no. ACa 58. Principal's Reports, 1903–33, 21 February 1906.

116 Ibid., 26 November 1906.

117 Shorney, *Teachers in training*, p. 86.

118 HCA Acc. no. ACa 58, Principal's Reports, 1903–33, 9 February 1907.

119 Ibid., 30 November 1908.

120 Ibid., 29 February 1912.

121 Ibid., 9 December 1912.

122 HCA Acc. no. 1192. Interview with a student, 1915–17.

123 HCA Acc. no. ACa 58. Principal's Reports, 1903–33, 9 February 1914.

124 Ibid., October 1921.

125 Ibid., March 1922.

126 HCA Acc. no. 1190, no. 22. Reply to questionnaire on Miss Allan from a student, 1925–7.

127 Homerton Association News, 1962.

128 HCA Acc. no. ACa 58 Principal's Reports, 1903–33, 19 July 1920, December 1926.

129 Vicinus, *Independent women,* p. 201.

130 HCA Acc. no. 1191, no. 5. Reply to questionnaire on Miss Allan from a student, 1932–4.

131 HCA Acc. no. 1191, no. 24. Reply to questionnaire on Miss Allan from a student, 1933–5.
132 HCA Acc. no. 1190, no. 16. Reply to questionnaire on Miss Allan from a student, 1929–31.
133 HCA Acc. no. 1508. Tributes at Miss Skillicorn's memorial meeting, 2 June 1979.
134 HCA Acc. no. 238. Obituary of Miss Skillicorn 1979.
135 Shorney, *Teachers in training,* p. 153.
136 HCA Acc. no. 1405. Interview with member of staff, 1952–64.
137 HCA Acc. no. 1406. Interview with member of staff, 1955–80.
138 HCA Acc. no. 1408. Interview with member of staff, 1953–75.
139 HCA Acc. no. 1421. Interview with member of staff, 1951–7.
140 HCA Acc. no. 1552. Interview with member of staff, 1943–75.
141 HCA Acc. no. 1410. Interview with member of staff, 1952–74.
142 HCA Acc. no. 1036. Interview with member of staff, 1961–71; HCA Acc. no. 1395. Reminiscences of member of staff, 1947–54; HCA Acc. no. 1404, no. 9. Reply to questionnaire on Miss Skillicorn from a student, 1939–41.
143 HCA Acc. no. 1422, Interview with member of staff, 1948–51.
144 Ibid.
145 HCA Acc. no. 1403, no. 25. Reply to a questionnaire on Miss Skillicorn from a student, 1947–9.
146 L. Grier, *The life of Winifred Mercier* (London: Oxford University Press, 1937), p. 254.
147 Ibid., p. 27.
148 Ibid.
149 Ibid., pp. 89–232.
150 Ibid., p. 256.
151 Ibid., pp. 257–8.
152 Ibid., p. 255.
153 Ibid., p. 39.
154 Ibid., p. 235.
155 See Stanley, *Romantic friendship.*
156 M. Vicinus, 'Distance and desire: English boarding school friendship 1870–1920', in Duberman *et al.*, *Hidden from history*, p. 228.
157 Grier, *Winifred Mercier*, p. 253.
158 Ibid., p. 18.
159 Ibid., p. 32.

6 The last days of the women's college

1 Board of Education, *Teachers and youth leaders: report of the Committee appointed by the President of the Board of Education to consider the supply, recruitment and training of teachers and youth leaders* (London: HMSO, 1944), p. 65.
2 J. Weeks, *Sex, politics and society* (London: Longman, 1981), pp. 256–7.
3 D. Shorney, *Teachers in training 1906–1985: a history of Avery Hill College* (London: Thames Polytechnic, 1989), pp. 181–3.
4 Ibid., p. 183.
5 A. Myrdal and V. Klein, *Women's two roles: home and work* (London: Routledge and Kegan Paul, 1956).
6 K. Ollerenshaw, *Education for girls* (London: Faber and Faber, 1961), pp. 182–3.
7 M. Pugh, *Women and the women's movement in Britain 1914–1959* (London: Macmillan, 1992), p. 288.
8 Report on the Social Insurance and Allied Service, Cd. 6404 (London: HMSO, 1942), pp. 52 and 49. quoted in Pugh, *Women and women's movements*, p. 294.

9 B. Spock, *Baby and Child Care* (1963), p. 460 quoted in Pugh, *Women and women's movements*, p. 296.

10 J. Bowlby, *Maternal care and mental health* (1951), p. 11 quoted in Pugh, *Women and women's movements, p. 296.*

11 Pugh, *Women and women's movements,* p. 296.

12 A. Myrdal and V. Klein, *Women's two roles*, p. 117.

13 J. Lewis, 'Myrdal, Klein, *Women's Two Roles* and postwar femininism 1945–60', in H. L. Smith (ed.), *British feminism in the twentieth century* (Aldershot: Edward Elgar, 1990), p. 167.

14 Pugh, *Women and women's movements*, p. 297.

15 Myrdal and Klein, *Women's two roles*, p. 126.

16 Ibid., pp. 165–7.

17 Ibid., p. 156.

18 Ibid., p. 157.

19 Ibid., p. 158.

20 Ibid., p. 163.

21 J. Hubback, *Wives who went to college* (London: Heinemann, 1957), pp. 4–5.

22 Ibid., pp. 5–6.

23 Ibid., p. 133.

24 Ibid., p. 7.

25 Ibid., p. 14.

26 Ibid., p. 10.

27 Ibid., p. 23.

28 Ibid., p. 54.

29 Ibid., p. 55.

30 Ibid., p. 54.

31 Ibid., pp. 101–3.

32 Ibid., p. 102.

33 Ollerenshaw, *Education for girls*, p. 134.

34 Ibid., p. 18.

35 Ibid., p. 19.

36 Ibid., p. 194.

37 Ibid., p. 146.

38 Ibid., p. 146–7.

39 Ibid., pp. 148–9.

40 Ibid., p. 149.

41 Ibid., pp. 150–1.

42 Ibid., p. 189.

43 Ibid., p. 195.

44 Women's Group on Public Welfare, *The education and training of girls* (London: National Council of Social Service, 1962), p. 109.

45 Ibid., pp. 6–7.

46 Ibid., p. 9.

47 Ibid., pp. 9–12.

48 Hubback, *Wives who went to college,* pp. 54–6.

49 Women's Group, *The education and training of girls*, p. 11.

50 Ibid., p. 38.

51 Ibid., pp. 71–2.

52 Ibid., p. 87.

53 Ibid., p. 88.

54 Hubback, *Wives who went to college*, p. 5.

55 Bishop Otter Archive (hereafter BOA) Bishop Otter Annual Report 1950–1.

56 Otter Memorial Paper no. 12. *Flints, ports, otters and threads: a tribute to K. M. Elisabeth Murray 1909–1998*, p. 38.

57 *Bishop Otter College Magazine*, 1956.
58 *Bishop Otter College Magazine*. 1954.
59 *Bishop Otter College Magazine*, 1950.
60 *Bishop Otter College Magazine*, 1953.
61 *Bishop Otter College Magazine*, 1955.
62 Bishop Otter College, Annual Report, 1955–6.
63 Bishop Otter College, Annual Report, 1957–8.
64 Bishop Otter College, Annual Report, 1958–9.
65 *Bishop Otter College Magazine*, 1959.
66 *Bishop Otter College Magazine*, 1960.
67 Ibid.
68 *Bishop Otter College Magazine* 1959.
69 Shorney, *Teachers in training*, p. 174.
70 Ibid., p. 175.
71 *Avery Hill Reporter,* Jubilee number 1957.
72 *Avery Hill Reporter*, 1955.
73 *Avery Hill Reporter*, 1952.
74 Shorney, *Teachers in training*, p. 161.
75 Avery Hill Governing Body minutes, 5 October 1953.
76 Ibid., 6 February 1956.
77 Ibid., 21 January 1952.
78 Ibid., 1 November 1954.
79 Ibid., 10 October 1955.
80 *Avery Hill Reporter* Jubilee number 1957, January 1929.
81 Shorney, *Teachers in training,* pp. 182–3.
82 *Avery Hill Reporter*, 1959.
83 Homerton College Archive (hereafter HCA) Acc. no. 1404, no. 29. Reply to questionnaire on Miss Skillicorn from a student, 1949–51.
84 HCA Acc. no. 1554. Interview with students, 1951–3.
85 HCA Acc. no. 1520. Interview with a student, 1953–5.
86 HCA Acc. no. 1403, no. 35. Reply to questionnaire on Miss Skillicorn from a student, 1953–5.
87 HCA Acc. no. 1245. Interview with students, 1949–51.
88 HCA Acc. no. 1690. Interview with a student, 1957–9.
89 HCA Acc. no. 1305. Interview with a student, 1958–60.
90 HCA Acc. no. 1690. Interview with a student, 1957.
91 HCA Acc. no. 1863. Reply to centenary questionnaire from a student, 1957–9.
92 HCA Acc. no. 1576. Interview with a student, 1956–8.
93 HCA Acc. no. 1305. Interview with a student, 1958–60.
94 HCA Acc. no. 1863. Reply to centenary questionnaire from a student, 1957–9.
95 *Homerton Association News*, 1956, p. 11.
96 HCA Acc. no. 1421. Interview with member of staff, 1951–7.
97 HCA Acc. no. 1404. Interview with member of staff, 1955–80.
98 See e.g. HCA Acc. no. 1504. Interview with member of staff, 1958–83.
99 HCA Acc. no. 1406. Interview with member of staff, 1953–75.
100 *Homerton Association News*, 1953, 1956, 1957.
101 HCA Acc. no. 1404. Interview with member of staff, 1955–75.
102 HCA Acc. no. 1504. Interview with member of staff, 1958–83.
103 *Homerton Association News*, 1959.
104 Myrdal and Klein, *Women's two roles,* p. 158.
105 Hubback, *Wives who went to college,* p. 102.
106 HCA Acc. no. 1245. Interview with students, 1949–51.
107 HCA Acc. no. 1554. Interview with students, 1951–3.

108 Supply teachers formed a pool from which schools in their locality could draw to cover temporary absences of members of staff.
109 HCA Acc. no. 1705. Interview with a student, 1943–5.
110 The term 'career break' was not in use at this period. Married teachers returning to work were usually referred to as 'married women returners' or working wives.
111 HCA Acc. no. 1675. Interview with two students, 1954–6.
112 Husbands' and wives' earnings were amalgamated at this period for tax purposes. See also Hubback, *Wives who went to college*, pp. 110–121 for a discussion of this issue.
113 HCA Acc. no. 1576. Notes on interview with a student, 1956–8.
114 HCA Acc. no. 1305. Notes of interview with a student, 1958–60.
115 HCA Acc. no. 1204. Interview with a student, 1959–61.
116 HCA Acc. no. 1305. Interview with a student, 1958–60.
117 *Avery Hill Reporter*. Jubilee number 1957.
118 *Homerton Association News*, 1960.
119 Hubback, *Wives who went to college*, pp. 54–5, 96.
120 *Homerton Association News*, 1956.
121 HCA Acc. no. 1554. Interview with students, 1951–3.
122 *Homerton Association News*, 1961.
123 *Bishop Otter College Magazine*, 1961.
124 Bishop Otter Annual Report, 1960–1, 1961–2, 1967–8.
125 Bishop Otter Annual Report, 1969–70.
126 Bishop Otter Annual Report, 1958–9, 1960–1, 1961–2, 1962–3, 1964–5.
127 Bishop Otter Annual Report 1956–7.
128 Bishop Otter Annual Report, 1961–2.
129 Bishop Otter Annual Report, 1962–3.
130 *Bishop Otter College Magazine*, 1961.
131 *Bishop Otter Guild Chronicle*, 1962.
132 *Bishop Otter College Magazine,* 1961.
133 BOA Uncatalogued Box 28.
134 *Bishop Otter Guild Chronicle*, 1963.
135 *Bishop Otter Guild Chronicle,* 1964.
136 Otter Memorial Paper, no. 12, pp. 49–50.
137 *Avery Hill Reporter*, 1964. Young men at this period were required to serve two years in the Armed Forces.
138 Shorney, *Teachers in training*, pp. 183–7.
139 Ibid., p. 187.
140 *Avery Hill Reporter*, 1960.
141 Shorney, *Teachers in training*, p. 187.
142 *Avery Hill Reporter*, 1962.
143 Avery Hill Governing Body minutes 4 April 1960.
144 *Avery Hill Reporter*, 1963.
145 *Avery Hill Reporter*, 1963.
146 *Avery Hill Reporter*, 1964.
147 HCA Acc. no. 1036. Interview with principal, 1961–71.
148 *Homerton Association News*, 1967.
149 HCA Acc. no. 1405. Interview with member of staff, 1952–64.
150 See. e.g. HCA Acc. no. 1619. Interview with member of staff, 1966–92.
151 *Homerton Association News*, 1961, 1964, 1967, 1969.
152 HCA Acc. no. 1504. Interview with member of staff.
153 HCA Acc. no. 1708. no. 3. Reply to centenary questionnaire from a student, 1960–3.
154 HCA Acc. no. 1405. Interview with member of staff, 1952–64.
155 HCA Acc. no. 1409 and 1619, Interviews with members of staff.

156 HCA Acc. no. 1409. Interview with member of staff.
157 Ibid.
158 HCA Acc. no. 1410. Interviews with members of staff, 1943–74 and 1952–74.
159 HCA Acc. no. 1409 Interview with member of staff.
160 HCA Acc. no. 1619. Interview with member of staff.
161 See C. Heward, 'Men and women and the rise of a professional society: the intriguing history of teacher education', *History of Education,* 22 (1), 1993, pp. 25–8 for further comment on the national picture.
162 Ibid.
163 HCA Acc. no. 1405. Interview with member of staff, 1952–64.
164 HCA Acc. no. 1409. Interview with member of staff.
165 HCA Acc. no. 1504. Interview with member of staff.

Bibliography

Published sources

Books

Addison, P. *The road to 1945* (London: Pimlico, 1994)

Beddoe, D. *Back to home and duty: women between the wars, 1918–1939* (London: Pandora, 1989)

Bell, A. O. (ed.) *The diary of Virginia Woolf. Vol. II. 1920–24* (London: Penguin, 1981)

Bingham, C. *The history of Royal Holloway College* (London: Constable, 1986)

Bishop Otter College *The Bishop Otter Permanent Art Collection* (London: West Sussex Institute of Higher Education, 1989)

Bland, L. *Banishing the beast: English feminism and sexuality 1880–1930* (London: Pandora, 1995)

Board of Education *Teachers and youth leaders: report of the Committee appointed by the President of the Board of Education to consider the supply, recruitment and training of teachers and youth leaders* (The McNair Report) (London: HMSO, 1944)

Brittain, V. *Testament of youth* (London: Gollancz, 1933)

Cadogan, M. and Craig, P. *You're a brick Angela* (London: Gollancz, 1978)

Cole, M. *Whitelands College: the history* (London: Whitelands College, 1982)

Cole, M. *Be like daisies: John Ruskin and the cultivation of beauty at Whitelands College* (St Albans: Brentham Press, 1992)

Collecott, N. *Peggles and primroses: a country childhood* (Lavenham: Terence Dalton, 1989)

Copelman, D. *London's women teachers: gender, class and feminism 1870–1930* (London: Routledge, 1996)

Dent, H. C. *The training of teachers in England and Wales 1800–1975* (London: Hodder and Stoughton, 1977)

Donoghue, E. *Passions between women: British lesbian culture 1688–1801* (London: Scarlet Press, 1993)

Duberman, H. B. *et al.* (eds) *Hidden from history: reclaiming the gay and lesbian past* (London: Penguin, 1991)

Dyhouse, C. *No distinction of sex? Women in British universities 1870–1939* (London: UCL Press, 1995)

Edwards, E. (ed) *Homerton 1894–1994: one hundred years in Cambridge* (Cambridge: Homerton College, 1994)

Faderman, L. *Surpassing the love of men* (London: Junction Books, 1981)

Faderman, L. *Odd girls and twilight lovers: a history of lesbian life in 20th century America* (London: Penguin, 1991)

Firth, C. B. *Constance Louisa Maynard: mistress of Westfield College* (London: Allen and Unwin, 1949)

Freeman, G. *Alma Mater: memories of Girton College 1926–29* (Cambridge: Pevensey, 1990)

Grier, L. *The life of Winifred Mercier* (London: Oxford University Press, 1937)

Hackman, D. W. *First year up* (London: Dent, 1951)

Homerton College: brief historical notes 1695–1945 (Cambridge: Homerton College, 1945)

Hubback, J. *Wives who went to college* (London: Heinemann, 1957)

Hunt, F. (ed.) *Lessons for life: the schooling of girls and women, 1850–1950* (Oxford: Basil Blackwell, 1987)

Hunt, F. and Barker, C. *Women at Cambridge: a brief history* (Cambridge: University of Cambridge, 1998)

Jackson, M. *The real facts of life: feminism and the politics of sexuality, c. 1850–1940* (London: Taylor and Francis, 1994)

Jeffreys, S. *The spinster and her enemies: feminism and sexuality, 1880–1930* (London: Pandora, 1985)

Jefferys, S. *Anticlimax: a feminist perspective on the sexual revolution* (London: Women's Press, 1990)

Jones, L. G. E. *The training of teachers in England and Wales: a critical study* (Oxford: Clarendon, 1923)

Kean, H. *Deeds not words: the lives of suffragette teachers* (London: Pluto, 1990)

Kitzinger, C. *The social construction of lesbianism* (London: Sage, 1987)

Lee, H. *Virginia Woolf* (London: Chatto andWindus, 1996)

McGregor, G. P. *Bishop Otter College and policy for teacher education 1839–1980* (London: Pembridge, 1981)

Montgomery, F. A. *Edge Hill College: a history 1885–1985* (Liverpool: Edge Hill College, 1985)

More, C. *The training of teachers 1847–1947: a history of the Church Colleges at Cheltenham* (London: Hambledon, 1992)

Myrdal, A. and Klein, V. *Women's two roles: home and work* (London: Routledge and Kegan Paul, 1956)

Nunn, P. G. *Victorian women artists* (London: Women's Press, 1987)

Ollerenshaw, K. *Education for girls* (London: Faber and Faber, 1961)

Oram, A. *Women teachers and feminist politics 1900–1939* (Manchester: Manchester University Press, 1996)

Otter Memorial Paper no. 12. *Flints, ports, otters and threads: a tribute to K. M. Elisabeth Murray 1909–1998* (Chichester: Chichester Institute of Higher Education, 1998)

Pugh, M. *Women and the women's movement in Britain 1914–1959* (London: Macmillan, 1992)

Report on the Social Insurance and Allied Service (The Beveridge Report) (London: HMSO, 1944)

Robinson, A., Purkis, J. and Massung, A. *A Florentine procession* (Cambridge: Homestead Press, 1997)

Shorney, D. *Teachers in training 1906–1985: a history of Avery Hill College* (London: Thames Polytechnic, 1989)

Simms, T. H. *Homerton College 1695–1978* (Cambridge: Homerton College, 1979)

Smart, R. *On others' shoulders: an illustrated history of the Polhill and Lansdowne Colleges, now De Montfort University, Bedford* (Bedford: De Montfort University, 1994)

Smith, H. L. (ed). *British feminism in the twentieth century* (Aldershot: Edward Elgar. 1990)

Sondheimer, J. *Castle Adamant in Hampstead: a history of Westfield College 1882–1982* (London: Westfield College, 1983)

Spock, B. *Baby and baby care* (London: Bodley Head, 1963)

Strachey, R. *The cause* (London: Bell, 1928)

Ten decades: exhibition of ten women artists born 1897–1906: Catalogue (Norwich: Norwich Institute of Art and Design, 1992)

Tropp, A. *The school teachers* (London: Heinemann, 1957)

Vicinus, M. *Independent women: work and community for single women 1850–1920* (London: Virago, 1985)

Webster, W. *Imagining home: gender, 'race' and national identity, 1945–64* (London: UCL Press, 1998)

Weeks, J. *Sex, politics and society* (London: Longman, 1981)

Widdowson, F. *Going up into the next class: women and elementary teacher training 1840–1914* (London: Hutchinson, 1983).

Wilkinson, A. M. *Ripon Training College 1862–1962* (Ripon: The College, 1963)

Women's Group on Public Welfare *The education and training of girls* (London: National Council of Social Service, 1962)

Woolf, V. *A room of one's own* (London: Hogarth, 1929)

Woolf, V. *Three guineas* (London: Hogarth, 1938)

Young, F. *Margaret Stansfeld* (Bedford: Bedford Physical Training College, 1956)

Zebedee, D. H. J. *Lincoln Diocesan Training College 1862–1962* (Lincoln: Lincoln Training College, 1962)

Articles

Alberti, J. The turn of the tide: sexuality and politics, 1928–31. *Women's History Review* 3 (2), pp. 169–89, 1994

Birmingham Feminist History Group. Feminism as femininity in the 1950s. *Feminist Review* 3, 1979

Dixon, A. Ruskin's rustic fantasies. *Country Life* 183, pp. 130–3, 1989

Dyhouse, C. Signing the pledge? Women's investment in university education and teacher training before 1939 *History of Education* 26, pp. 207–23, 1997

Edwards. E. The friendly societies and the ethic of respectability in nineteenth century Cambridge (unpublished PhD thesis, CNAA, 1987)

Edwards, E. Educational institutions or extended families? The reconstruction of gender in women's colleges in the late nineteenth and early twentieth centuries *Gender and Education* 2, pp. 17–35, 1990

Edwards, E. Alice Havergal Skillicorn, principal of Homerton College, Cambridge, 1935–60: a study of gender and power. *Women's History Review* 1 (1), pp. 109–29, 1992

Edwards, E. The culture of femininity in women's teacher training colleges 1900–50. *History of Education* 22 (3), pp. 277–88, 1993

Edwards, E. The culture of femininity in women's teacher training colleges 1914–1945. In S. Oldfield (ed.) *This working-day world: women's lives and culture(s) in Britain 1914–1945* (London: Taylor & Francis, 1994), pp. 54–67

Edwards, E. Homoerotic friendship and college principals, 1880–1960. *Women's History Review* 4 (2), pp. 149–63, 1995

Edwards, E. Revisiting Miss Skillicorn: a journey in auto/biography. *Auto/Biography* 1, 2, and 3, pp. 95–103, 1997

Forrest, L. Femininities and friendship in a College of Education. *Gender and Education* 5 (2), pp. 211–15, 1993

Heward, C. Men and women and the rise of professional society: the intriguing history of teacher educators. *History of Education* 22, pp. 11–32, 1993

Knights, L. C. Will training colleges bear scrutiny? *Scrutiny* 1, pp. 247–63, 1932–3

Lewis, J. Myrdal, Klein, *Women's two roles* and postwar feminism 1945–1960. In H. L. Smith *British feminism in the twentieth century* (Aldershot, Edward Elgar, 1990), pp. 167–88

Mackinnon, A. Educated doubt: women, religion and the challenge of higher education, c. 1870–1920 *Women's History Review* 7 (2), pp. 241–59, 1998

Oram, A. Embittered, sexless or homosexual: attacks on spinster teachers 1918–39. In Lesbian History Group *Not a passing phase: reclaiming lesbians in history 1840–1985* (London: Women's Press, 1989), pp. 99–118

Oram, A. Repressed and thwarted or bearer of the new world? The spinster in inter-war feminist discourses. *Women's History Review* 1 (3), pp. 413–34, 1992

Purvis, J. A national library for women in Britain.*Women's History Review* 7 (3), p. 293, 1998

Rupp, L. J. Imagine my surprise: women's relationships in mid-20th century America. In *past* M. B. Duberman and others (eds) *Hidden from history: reclaiming the gay and lesbian* (London: Penguin, 1991), pp. 395–410

Schoolmistress 27 February 1892

Smith-Rosenberg, C. The female world of love and ritual: relations between women in nineteenth-century America. *Signs* 1, pp. 1–29, 1975–6

Stanley, L. Romantic friendship: some issues in researching lesbian history and biography. *Women's History Review* 1 (2), pp. 193–216, 1992

Summerfield, P. Cultural reproduction in the education of girls: a study of girls' secondary schooling in two Lancashire towns. In *Lessons for life: the schooling of girls and women 1850–1950*, F. Hunt (ed.) (Oxford: Blackwell, 1987), pp. 161–70

The Times, 17 February 1998. Obituary E. Murray

Vicinus, M. 'One life to stand beside me': emotional conflicts in first-generation college women in England. *Feminist Studies* 8 (3), pp. 603–27, 1982

Vicinus, M. Distance and desire: English boarding school friendship 1870–1920. In M. B. Duberman and others (eds.) *Hidden from history: reclaiming the gay and lesbian past* (London: Penguin, 1991), pp. 212–29

Vicinus, M. 'They wonder to which sex I belong': the historical roots of the modern lesbian identity. *Feminist Studies* 18 (3), pp. 467–97, 1992

Archival sources

Avery Hill College

Avery Hill Reporter. 1907–16; 1924–38; 1948–64

Acc. no. E.2.1. Reminiscences of a student, 1912–14

Acc. no. E.2.2. Reminiscences of a student, 1912–14

Acc. no. E.2.3. Reminiscences of a student, 1918–20

Acc. no. E.2.4. Reminiscences of a student, 1922–4
Acc. no. E.2.5. Reminiscences of a student, 1925–7
Acc. no. E.2.6. Reminiscences of a student, 1926–8
Acc. no. E.2.7. Reminiscences of a student, 1926–8
Acc. no. E.2.8. Reminiscences of a student, 1927–9
Acc. no. E.2.9. Reminiscences of a student, 1927–9
Acc. no. E.2.10. Reminiscences of a student, 1927–9
Acc. no. E.2.11. Reminiscences of a student, 1927–9
Acc. no. E.2.12. Reminiscences of a student, 1928–30
Acc. no. E.2.13. Reminiscences of a student, mid-1930s
Acc. no. E.2.14. Reminiscences of a student, 1934–6
Acc. no. E.2.15. Reminiscences of a student, 1935–7
Acc. no. E.2.16. Reminiscences of a student, 1936–8
Acc. no. E.2.17. Reminiscences of a student, 1944–6
Acc. no. L.1.1. *Governing Body Minutes*, 1945–64

Bishop Otter College

Bishop Otter College Magazine, 1900–61
Bishop Otter Guild Chronicle, 1951–75
Acc. no. MS17. *College Register,* 1897–1938
Acc. no. MSA7. *Council Minutes*, 1917–30
Acc. no. A42. *Council Minutes*, 1931–7
Acc. no. A44. *Council Minutes,* 1943
Acc. no. A46. *Council Minutes,* 1947
Acc. no. A75. *Reports of Finance Committee*, 1935 and 1936
Acc. no. G78. Reminiscences of a student, 1920–2
Acc. no. G82–86. Memorabilia of a student, 1925–7
Acc. no. G87–88. Memorabilia of a student, 1932–4
Acc. no. G94. Letters from former students in response to newspaper appeal by archivist December 1988. Includes interview with domestic bursar 1945–60.
Acc. no. 95–96. Memorabilia of a student, 1940–2
Acc. no. G89. Memorabilia of a student, 1927–9
Acc. no. G90. Memorabilia of a student, 1946–8
Acc. no. G93. Memorabilia of a student, early 1940s
Acc. no. G97. Memorabilia of a student, 1943–5
Acc. no. G98. Memorabilia of two students, 1918–20 and 1919–21
Acc. no. L1/2/15. *Annual reports*, 1883–1970
Louisa Hubbard Archive
Daisy Read Archive
Uncatalogued Box 28. E. Murray's archive file.
Uncatalogued Box. 35. G. P. McGregor's notes for his book *Bishop Otter College*; F. Johnson's memorandum to governors about her bathroom

Homerton College

Homerton Association News, 1949–62
Homerton News Letter, 1909–47
Homerton Roll News, 1987–90

Homertonian 1896–9, 1909–16, 1932–5, 1940

Acc. no. ACa 58. Principal's reports 1903–33

Acc. no. ACa 61. Reports of Trustee's Finance and General Purposes Committee 1935–60

Acc. no. ACa 1320. Principal's reports to Trustees 1933–60

Acc. no. ACc 1511. Register of college staff

Acc. no. 4. Letter from prospective student to her college mother, 1899

Acc. no. 238. Obituary of Miss Skillicorn 1979

Acc. no. 417. Annotated snapshots belonging to student, 1925–7

Acc. no. 444. Notes towards an obituary of Miss Skillicorn by Chairman of Trustees, 1970s

Acc. no. 630. 50 years of the Homerton Association

Acc. no. 807. Reminiscences of a student, 1920–2

Acc. no. 808. Reminiscences of a student, 1925–7

Acc. no. 810. Reminiscences of a student, 1927–9

Acc. nos. 888–900. Letters home from a student, 1928

Acc. no. 945. Reminiscences of a student, 1940–2

Acc. no. 967. Record of a discussion with four students, 1946–8

Acc. no. 1026. Reminiscences of a student, 1920–2

Acc. no. 1028. Reminiscences of a student, 1932–4

Acc. no. 1036. Interview with principal, 1961–71

Acc. no. 1189. Replies to questionnaire on Miss Allan from students, 1904–19

Acc. no. 1190. Replies to questionnaire on Miss Allan from students, 1920–9

Acc. no. 1191. Replies to questionnaire on Miss Allan from students, 1930–5

Acc. no. 1192. Interview with student, 1915–17

Acc. no. 1204. Interview with student, 1959–61

Acc. no. 1214. Reminiscences of a member of staff, 1949–74

Acc. no. 1229. Reminiscences of a student, 1947–9

Acc. no. 1230. Papers concerning librarian

Acc. no. 1241. Homerton Union of Students. Minute and record book, 1940–54

Acc. no. 1245. Interview with class of 1949

Acc. no. 1270. Interview with student, 1951–3

Acc. no. 1305. Reminiscences of student, 1958–60

Acc. no. 1395. Reminiscences of member of staff, 1947–54

Acc. no. 1403. Replies to questionnaire on Miss Skillicorn from students, 1935–60

Acc. no. 1404. Replies to questionnaire on Miss Skillicorn from students, 1935–60

Acc. no. 1405. Interview with member of staff, 1952–64

Acc. no. 1406. Interview with member of staff, 1955–80

Acc. no. 1408. Interview with member of staff, 1953–75

Acc. no. 1409. Interview with member of staff

Acc. no. 1410. Interview with two members of staff, 1943–74 and 1952–74

Acc. no. 1411. Interview with member of staff, 1937–45

Acc. no. 1412. Interview with member of staff, 1942–6

Acc. no. 1419. Reminiscences of students, 1930s

Acc. no. 1420. Reminiscences of students, 1940s

Acc. no. 1421. Interview with member of staff, 1951–7

Acc. no. 1422. Letter from Miss Skillicorn to member of staff, 1949–51 and interview

Acc. no. 1441. Interview with twelve students, 1940–2

Acc. no. 1465. Reminiscences of students in 1920s and 1930s

Acc. no. 1488. Interview with member of staff, 1946–51

Acc. no. 1504. Interview with member of staff

Acc. no. 1508. Tributes at Miss Skillicorn's memorial meeting, 2 June 1979

Acc. no. 1520. Reminiscences of a student, 1953–55

Acc. no. 1533. Papers concerning Miss Skillicorn's early life and background from Manx Museum, Isle of Man

Acc. no. 1552. Interview with member of staff, 1943–75

Acc. no. 1554 Interview with class of 1951

Acc. no. 1574. Interview with member of staff, 1948–51

Acc. no. 1576. Interview with student, 1956–8

Acc. no. 1592. Interview with four students, 1949–51

Acc. no. 1619. Interview with member of staff

Acc. no. 1628. Reminiscences of Nan Youngman, 1992

Acc. no. 1629. Memoir of Kay Melzi by Nan Youngman

Acc. no. 1636. Interview with student, 1924–26

Acc. no. 1663. Kay Melzi's 80th birthday tribute book

Acc. no. 1675. Interview with two students, 1954–56

Acc. no. 1687. Interview with two students, 1936–8 and 1937–9

Acc. no. 1690. Interview with student, 1957–59

Acc. no. 1705. Interview with student, 1943–45

Acc. no. 1708. Replies to centenary questionnaire from students, 1960s and 1970s

Acc. no. 1863. Reply to centenary questionnaire from students, 1950s

Acc. no. 1892. Correspondence from Henry Lamb concerning Miss Skillicorn's portrait

Acc. no. 1979. Interview with class of 1943

College registers of students, 1909–1960

Index